Exploring
Underwater

THE SIERRA CLUB OUTDOOR ACTIVITIES GUIDES

EXPLORING UNDERWATER

The Sierra Club Guide to Scuba and Snorkeling

John L. Culliney and Edward S. Crockett

Illustrations by Rita Kempf

SIERRA CLUB BOOKS   SAN FRANCISCO

The Sierra Club, founded in 1892 by John Muir, has devoted itself to the study and protection of the earth's
scenic and ecological resources—mountains, wetlands,
woodlands, wild shores and rivers, deserts and plains.
The publishing program of the Sierra Club offers books to
the public as a nonprofit educational service in the hope
that they may enlarge the public's understanding of the
Club's basic concerns. The point of view expressed in each
book, however, does not necessarily represent that of the
Club. The Sierra Club has some fifty chapters coast to
coast, in Canada, Hawaii, and Alaska. For information
about how you may participate in its programs to preserve
wilderness and the quality of life, please address inquiries
to Sierra Club, 730 Polk Street, San Francisco, CA 94109.

Library of Congress Cataloging in Publication Data:

Culliney, John L   1942–
Exploring Underwater

Bibliography: p.
Includes index.
1. Diving, Submarine. I. Crockett, E. S.
II. Sierra Club.   III.   Title.
GV840.S78C79   797.2'3   79-21944
ISBN 0-87156-270-7

Cover design by Pushpin Studios
Book design by Jon Goodchild
Illustrations by Rita Kempf

Printed in the United States of America
10 9 8 7 6 5 4 3 2

For Aaron, who loves the water.

Contents

Acknowledgments

A large number of friends and colleagues have influenced the making of this book. Most deserving of appreciation are the intrepid diving partners—Carl Burger, Frank Perron, Eric Radack, Steve Kempf, Gary McDaniel, and Barry Griffin—in whose company many personal underwater frontiers were crossed, some rare discoveries made, and numerous thoughts evolved that have found expression in this book.

Doctors Richard Cooper, Larry Harris, Tuck Hines, Bill Kirby-Smith, and Ruth Turner also deserve thanks for invaluable assistance and/or memorable companionship on expeditions into the ocean wilderness.

Paul Boyle cheerfully provided surface support, often in dismal weather, during a series of highly instructive underwater exercises in Massachusetts Bay.

This book, in part, has grown out of marine biological research experiences in association with the Duke University Marine Laboratory, Harvard University, Northeastern University, and the United States Office of Naval Research. The friendly support and encouragement of numerous staff members of those institutions are gratefully acknowledged.

A special thanks to Diana Landau and Wendy Goldwyn at Sierra Club Books and to their independent editorial colleague, Suzanne Lipsett. Their enthusiastic and expert guidance helped bring the manuscript through surges of revision to a graceful emergence.

Finally, our thanks to staff at the professional diving agencies, NAUI, YMCA, and SSI, who responded to our requests for recent instructional guidelines.

Preface

T HIS BOOK HAS BEEN WRITTEN from two main
points of view. One of us is a professional scuba
instructor, the other a professional marine biologist.
We have tried to combine the basic elements of diving, practical and experiential, in one volume. A third
essential theme is one that pervades both of our
thinking about diving: conservation. Unless current
efforts to preserve the underwater wilderness are
strengthened and expanded, our most cherished diving areas will be lost one by one and the few sites that
escape degradation will be overrun with divers.
Hence our concern and hope that all who enjoy the
underwater wilderness will participate privately and
publicly in its protection.

The practical sections of the book are aimed
primarily at beginning divers and people who are
thinking of learning to dive. But we wish to emphasize that while you will learn a lot about diving
from this book, you should not expect to learn how to
dive here. No book can substitute for a basic course in
diving taught by a professional instructor affiliated
with one of the accredited scuba-diver-certifying organizations. Five such organizations exist in the
United States: NAUI (National Association of Underwater Instructors), PADI (Professional Association of
Diving Instructors), NASDS (National Association of

Scuba Diving Schools), SSI (Scuba Schools International), and the familiar YMCA. Comparable organizations whose certifications are generally recognized in the United States are found abroad, for example, the British Sub-Aqua Club. Proof of basic certification in the form of a valid "C-card" ("C" for certification) in the holder's name is now required before an individual can obtain airfills, rent or even purchase equipment, or engage in charter-boat or resort-affiliated diving.

Divers by nature are an opinionated lot, voicing strong preferences for certain types and even brands of equipment, as well as fervent adherence to certain techniques. A nationwide survey would surely reveal that the "best," "safest," and "only" ways to dive are legion, depending on such factors as geographic location, age of the diver, and the particular organization and even dive shop with which one's instructor is affiliated. In writing about diving, we are in a position to be insufferably opinionated ourselves. We have partially resisted this impulse by trying to avoid mentioning brand names and to couch our prose in an advisory rather than a dictatorial tone. Some readers may still find passages that rankle, but we would like to remain friends and even hear from those who disagree with us on specific points. While, between us, we have enjoyed diving in many of the popular areas in North America and in other places that are not so well known, we are still seekers, and we rarely fail to be impressed when someone introduces us to his or her local underwater beauty spot. No one has tried, done, or seen it all. A little humility, like saliva in the mask, serves to clarify the view of one's position down below.

If we were asked to list the main reasons why people dive, or why the popularity of recreational diving is growing so rapidly, and why committed divers find their sport so compelling, we would begin with simple answers. Diving is fun; diving is healthful; diving is physically adventurous and mentally challenging. But we think that behind these answers lies a deeper motivation. Divers, as true explorers, participate directly in one of the great traditions of humankind. Two great physical frontiers are left to test the human spirit: the ocean and outer space. In the early stages of exploring the two, rough parallels have shown themselves in technological development and in the level of training demanded of the explorers themselves. But ironically, though the ocean is infinitely more palpable, fathomable, and accessible than outer space, at least until very recently astronomy has been favored above marine science and has remained well ahead developmentally.

People looked outward to the planets and stars before they became intrigued by the sea and expert at observing in even its shallow depths. Why? Historically, one finds a strong religious impetus to explore the heavens. But an earlier advent of pleasure diving might have changed all that. Before explorers entered the sea, little did anyone imagine the sublime, majestic, and boundless halls of the deep and the alien sounds of choirs of whales. Nor, perhaps, could seekers have anticipated the rapturous states of mind attainable by pilgrims to the oceans, the source of all the life and consciousness we are aware of so far. Perhaps heaven does lie in the other direction.

JLC
Waimanalo, Hawaii
August 1979

ESC
Weymouth Landing,
Massachusetts

The Craft of Diving

Chapter 1

Snorkeling: Tools and Techniques

T HE ADVENTURE BEGINS at the water's edge. You stand facing a veiled terra incognita, a deceptively quiet frontier that you know teems with life. Today you are scouting a new area. There is a good chance that no human has plunged into these particular wilds before you.

As an explorer, you attend to your equipment carefully and prepare yourself methodically, without haste. On this trip you are traveling light. You spit into your mask and, using a forefinger, spread the saliva over the whole inner surface of the faceplate. Then you rinse the mask in the water, put it on, and push the snorkel tube up under the strap just in front of your ear. The mask is comfortable and the seal is tight. You wade into the water, float free, and slip on your fins in weightless ease. The fins are snug but not tight, and you are ready. You turn and push off into a fluid third dimension and out over the immense trackless wilderness of the water planet.

Snorkeling is among the most satisfying recreational activities. It offers one the opportunity to make an excursion within the mind as well as the sea. Distances covered and depths reached by snorkelers—or free divers, as they are sometimes called to indicate lack of dependence on scuba gear—vary enormously according to experience and level of physical fitness. For most aficionados, visibility under water usually defines a limit to offshore excursions. The world below becomes less interesting and more lonely when one can no longer see the bottom from the surface. In familiar waters and in the absence of strong or unpredictable currents, a highly experienced few go out well beyond the point at which the bottom vanishes. The best of them dive for periods approaching two minutes on a single breath to find hidden terrain at depths of 75 feet or more.

Even with the purchase of an insulating suit to ward off the chill of a winter sea, snorkeling is fairly inexpensive as outdoor sports go. In the modern world, where the natural environment is receding, where adventure is hard to find, and where healthful exercise is a prescribed necessity, snorkeling offers something for almost everyone. Often, the snorkeler can reach wild, scenic, and silent places without burning up gasoline for hours on highways and byways. In taking off from a corner of their local beach, snorkelers enter a dimension unavailable to the mere swimmer. For a little while, they become part of a primeval world, where they do not always represent the dominant species. Finally, snorkeling calls into play nearly every muscle in the body and serves to condition the lungs. And the weight-conscious are generally glad to learn that a minute or two of exposure to what passes for warm water in many localities loses a snorkeler more calories than a jogger sweats away in a long mile.

To begin, one should be in good health, but need only be able to float and move comfortably in the water. Speed swimming and fancy strokes are not called for. After a while, increased grace and efficiency of movement seem to evolve naturally. Perhaps the snorkeler acquires aquatic skills subconsciously from watching the fish.

Snorkeling Equipment

The easiest way to get started in snorkeling is to borrow the equipment and make your first excursion with an experienced friend. Professional instruction at this stage of diving is seldom necessary although it is available from the major scuba instructional organizations. Once you have glimpsed the world below the water's surface, you will probably be eager to get your own equipment.

The Mask

The mask is usually the first piece of gear a new snorkeler considers. Having a clear and comfortable view of the scene below is so important to the overall quality of the diving experience that the choice of a mask can be more critical than that of a snorkel or pair of fins. Our recommendation is that you visit a professional dive shop. You will probably be astonished by the variety of masks available, and you will be pleased by the attention you receive from the personnel, themselves experienced underwater explorers.

A good face mask can be viewed as an investment, especially if you plan to advance from snorkeling to scuba diving. Because it encloses your nose, a mask permits you to maintain a comfortable pressure in the depths within your air-filled window. You do this by exhaling gently through your nose into the mask as you descend. At any depth, the mask need feel no tighter than it did at the surface—which leads to a word or two about goggles. Avoid them! When a person wearing goggles dives downward from the surface, increasing water pressure forces the goggles ever more tightly against the face and can cause the eyes to bulge outward and become bloodshot. There is no way to adjust the pressure in the air space enclosed by goggles, and serious injuries to the eyes can result when the pressure grows too great.

Regarding the size of the air space, we join most diving instructors in recommending that a beginning snorkeler or scuba diver purchase a "low-volume" mask, recognizable by its relatively flattened profile. The term "low-volume" refers to the volume of air enclosed by the mask when in position on the face. Naturally, a low-volume mask is much easier to clear

1.1. *Popular styles of modern, low-volume diving masks. Such designs allow manual pinching of the nostrils, a maneuver that greatly aids in balancing pressure in the ears (see text).*

after flooding—the diver merely displaces the water by exhaling air—than a mask with a large internal volume.

You should check several particulars in choosing a mask. First, look at the faceplate and make sure it bears the inscription "Tempered," usually located along one edge. Some cheap masks with plastic faceplates are sold by discount department stores. Avoid these masks. After a few encounters with sand, their faceplates become blurred by scratches inside and out. Also, exposure to sunlight can cause clear plastic to turn annoyingly milky and, after a while, hopelessly opaque. Heavy-duty tempered glass in a faceplate will not scratch easily. Nor will it shatter into piercing daggers and slivers if you fall on the rocks.

Next, look at the rubber, especially around the flange, the part that fits against your face. Do you see any small cracks or dry, scuffed-looking areas that leave flecks of rubber on your fingers? Rubber showing such signs might be old and dried out, or might have been chronically exposed to sunlight or certain damaging chemical fumes. If the rubber shows any hint of deterioration, look for another mask. Point out the defective equipment to a salesman, but don't be talked into buying it. Sometimes, old equipment with bad rubber is found on special sale, but it is usually no bargain. Decaying rubber might hold up for a little while, but it will crumble faster than ever with use.

In most masks now on the market, the rubber is recessed on either side of the nose. This design feature is a definite advantage, since it aids a diver in alleviating the effects of water pressure on the ears. We will return to this topic later.

After checking the rubber fittings, try the mask on for size. Choosing a mask to match the width of your face is important to prevent a cramped feeling from developing around the eyes. Your first view through a face mask will probably bring a sense of tunnel vision anyway, but if your eyes feel abnormally constricted, as if your visual pathway is being forcibly shifted toward the center of your face, choose a wider mask. Then, test the seal of the mask by placing it on your face without using the strap. Try to inhale through your nose. The suction alone, created by the effort to inhale, should hold the mask in position. The seal should be firm and comfortable, and you should not be able to feel the suction slipping even slightly due to air being drawn into the mask.

Finally, check the strap. Be sure that it is of good-quality, flexible rubber, and that it is long enough to allow the mask to fit comfortably, not tightly. Remember that if you plan to do any cold-water exploration, the strap will have to go on over a wetsuit hood at least a quarter-inch thick all around.

Ideally, your underwater visual acuity through the mask should be about what you are used to, within a range of a few meters, in the rest of your daily life. However, achieving this ideal poses some problems for people who wear glasses or contact lenses. Occasionally, divers we talk with report that their contacts somehow stay on, even when they accidentally open their eyes directly to the water after the mask has been flooded or removed. A few underwater contact wearers trust either to luck or to their extreme vigilance in the effort to avoid the problem of a flooded mask altogether. Relying on luck is risky, however, and continuous vigilance regarding contact lenses undoubtedly detracts from the enjoyment of diving. Fortunately, the diver who wears lenses or glasses has two good options for maintaining unimpaired visual acuity behind a face mask.

For a person whose vision is impaired to about the same extent in both eyes, a line of masks with pre-ground lenses is available. These masks are generally sold off the shelf or on short notice from most well-equipped dive shops. They are of high quality and cost about twice as much as a standard mask. The grades of lenses cover a wide range of visual corrective power (from 1 to 10 diopters). If you have any doubts, arrange to try a piece of prefashioned optical equipment in the water before you invest in it.

The second option is to order a pair of flat-ground lenses made to your prescription to be bonded with a clear sealant into the mask of your choice. Check with your local dive shop for details of this process. Chances are the personnel there can arrange for the work to be done.

The Snorkel

Choosing a snorkel should be easy after you have decided on a mask. Snorkels come in a variety of styles. Some have funny twists, designed to wrap around the approximate contours of the head and aim the opening at the top to one side of the swimmer so that forcibly exhaled gouts of water do not fall back on one's head. Apparently some snorkelers become sensitive to this self-inflicted form of water torture.

The snorkel mouthpiece, virtually identical to that of a scuba regulator, is inserted fully into the mouth and gently adjusted until the rubber "bits" rest comfortably on either side of the mouth between lightly clenched teeth. With the mouthpiece in this position, the lips can extend over the smooth, curving outer surface of the rubber, forming a seal. Mouthpieces vary in shape and size; comfort is probably the prime consideration. Hard rubber pressing against the gums may be annoying and even cause bleeding. People who wear braces on their teeth may wish to consult their orthodontists about the effects of a diving mouthpiece.

There is a controversy over the comparative efficacy of large- and small-bore tubes in snorkels. Large bores are said to reduce the frictional resistance of breathing, perhaps important during prolonged and strenuous swimming. However, it has been demonstrated that small-bore snorkels enclose significantly less dead air space than their large-bore counterparts. "Dead air space" refers to the volume within the respiratory passage at the time of each inhalation that is taken up by exhaled air with a low oxygen content. The snorkel, being a continuation of the body's respiratory passage, represents an extension of the dead air space. The effect of a greater than usual dead air space is more rapid breathing, or panting, in order to obtain a normal amount of oxygen to support bodily activity and to eliminate carbon dioxide generated by that activity. Therefore, one's choice in tube diameter presents a trade-off: easier breathing, or minimal dead air space. To our knowledge, it has not been resolved which option is more beneficial to a snorkeler.

Swim Fins

The last essential item of equipment for the serious snorkeler is a pair of swim fins. Although one can move through the water without them, fins boost the

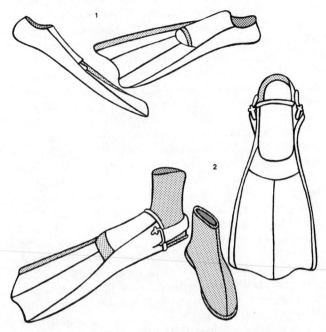

1.2. *Two styles of fins: 1, slipper type for light snorkeling. 2, adjustable, heelstrap type with neoprene booties, a better choice for scuba diving.*

swimmer's speed and power enormously. These considerations may not interest those content to paddle around in calm and very shallow water, but they become important to the snorkeler who wants to descend smoothly and efficiently more than a few feet to view closely something seen from the surface. Fins are absolutely necessary for anyone who ventures into water where any noticeable current flows or where swells and surge meet a rocky coast. With the control and power that fins bestow, a swimmer can avert such disasters as being carried out to sea or swept into rocks or reefs, and sustaining serious bodily injury.

Like other diving paraphernalia, fins come in a variety of styles and sizes. We recommend the heelstrap, or adjustable, style of fin. Avoid floppy fins, usually of the slipper type. These provide very little thrust and speed relative to the swimming effort applied, and to experienced underwater explorers they are a source of pure frustration. The heelstrap fins typically come in three sizes for adults; as a first approximation, choose the size that seems appropriate for the strength of your legs. Large fins will perform well only for the muscular individual; slender and less athletic persons should choose the small or medium size. These fins are nearly always worn with special neoprene booties that have both an insulating and a cushioning effect. Booties are worn even in warm water to prevent the fins from chafing the feet. Booties together with the adjustable strap permit one of the three sizes of fin to fit just about anyone.

A word about the stiffness of fins: if you are on the slim side, you may be dismayed at first by the muscular effort it takes to move your fins in the water. Try using slow and easy strokes. You will move through the water nicely, and your legs will get stronger the more you use your swim fins. Avoid the novice's tendency to flutter kick with fins; this bad habit results in little thrust and will tire you out.

Before you buy fins, check the rubber for any signs of deterioration, just as you did with the mask. Small cracks or chips along the sides of the flat portion, or blade, of the fin can spread across the blade with the normal stress of swimming, destroying the fin's rigidity and making it useless in a short time.

Wetsuits

With the purchase of mask, snorkel, and fins, you are basically equipped for excursions into the aquatic wilderness. Depending on your hardiness and the water temperature in your diving area, you may also want to get a wetsuit. Such a suit consists of booties, pants, jacket, gloves or mitts, and a hood. Modern wetsuits are made of a synthetic, rubberlike material called closed-cell neoprene foam. The term "closed-cell" refers to millions of tiny bubbles of nitrogen gas within the neoprene material. The trapped gas accounts for the thermally insulating property of the wetsuit and also causes it to be highly buoyant.

In all but the coldest water, most people find that a well-fitting wetsuit of one-quarter-inch thickness is sufficient for at least a few minutes of snorkeling. The best wetsuits are lined inside and out with a tough, wear-resistant nylon fabric. Nylon on the inside allows the suit to be slipped on far more easily than if the naked, clinging, rubbery neoprene were in contact with the skin. Nylon on the outside resists abrasion and contact with sharp edges, such as coral, that would slice readily into soft neoprene. In better makes of suits, the pants extend upward to cover the chest and back, the whole garment being held up by broad neoprene straps over the shoulders. The get-up resembles a pair of bib overalls, hence the common name for this style of diving dress: farmer-john. The jacket goes on over the extended "overalls," covering the core of the body (chest and abdomen) with a double thickness of insulation—in effect, one-half inch in a quarter-inch suit. Farmer-john suits are more expensive than ones with simple, waist-high pants, but they keep you much warmer and permit more extensive cold-water exploration.

Neoprene hoods also come in two basic styles. The so-called cold-water hood, or winter hood, extends downward in a wide flange to the upper chest and back, and partway out over the shoulders. (See Figure 9.1.) This helps to slow down the exchange of outside cold water with the thin layer of warmed water around the core of your body. A summer hood covers the head and neck only.

If you wear a wetsuit, you will also need a weight belt to counteract the buoyancy of the material. Weight belts are made of strong nylon webbing, with a buckle that operates on a friction principle. There are only two settings: open, the buckle allows the free end of the belt to slide freely; closed, it holds the free end fast at any point. Such a buckle is called a quick-release type. Lead weights, typically available in 2, 3, 4, 5, 6, and 10-pound sizes are threaded on the belt as needed. The average fully-wetsuited person needs about 18 to 20 pounds of lead weights on the belt in order to become *neutrally buoyant*, or weightless, at the surface. In a state of neutral buoyancy, a diver floats with a full inhalation and just begins to sink with a full exhalation. Proper fit in a wetsuit is also important. A snug fit without sacrifice of freedom of movement is ideal, but in lieu of a complicated and wordy description or a cryptic illustration, we advise you to try on suits with the expert advice of the staff at a professional dive shop.

Upon entering cold water, the wetsuited body finds that the first minute or two is the worst, as icy tricklings enter the suit at several points. The principle of a wetsuit is not to exclude water, but to prevent the continual influx of new cold water around the skin. The body quickly warms the very thin layer of water within the suit, and after about the first minute this layer reaches a comfortable temperature and remains there.

For prolonged exposure in cold water, a one-quarter-inch thick suit is not enough. Additional measures, such as wearing thermal underwear or a neoprene vest inside the suit, will help conserve warmth, but the increased bulk and stiffness will noticeably restrict a swimmer's ease of movement. Extended winter diving in northern seas or exploration of the world of lakes under ice demands more efficient insulation. Highly sophisticated suits that keep a diver dry and warm indefinitely are now available. We will discuss these in Chapter 3.

Accessories

Most dive shops feature a wide variety of underwater gadgets and ancillary equipment, from underwater lights and compasses to power sleds and fancy photographic equipment. Most of these items are more appropriate for the scuba diver than the snorkeler, and we therefore cover them in later chapters.

The snorkeler may have use for some limited extra equipment, however. If you plan to forage for seafood, such as lobsters, or collect shells, unusual rocks,

1.3. *The complete snorkeler with wetsuit, low-volume mask, snorkel, buoyancy compensator, gloves, fins, and catch bag.*

aquarium specimens, and so on, a bag made of nylon mesh will be useful. Such bags are sold in every dive shop.

As you fill your collecting bag with lobsters, shells, rocks, lost fishing lures, and other treasures from the shallow sea floor, you will find that the bag tends to drag you down. One solution to this problem is to wear an inflatable vestlike device called a *buoyancy compensator* (BC for short), and use it to support any extra weight you end up carrying. Alternatively, you may just want to attach a float of some kind to the bag itself. However, the advantage of a BC is that it buoys your body and allows you to rest at the surface without treading water. We strongly recommend a BC for any serious snorkeler getting away from lifeguard-protected beaches and heading into the aquatic wilderness.

Once you have your equipment, you may want to experiment with it in a swimming pool before entering more challenging waters. Or, if you start at the beach, a good way to learn to use mask and snorkel is simply to wade without swim fins into calm water up to your belly or chest and bend down with your face in the water. You'll be able to watch small fish, shrimp, and other creatures jumping ahead of your feet without worrying about propelling yourself around.

Underwater Vision

Your mask is a portable window giving you a clear view of the underwater world. When you look through it, you see as if through the side of an aquarium. By contrast, if you open your eyes under water without using a mask, the scene before you will be hopelessly blurred.

As on land clear vision under water requires that reflected light from an object in view be focused on the retina at the back of the eye. The eye is a kind of organic camera, with the tissue-thin retina serving as film. If an image is not precisely focused on the film, or on the retina, the picture will be fuzzy. In both eye and camera, focusing is accomplished by the bending, or refracting, of light rays, which normally diverge in straight lines from the object in view. The difference between a person's natural eyesight in air and that in water is due to the degree of refraction that takes place as light enters the eye.

Anyone who took physics in high school may remember that light refracts greatly as it moves between water and air. Beginning at the outer surface of the eye is a fluid-filled layer of tissue called the cornea. Light rays traveling in air bend sharply when they enter the cornea. And because the cornea is curved, the rays naturally bend toward one another. They

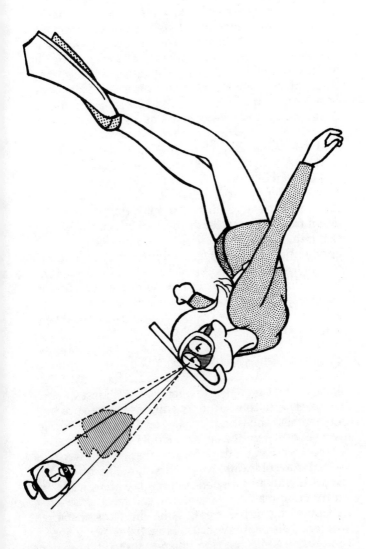

1.4. *Visual distortion under water. The fish appears one-fourth closer, hence one-fourth larger, than it really is.*

converge inward toward the retina at the back of the eye, and in a normal eye fine adjustments in the lens result in a razor-sharp focus.

However, when the naked eye is immersed in water, the laws of physics no longer aid good vision. Rays of light in the water no longer bend appreciably as they pass into the fluid-filled eye, and the lens by itself is incapable of bending the rays into focus on the retina. Only when a layer of air is placed in front of the eyes can a human diver achieve a sharp focus. A mask or goggles restores the necessary degree of refraction.

Underwater vision has other surprises for the novice. A bold or foolish fish may appear to hover 3 feet in front of your mask; you reach out to touch it and discover that it is nearly 4 feet away. Your hand looks a fourth larger than it should. As you look down from the surface, the bottom appears a fourth closer than it really is. Altered depth perception and apparent magnification are other results of the refraction of light by water. As many a trout fisherman can attest, distortion in the location and size of an underwater object is experienced by a person looking into water from above the surface as well as by the diver below.

The First Plunge

For your first plunge into open water, choose a familiar beach with calm water conditions. Make sure that any clothes, shoes, duffel bags, and other belongings you set down on the beach are out of reach of the highest waves and the tide. If you are going wetsuited into cold water for the first time, be prudent. Snorkel with an experienced friend. Choose your entry point mainly by exercising common sense— avoid strong surf, currents, concentrations of sharp oyster shells or spiny sea urchins, fishermen's lines, and reckless surfers. Don't plan to go too far offshore. And at the first sign of a real chill—that is, when you begin to shiver noticeably—head for the beach. You'll bless a friend who has a fire going on the sand when you return in such an instance, and a thermos of hot coffee, cocoa, or soup will be welcome too. You are likely to appreciate such aids to warming up after a long swim at any time of year.

Just before entering the water, most divers perform the slightly macho-seeming ritual, mentioned earlier, of spitting into the mask. This mysterious little habit actually helps to prevent fogging on the inside of the mask. To achieve this effect, first smear the saliva around with your finger so that it covers the whole inner surface of the glass; then rinse the mask in the water until the glass is clean. A clear film from the saliva will remain, usually for the duration of the dive, and will inhibit annoying condensation. Also, dive shops sell a liquid preparation claimed by some to be superior to the saliva remedy for inhibiting fogging inside the mask. We'll take saliva anytime.

With your mask properly treated and your snorkel secured (either pushed up under the mask strap or held to the strap by a rubber loop), you are ready to enter the water. In many situations it is a good idea to carry your fins in with you and put them on when you reach waist-deep water. If you don your fins on a coarse sand or gravel beach, you may end up with sharp pieces of grit chafing horribly around your instep, and you'll probably have to take off the fins again in open water to clear out the sand. Furthermore, trying to walk on slippery rocks while wearing fins is not only difficult; it can be dangerous. However, in a situation where you can jump directly into deep water, as from a boat or a ledge, wear your fins in. When you jump, use one hand to hold the mask in position against your face. Otherwise it will be torn off when you hit the water.

The Surface Dive

As a beginning snorkeler, you will undoubtedly glide out over the seascape enthralled. Rocky bottom, reefs, or areas of extensive seaweed cover are unlike familiar landforms. Even sandy terrain dappled by shifting patches of sunlight and shadow looks exotic and mysterious. You'll see a fish dive into a waving canopy of vegetation, and colorful starfish splayed out on a rock will invite closer inspection. An interesting-looking shell half hidden in the sand will intrigue you, and you'll arch beneath the surface, flipper down, and pick it up. In doing so you'll be performing the technique known as *surface diving*, important to both snorkelers and scuba divers.

A surface dive is a smooth descent started from a floating position. Surprisingly, many people have trouble getting themselves under water and expend a lot of energy thrashing about before they are headed down toward the bottom. To perform the simplest and most efficient surface-diving technique, start from the normal prone swimming position. Hold your breath and bend straight downward from the waist so that the forward part of your body is pointing at the bottom. Next, with a quick snap, bring your legs straight up into the air. Your whole body will again be fairly straight, but aimed downward, and the weight of your legs in the air will begin to push you toward the bottom. A whale sounds in a similar manner, using the weight of its huge tail to start its body downward. To complete the maneuver, perform a powerful breaststroke with your arms. This will bring your fins completely below the surface where kicking will take over as the main propulsive force.

An Introduction to Pressure Physics

If you are going down more than 6 or 8 feet, you will notice a sensation of pressure in your ears. This feeling usually begins to register as pain by about 10 feet. If left unattended, the pain will rapidly become excruciating as you continue to descend. Such pain is caused by an unrelieved pressure difference between the surrounding environment and the space in the middle ear, just inside the tympanic membrane, or eardrum. This pressure imbalance results in the condition known as *ear squeeze*, and in extreme cases the eardrum can be ruptured. Ear squeeze, along with such secondary effects as bleeding and damaged membranes, is the most common malady treated in hyperbaric, or high-pressure, medicine.

To obtain relief from squeeze, you only have to equalize the pressure in the middle ear with that of the environment, or ambient pressure. You can accomplish this equalization by yawning, working the jaw back and forth, or swallowing. But the most effective technique is simply pinching the nose shut and trying to blow it as if into a handkerchief. No air is expelled, but the blowing effort is transmitted from the nasal passage through the connecting Eustachian tubes to the middle ears. The effect is to increase the air pressure within the middle-ear spaces, and thus eliminate the pain.

In this context, the functional design of the part of the face mask that fits around the nose becomes clear. It allows you to pinch your nose with thumb and forefinger without taking off the mask. Once you get used to it, clearing, or balancing, your ears will become nearly automatic. You will also learn to do it before the sensation of increased pressure becomes painful. Beginners often wait until they are fairly deep before blowing against their pinched noses, and then blow until they are blue in the face without getting any relief. Usually, if they move up a few feet closer to the surface and try again to clear their ears, they will be successful. Experienced divers clear their ears several times, eliminating any occurrence of pain, while descending the first 30 feet, where squeeze is most severe.

Sometimes a person will find that a cold or allergy interferes with clearing the ears. In mild cases, a nasal decongestant used a few minutes before the diver enters the water will expand the Eustachian tubes to the middle-ear spaces, as well as other airways to facial sinuses, so that diving will be comfortable.

One of the most serious hazards concerning a snorkeler's or a diver's ears involves a seemingly innocent gadget, the earplug. A simple rule applies: *never* wear earplugs. A surface dive to just 12 or 15 feet can cause earplugs to suddenly implode into the auditory canal, burst through the eardrums, and penetrate into the delicate inner ear.

If you snorkel with a wetsuit, you will soon learn another interesting, but nonpainful, lesson in high-pressure physics. At the surface, the gas in the cells of an average person's full wetsuit will buoy up the roughly 20 pounds of lead weight that must be attached to a snorkeler's belt to permit him or her to submerge easily. However, as a person dives downward from the surface, a progressive squeeze is exerted on the wetsuit. Compression shrinks the millions of tiny gas cells in the suit, and the diver loses buoyancy. At 33 feet, half the buoyancy possessed by the snorkeler at the surface has been lost. This phenomenon is reversible, since the wetsuit's gas cells expand again during ascent. But at the beginning of the upward swim from 33 feet, one starts up with the equivalent of 10 pounds of lead acquired in the descent. The deeper one goes, the greater is the temporary weight handicap. Many experienced snorkelers choose to compensate somewhat by underweighting themselves slightly at the surface. Thus, they start out as positively buoyant—lighter than water—which means getting below requires a bit more effort than otherwise, but they will be carrying less dead weight on a relatively deep excursion to the bottom.

Surfacing

The snorkeler returning to the surface is often in a hurry. The urge to breathe becomes extremely powerful. The most important thing to remember at this stage is, Look up. This simple precaution will keep you from crashing into floating objects such as boats, logs, or other snorkelers. In tropical waters, where stinging Portuguese men-of-war or similar creatures exist, looking up during ascent can help you avoid a painful experience. The undersurface and tentacles of the man-of-war are a deep blue color and stand out surprisingly well when viewed against the silvery ceiling of the underwater world.

Tilting your head back as you ascend will not only afford you a view of the surface, but also it puts you in position to clear water from your snorkel in the most efficient and effortless way. Clearing a snorkel full of water takes some effort if you wait until you reach the surface. And even after you spout like a miniature whale in the attempt, the annoying thimbleful or two of water will usually remain to be sucked into your mouth on the next breath. Instead, try this: with your head tilted back so you are looking straight up, begin to exhale just before you break the surface. You will feel almost no resistance, since your head will be so far back that the snorkel will be pointing down at a slight angle, and water will run out of it with the aid of gravity as you exhale. Continue to exhale as you surface, bringing your head forward to the face-down position, and you will end up with a very dry snorkel. Your body automatically returns prone to the surface.

Hyperventilation

Experienced snorkelers adopt habits that contribute to increased ease and efficiency in the water. One of the most important is hyperventilation before a surface dive. Hyperventilation can greatly extend a snorkeler's underwater excursion time, but it can also be dangerous.

When you take several deep breaths in rapid succession, the effect is to slightly increase the lungs' oxygen content (called *partial pressure of oxygen* by physiologists) and, to a much greater extent, to decrease the amount of carbon dioxide present. The stimulus to breathe is provided by a small part of the brain, the respiratory center, which senses the levels of oxygen and carbon dioxide in the blood. Thus, after hyperventilating, snorkelers can hold their breath for an abnormally long period, since the stimulus to breathe—carbon dioxide—is greatly reduced for a time. After a while, a combination of rising carbon dioxide and falling oxygen during breath holding triggers the urge to breathe again.

The respiratory center, however, is more sensitive to rising carbon dioxide levels than to falling oxygen levels. The danger in breath holding after hyperventilation is that the oxygen level in the blood can become so low that the person can black out before feeling the strong urge to breathe. Thus, a snorkeler can feel normal on a deep dive after hyperventilation, but suddenly slip into unconsciousness during the ascent. This happens because the ascent lowers the partial pressure of carbon dioxide in the blood, creating a false relief from the urgent "resume breathing" signals emanating from the respiratory center. At the same time, the oxygen level diminishes drastically below the danger level. Recent medical literature contains reports of a number of fatal and near-fatal drownings in underwater swimming contests. Nearly every one of these accidents was a direct result of hyperventilation. Currently, physicians recommend that snorkelers take no more than two deep breaths prior to descent.

With practice, a snorkeler can stay down for a minute at a time without danger. The Ama, women skin divers of Japan, make repetitive dives lasting about a minute each while they collect shellfish on the sea floor 50 or 60 feet down. Exceptional instances of underwater breath holding (using surface air with no extra oxygen) exceeding two minutes have been reported, but according to physicians, such efforts for the record books involve a risk of potential brain damage due to oxygen starvation.

Snorkelers in good physical condition can make surprisingly deep dives. Some professionals hold a heavy weight during a deep descent and let themselves be carried down quickly and passively, thereby saving swimming energy. The weight is attached to the diver's boat by a rope and can be retrieved by a nondiving partner in the boat after the diver reaches the desired depth and lets go. Captain Jacques Cousteau has observed breath-holding Arab sponge divers on the bottom at 130 feet. In Hawaii, fishermen set giant nets in 60 to 70 feet of water, and then free dive routinely to the bottom to guide the nets over coral blocks and other obstructions as they are being pulled in. The lung capacities of people able to make such dives are enormous. At 130 feet, the weight of the overlying water collapses the air-filled chest to one-fifth of its volume at the surface. The inward flexure of the rib cage in an average person would cause intolerable pain long before such extreme depths were reached.

A Few Precautions

If one is a competent swimmer and is careful about hyperventilation, the dangers inherent in snorkeling are few. Minor accidents consist primarily of contusions and abrasions sustained in contact with rocky bottom and noxious creatures. Snorkelers who have respect for rough water acquire finesse in their bodily movement, have an awareness of local marine biology, and wear protective clothing, especially gloves, can avoid most common injuries. A meeting with a large predatory shark, the most fearsome image in the mind of many an underwater explorer, is extremely unlikely within the shallow depths inhabited by snorkelers. An exception may be where seals and sea lions attract great white sharks that could mistake a human for their natural prey.

The most bizarre snorkeling accident we have heard of occurred on the French Riviera. A man inhaled a bee which had landed on the tip of his snorkel as he was swimming a short distance offshore. The bee stung the man well back in the throat, and the swelling of sensitive tissue blocked his windpipe. Only an emergency tracheotomy could have saved him. Although he reached shore, he collapsed and died of suffocation on the beach.

Barring bees landing on your snorkel (if they persist, screen the opening), you can spend a long lifetime exploring the underwater wilderness just off your favorite beaches. The ocean is the last frontier on earth. Finding perfect solitude and untrammeled wilderness is still easy off many shores. And it may be true that the sea can absorb more wilderness sightseers than the spectacular areas on land. Sometimes an acre of reef or algal forest, with its dreamlike strangeness, can be as fascinating as an entire mountainside or a wild river. Some of the most exotic wild country in the world is under water. Once you have mastered snorkeling and have sensed the immensity, complexity, and beauty of the undersea world, you are likely to be drawn to scuba. In the next two chapters we turn to the fundamentals of scuba diving.

Chapter 2

Getting Started with Scuba

S O YOU THINK you would like to be a scuba diver? If you enjoy being in the water, if you feel psychologically comfortable in open water (an ocean or lake, as opposed to a swimming pool), and if you are a reasonably competent and confident swimmer, you are probably ready for scuba training. The old image of diving as a sport for the gorilla-chested male animal is now old and wrinkled. Nearly anyone who can swim and who learns the proper techniques and ways of the underwater world can become a good diver.

These same qualifications also apply to an open-water snorkeler. Snorkeling proficiency is certainly an aid in learning to scuba dive, but it is not absolutely necessary. If you have never snorkeled, expect to learn this skill along with the others covered in introductory diver instruction.

Diving is physically demanding, and better than average fitness is an asset. A scuba diver is assumed to be in general good health, but especially must be free of heart and lung disorders. Most divers are nonsmokers, and we advise smokers who plan to take up diving to kick this lung-impairing habit (more on smoking as a health risk to divers in Chapter 4). Most diving-instruction organizations now require that students have a physical examination before they begin a dive course. If a specific medical condition, perhaps one that turns up in a routine physical, makes diving questionable for you, consult a diving physician. Referrals usually can be arranged through a local professional diving instructional and equipment center.

Where to Find Scuba Instruction

You should contact one or more of the nationally recognized scuba-instruction organizations in your area. Usually these organizations—NAUI, NASDS, PADI, YMCA, and SSI (see the Preface for full identification)—are affiliated with local diving equipment stores, known everywhere as dive shops. And among the people who sell the equipment in dive shops (*not* in discount department stores) are professional instructors certified by one or more of the agencies listed above. It's wise to shop around, since types of courses offered, schedules, cost of instruction, equipment provided for a given course fee, and subsequent discounts and deals for students on equipment purchase do vary considerably.

We emphatically recommend *against* starting to scuba dive with an "experienced" friend as instructor. Imagine the impact on your friend (husband, wife, lover, parent) in the event of a serious accident if even the slightest possibility of negligence existed. Safe, trouble-free, and enjoyable scuba diving involves learning an intricate series of intermeshing theoretical and practical skills. If that description sounds dry and academic, remember that the environment explored by a scuba diver does not naturally support human life. To use a slightly rarified parallel: would you expect to join an Apollo crew as copilot of the lunar lander, learning as you go?

What to Expect in a Basic Scuba Course

Modes of Instruction and Swim Test

All modern diver training combines classroom teaching with in-the-water learning and practice. A good scuba course offers 25 to 30 hours of instruction with more than half this time devoted to work in the water. The first wet session commonly consists of a swimming test without equipment, typically in a pool, although, where available, warm and calm natural waters close to shore are fine. You will be asked to swim as far as 300 yards without stopping. The type or quality of stroke is not important to most instructors; moving steadily through the water is all-important. An underwater swim without fins also is required by most agencies and instructors. Demonstrating that you can stay afloat under your own power for up to 30 minutes is another typical requirement.

Classroom Phase

Most basic scuba courses involve at least ten hours of instructor–student contact in the classroom, plus extra, out-of-class reading and perhaps simple problem solving. Topics covered in basic diving classes should include the following, which we have annotated to provide definitions of terms that will be used or discussed in greater detail later in this book.

Diving Physics

Atmospheric pressure. This is the force exerted by air in the atmosphere. Air at sea level has a pressure of 14.7 pounds per square inch, or 1 *atmosphere*, and most humans live at this ambient pressure. At elevations above sea level, air pressure becomes less than one atmosphere. Below sea level, a pressure greater than one atmosphere is exerted on air spaces in the body by the weight of overlying water.

Hydrostatic pressure. This is the force exerted by water, and it steadily increases with depth.

Buoyancy. This term refers to the tendency of an object under water to move up or down, or to remain at rest at a given depth in a delicate equilibrium.

Diving gases. These are the major gases that make

up the air breathed by the diver. They include nitrogen, oxygen, carbon dioxide, and rarely carbon monoxide as a severely toxic contaminant.

Gas laws. These are laws of physics that describe the effects of pressure and temperature on gases.

Heat transfer and insulation. These topics lead into discussions of how water conducts heat away from the human body and the heat-conserving properties of diving garments.

Diving Physiology and Medicine

Effects of pressure on air spaces in the body. This discussion will emphasize avoiding often painful pressure imbalances in the middle-ear spaces and facial sinuses (as discussed in Chapter 1), and especially eliminating the possibility of overpressurization of air in the lungs.

Decompression sickness (the bends). This is a condition that develops when an excess of nitrogen has dissolved in body fluids and comes out of solution as bubbles of gas when a diver surfaces.

Nitrogen narcosis. The instructor will describe (probably from personal experience) the intoxicating effects of nitrogen at relatively high pressure, corresponding to depths in excess of 100 feet.

Consequences of heat loss. You will learn how the body reacts to cold, and how to recognize and treat hypothermia, a deep chilling of the body that numbs physically and mentally and can ultimately prove fatal.

Diving psychology. Exploring this subject can contribute immeasurably to safe and enjoyable diving. Recognizing the occasions of overconfidence, unreasoning timidity, and panic is as important as knowing how to use your equipment properly.

Rescue and resuscitation. You will encounter the theory and practice of modern aquatic lifesaving, first aid, and cardiopulmonary resuscitation.

Diving Technique and Environment

Nondecompression diving. This is relatively shallow and short-to-moderate-duration diving that avoids the accumulation of excess dissolved nitrogen in the body and permits surfacing directly.

Decompression diving. This is diving that requires stopping and waiting for prescribed intervals at prescribed depths while approaching the surface, to allow excess nitrogen accumulated under pressure during the dive to leave the body gradually without forming bubbles and causing the bends.

Repetitive diving. This is diving that involves two or more descents within a 12-hour period. Repetitive dives may involve decompression or not.

Anatomy and function of diving equipment. You will be introduced to modern scuba gear: what it looks like, how it goes together, how it works.

Diving environments and aquatic life. This is usually local in scope. You may be able to preview the underwater scene in your area if your instructor has access to underwater photographs.

Underwater communications. These consist primarily of various hand signals and gestures used by divers. The idea is to practice them until the common ones become instantly recognizable.

How to plan a dive. You will learn the effective use of your equipment, proper techniques and special considerations for different diving environments, and safety aspects in both shore- and boat-based diving.

In-The-Water Training

Pool or Protected-Water Sessions

Wearing and manipulating diving equipment. You will learn how to assemble, adjust, wear, and carry diving gear in and out of the water. At first you may feel all thumbs and be disturbed by not being able to see what you have to do with your hands. Don't worry; after some practice your sense of touch will develop to accommodate new tasks, such as adjusting out-of-sight straps and fasteners, and you will be able to perform these manipulations as easily as you can tie your shoes in the dark.

Proper weighting and buoyancy control. You will learn whether you are a "sinker" or a "floater" (how easily you remain on the surface without the aid of buoyancy equipment). Then at the shallow end of the pool you will experiment with a wetsuit which insulates you from cold and at the same time, as discussed in Chapter 1, greatly increases your tendency to float. Wearing all your diving gear, you will find out how much lead you must carry on the weight belt to compensate for your floating tendency. Under water, you will learn to use a buoyancy control device that enables you to move effortlessly up or down or to hover absolutely weightless at any depth.

Entry and exit techniques. In full gear you will learn efficient and safe ways to get in and out of the water.

Removing and replacing diving gear in the water. Both at the surface and fully under water, you will learn to clear your mask of water, an essential skill in the event it becomes accidentally flooded during a dive (see Chapter 5, Figure 5.3, for one technique). Retrieving your breathing unit, should it be accidentally dislodged from your mouth is also practiced. Unbuckling, removing, and redonning the assembly holding your air tank, as you continue to breathe from it, is another exercise. This is simply done and even easy once you have practiced it on dry land or standing at the shallow end of a pool, and once your sense of touch has become educated around scuba equipment. Finally, you will learn the proper way to ditch a weight belt (see Chapter 5), if you ever have to make an emergency ascent from fairly deep water to the surface.

Emergency ascents. The controlled emergency ascent involves coming to the surface with all equipment in place as you slowly release a single breath of air. The ascent is first practiced in the pool from perhaps 10 feet down. You must exhale on the way up to avoid dangerous overpressurization. Some instructors have students practice controlled emergency ascents in open water (out of the pool). In a basic diving course, we do not recommend conducting exercises such as weight belt ditching and emergency use of buoyancy devices in open water, as they can lead to dangerous uncontrolled ascents. An *uncontrolled ascent*, by definition, is one in which the diver is forced to rise, often rapidly, to the surface.

The buddy system. You will learn the ways in which diving partners can help each other before, during, and after a dive. Especially important is the concept that diving buddies stay together in the water, both at the surface and below. You will probably practice the technique of *buddy breathing*—sharing a single breathing unit and air supply by passing the unit back and forth in an orderly manner. You will come to appreciate the physical difficulties of buddy breathing, for example, if you had to coordinate swimming with your buddy while sharing the same air supply. You should also become aware of the psychological difficulties and anxiety that can accompany this exercise. We will have more to say about the buddy system in later chapters as we discuss practical diving experiences.

Open-Water Sessions

A good basic scuba diving course should include at least two dives in open water. Typically students are able to go deeper than in a pool, but initial open-water dives, widely known as *checkout dives*, almost never extend deeper than about 30 feet. Instructors usually devote considerable individual attention to students in the open-water checkouts. This is where you enter the real underwater world to practice skills learned in the pool.

At the end of the course you will have a certificate and wallet-sized card, issued by your instruction organization, stating that you have qualified as a basic scuba diver. As a certified diver, you are recognized as someone who has mastered the essential skills of diving, rather than an unknown quantity who professes to know how to dive but might be a poor risk as a buddy. In practical terms, the possession of a certification, or "C-card," allows you to rent scuba gear wherever you may travel in the United States and most other places. Traveling divers usually pack small items (the regulator, for example) but rent heavy and bulky items such as air tanks from a local dive shop or resort near where they intend to dive. Unless you present a C-card, most responsible shops will not rent you equipment, except for snorkeling gear. Even airfills of your tank or purchases of scuba equipment are now sometimes disallowed to persons lacking a card.

Quickie Diving Courses

Occasionally would-be divers come across instructors or organizations that offer drastically abbreviated scuba training. "Learn to dive in half an hour" is the slogan of these back-alley gamblers, who are indeed gambling with the health and safety of their students. Some quickie courses that we know of are associated with resorts in the Caribbean, and they can also be found in other popular diving areas. Such programs for beginners are never sanctioned by the major agencies, and the consequences of incomplete training have included fatalities.

One documented case in the Caribbean involved the following problems.* A language barrier made it difficult for the English-speaking students to understand the instructor. The group being guided by the instructor included both beginners and experienced underwater photographers, and the divers were led to a depth of 40 feet to satisfy the experienced people. A buddy system was not in use. The victim, who was

---

*NOAA, et al. United States Underwater Fatality Statistics 1975. U.S. Department of Commerce (March 1977).

not wearing a BC, was seen to go off by himself, then to surface and cry for help. Inexplicably, no rescue attempt was made for ten minutes after the cry was heard. Finally, no police investigation was made and no autopsy performed. According to witnesses, the victim was a complete novice and had received only twenty minutes of instruction prior to the dive.

We believe that such "courses" should be outlawed. Anyone anticipating a diving vacation owes himself, as well as loved ones, friends, and potential diving partners, the security and peace of mind that comes only with thorough training and professional certification.

After taking a basic scuba course, you are equipped with the skills and safety practices to live for a short time just below the edge of an enchanting world whose nearly infinite newness and beauty wait to be explored. To unlock the deeper secrets of the sea there are more advanced skills and techniques: underwater navigation, photography, search and recovery. Many of these specialties, as well as training for deeper and more prolonged diving, are offered in the form of higher-level courses by the same professional instruction agencies that conduct basic diving courses. But now you are on your way, and we urge you to plunge ahead.

Chapter 3

Scuba Diving: The Basic Equipment

D IVING WITH THE AID of Self-Contained Underwater Breathing Apparatus—from which is
drawn the acronym "scuba"—has been described as
part space mission and part wilderness backpacking
trek. The parallel with astronautics comes from the
preparations necessary for a dive and the fact that
diving, like space travel, makes use of a special
technology to enter a medium in which humans cannot exist without an artificial life-support system.
Perhaps more fully than a space traveler, however,
experienced divers once submerged focus most of
their awareness away from their equipment and on
the exotic world they are privileged to explore.

At first glance, basic scuba equipment looks complex and arcane. The heavy tank, with its highly
compressed air, seems a formidable—and perhaps
even dangerous—burden to fasten to one's shoulders. Before entering the water, one might imagine
that the weight of the tank and lead-studded belt will
cause him to sink like a stone. One might also envi-
sion the regulator malfunctioning in deep water, or
the air hose accidentally being cut in two by sharp
coral. Most of these concerns can be assuaged once
the diver gains a secure knowledge of the way the
equipment works and proper methods of carrying
and using it. In this chapter, we cover these funda-
mental topics.

The integrated life-support system of the free-swimming diver consists of equipment necessary for three main underwater functions: *breathing*, *buoyancy control*, and *body-heat conservation*. It is easiest to get an overview of the nuts and bolts of scuba diving by considering these functions one at a time, even though some items of equipment perform more than one function, contributing, for example, to both buoyancy and heat conservation.

The Tank

Obviously, breathing is the function of most immediate concern to a diver. As he sinks beneath the surface, he is usually carrying about 72 cubic feet of air compressed into the small space within the tank on his back. (The figure represents the volume the compressed air would occupy if released at surface pressure.)

Tanks are made of steel or aluminum alloys. Aluminum tanks weigh about the same as steel ones of comparable internal volume; however, they are noticeably longer and bulkier than their steel counterparts. All tanks conform to strict federal manufacturing standards on containers for high-pressure gas set by the U.S. Department of Transportation. Stamped near the top of every regulation tank are several rows of letters and numbers containing important information, including the manufacturer's serial number, the Department of Transportation inspection code, and the dates on which the tank was pressure-tested. The date preceded by a plus (+) sign is that on which the first pressure test was performed and thus when the tank was manufactured. The plus sign indicates that the tank will safely sustain an internal pressure of 10 percent over its rated capacity, a convention routinely recognized at commercial air stations.

Scuba tanks come in a variety of sizes, ranging from 50 cubic feet to 94 cubic feet. Two tanks can be rigged together with a single valve; such a "doubles" rig greatly increases the capacity for deep diving, where air is used very rapidly. The most popular tanks in current use are singles: the galvanized steel 72 and the aluminum 80, the numbers referring to the volume of air in cubic feet held by these tanks when full. The steel 72 is routinely filled to a pressure of 2500 psi (pounds per square inch); this number includes the 10 percent overpressure allowance. The aluminum 80 is filled to 3000 psi. Imagine the volume of air inside a fairly large telephone booth and you will have a mental picture of approximately how much air a diver has bottled up inside a 72- or 80-cubic-foot tank at the beginning of a dive. We recommend always having your tanks filled at a professional dive shop, where high-quality air at a nominal cost is guaranteed. At most shops, it takes no more than five minutes to fill a standard tank.

Steel versus Aluminum

A continuing controversy prevails over the advantages of steel versus aluminum tanks. Both of us prefer steel tanks. One good reason for this preference is that aluminum tanks are relatively soft and may be dented if dropped on rock, metal surfaces, hard wooden piers, and the like. Dents weaken a tank, and a large dent can render one unserviceable. Also, aluminum tanks are subject to electrolysis or corrosive disintegration when in contact with a dissimilar metal. For this reason, the stainless steel bands of backpacks that hold aluminum tanks are lined in rubber. Clearly, an aluminum tank should never be left leaning against pipes or other metal objects. A brass or stainless steel valve on an aluminum tank will also initiate electrolysis where it contacts the aluminum, welding itself into the mouth of the tank or destroying the aluminum threads. Valves of dissimilar metals should be removed from aluminum tanks every six months and lubricated. Occasionally, corrosion occurs inside an aluminum tank, often resulting in loose dust—potentially very bad for small orifices of the regulator and for the lungs.

Aluminum tanks should be filled more slowly than steel ones. Both types of tanks are placed in a cooling bath to be filled, but a steel tank, which has a thinner wall, sheds the heat of the compressed air faster. The aluminum tank fills at the same rate to 3000 psi, but it retains more heat at the time. Later on, when the air cools, the pressure in the aluminum tank drops significantly.

Tank Maintenance

It is true that steel tanks, though they present fewer problems than aluminum tanks, can corrode internally if not properly cared for. To prevent corrosion in steel tanks, at least 100 psi of air should remain in a tank at all times. Outside moisture, the cause of corrosion, cannot enter a tank against substantial pressure. Another safeguard against moisture is to fill tanks only with "dry" air, guaranteed to be moisture-free by a pro dive shop.

By federal law, tanks must be pressure-tested every five years. The procedure is called *hydrotesting*. A tank being hydrotested is filled with water and subjected to a pressure of five-thirds over its rated capacity, and the date of the test is stamped near the top of the tank. No commercial air station will fill an out-of-date tank. Hydrotests can be arranged through local pro dive shops. It is important to realize that hydrotesting stretches and weakens a tank, actually shortening its life. Thus, you should not have your tank hydrotested more frequently than every five years.

The focus of the law notwithstanding, we feel that an annual visual inspection of the inside of scuba tanks—whether steel or aluminum—is far more important than hydrotesting. This service is now available at every professional dive shop. For a very small charge an expert will remove the valve and "scope" the tank's interior using a small lighted probe. If the inside of the tank is slightly rusty, it can be scour-cleaned, or "sand-blasted," at the shop. But if extreme corrosion or structural defects are found, the tank will be condemned. We predict that the law specifically directed at scuba tanks will change, and that visual inspections will be made mandatory, perhaps with the effect of rendering hydrotesting obsolete. As the law stands now, during the current five-year interval between tests, a tank can completely rust through from the inside, often with no external indication that it is a bombshell waiting to be filled. More and more dive shops nationwide are reserving the right to refuse to fill a tank without a current visual inspection sticker (within one year of date).

Tank Valves

Tank valves are of two types, the simple *K valve* and the nearly outmoded reserve valve, or *J valve*. The J valve incorporates a special spring-tensioned device, which, when positioned before a dive, provides a warning when the air supply is getting low and makes a reserve of air available. A diver carrying a single tank with a J valve will begin to experience

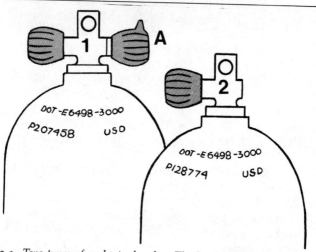

3.1. *Two types of scuba tank valve. The J valve (1) incorporates an air-reserve device operated by rotating the knob (A) downward, usually via an accessory pull-rod. The simpler K valve (2) allows for no air reserve but is less prone to malfunction.*

more effort in breathing as the tank's pressure drops to close to 300 pounds psi. Noticing the growing resistance to inhalation, he or she trips the spring valve manually, thereby gaining access to the air reserve and ascertaining that only 300 psi is left in the tank and that it is time to head for the surface. Unfortunately, J valves are prone to mechanical problems: rubber gaskets can erode and fail, causing leakage of air. Also, the J valve can be accidentally tripped or left in the wrong position by the forgetful diver. For these reasons, the J valve, with its manual air-reserve mechanism, has rapidly declined in popularity, giving way to a submersible pressure gauge, which, used in conjunction with the simple K valve, continuously monitors the air supply, allowing a diver to check the reserve at any time. The precise knowledge of the amount of air in the tank at any given time not only affords divers more peace of mind; it also gives them a greater ability to judge time and distance limits for underwater excursions than does trying to guess when the 300-psi warning will appear.

The tank valve, made of chrome-plated brass, has a safety plug in the form of a metal wafer designed to release if tank pressure should become dangerously high. Valve plugs for a steel 72-cubic-foot tank blow out at roughly 3200 psi; those for an aluminum 80 blow out at around 3600 psi (again, these tanks are normally filled to 2500 and 3000 psi respectively). Blowouts can occur if the tank is accidentally overfilled by an air compressor that lacks an automatic switch to stop it at the proper pressure. They have also been known to occur when filled tanks are left lying around in the hot sun. When a safety plug blows, it disintegrates harmlessly, but the terrific noise, accompanied by the kicking and spinning of the tank on the ground, is impressive and momentarily frightening.

In deference to the tremendous potential energy contained in them, diving tanks should be carried with a firm grip on the valve or the cylinder itself, not by the straps or backpack assembly, which might slip. Tanks being transported by car should be secured and padded to prevent them from rolling and bumping against anything. While there is practically no danger that a dropped tank can rupture and explode, these precautions are important simply because tanks are heavy and if unsecured can damage people and other sensitive objects.

Where Diver Meets Tank

A scuba tank is attached to the diver by a frame or harness rigged with shoulder and waist straps. The entire assembly, minus the tank itself, is usually called a *backpack*. Many variations of the backpack are on the market. Some backpack frames are contoured to match roughly the humps and hollows of human anatomy; some frames are merely flat and may feel better on your back than an elaborately contoured one. Try on different backpacks for relative comfort. If you are like the princess in the fairy tale who felt the pea through thirteen mattresses, you may not find any backpack that satisfies you in the dive shop. But once you enter the water you will scarcely notice the pressure of the frame.

We prefer backpacks with a quick-release mechanism for removing and replacing the tank. You will appreciate this feature too, after you have once struggled with corroded hose clamps or tenacious wing nuts in the hot sun on a rocking boat while your buddies wait, having replaced tanks in their own backpacks in seconds. It is of course mandatory, in case of underwater emergency, that the buckles securing the backpack straps to you are free of corrosion and are of a type that releases quickly.

The Regulator

It is the function of the *diving regulator* to deliver the high-pressure air in the tank to the diver's lungs at the ambient, or surrounding, water pressure. The diving regulator, invented by Emile Gagnan and Jacques Cousteau in 1943 in France, is the keystone of the underwater life-support system. At first glance and use, the regulator may seem too simple and delivery of air to the lungs from the enormously pressurized reservoir in the tank too easy. How great is the chance that this small metallic contrivance, linking the diver to the air supply via a fragile-looking rubber hose, will malfunction or rupture under water? How well is the thing put together? How does it work?

All diving regulators now in use are known as *two-stage regulators*. They are ingenious devices, simple in design and function, but rugged in construction. Basically, two styles of the two-stage regulator exist, the single-hose and the older, almost obsolete double-hose style. (The twin hoses are cumbersome and relatively fragile, and the mechanism imparts a high breathing resistance. Double-hose regulators are not generally available today and will soon be found solely in the realm of antiques.) The two-stage regulator is designed to reduce the pressure of air delivered to the diver to a level that matches the pressure of the immediate environment. It works through an arrangement of valves whose opening and closing are controlled by powerful springs triggered by the small pressure changes created by breathing.

The flow of air through a modern regulator passes two pressure-reduction stages, with the greatest reduction occurring in the first stage. Both stages oper-

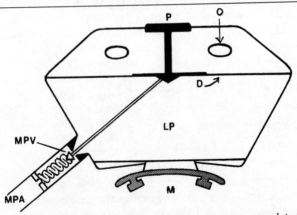

3.2. *Second-stage assembly of a single-hose, two-stage regulator:* M, *mouthpiece;* LP, *low-pressure chamber;* D, *diaphragm;* O, *opening to ambient pressure;* P, *manual purge button;* MPV, *medium-pressure air inlet valve;* MPA, *medium-pressure air from first stage.*

ate in tandem on demand as a diver inhales. In a single-hose regulator, the first stage receives high-pressure air from the tank and transmits medium-pressure air through rugged, synthetic-rubber tubing to the second stage, attached to the diver's mouthpiece (see Figure 3.2). The second stage incorporates a large flexible-rubber diaphragm whose center is reinforced by a lightweight metal disk. The diaphragm flexes during inhalation toward the mouthpiece, depressing a metal linkage to the second-stage valve and thus allowing medium-pressure air to enter the low-pressure (LP) chamber. After an inhalation, the diaphragm returns to its resting position and the valve closes.

Exhaled air passes through a grated opening covered on the outside by a flap of soft rubber. The rubber flexes freely outward to let air escape, but seals the opening in the return direction so that water cannot flow back into the LP chamber. The scuba mouthpiece is made of flexible rubber. In construction it is usually identical to the mouthpiece of a snorkel.

Some regulators have a manual adjustment in the second stage, allowing a diver to change the tension of the valve that admits air to the low-pressure chamber. The manual adjustment helps to eliminate the escape, or free flow, of air when the regulator is not in the mouth. In use, the airflow of your regulator should always be adjusted to allow for a minimum of effort in inhalation. If you notice any resistance to breathing, have your regulator tuned up at your dive shop.

Buoyancy Control

The control of buoyancy is one of the fine arts of diving. All modern instruction in scuba should include sessions on buoyancy control. This technique greatly conserves swimming energy, is important for underwater photographers and spearfishermen, and can be an aid in the performance of any underwater work. The experienced diver continually uses this technique to remain in control of forces that tend to make the diver rise or fall in the water. We recommend that all divers, including snorkelers, routinely wear a buoyancy-compensating device.

Buoyancy-Compensating Devices

The least expensive buoyancy-compensating device (BC) is a small vest donned over the head and secured around the waist by a strap and buckle. The vest features a small (typically 12-gram) replaceable cartridge containing pressurized carbon dioxide. By pulling a short rip cord, the diver trips a metal lever that pierces the base of the carbon dioxide cartridge; the

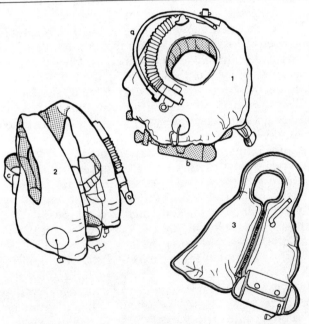

3.3. *Three popular styles of buoyancy compensators: Type 1 shows a mechanical, or auto-, inflator (a) combined with an auxiliary air bottle (b). Type 2 combines the functions of a BC and backpack. The tank is attached by means of the metal band (c) in the rear. Type 3 usually employs large carbon dioxide cylinders to provide emergency inflation.*

gas released inflates the vest. This sort of vest has long been touted as an essential safety device, but a diver who uses a small-volume vest should be aware that below 30 or 40 feet emergency use of the carbon dioxide system alone will have little buoyant effect. The amount of gas in the cylinder is too small to inflate the vest significantly against the pressure below these depths. We suggest that the small vests be relegated to minimal use in snorkeling only.

In addition to the carbon dioxide cartridge, vests and other types of BCs also incorporate a mouth inflator—a tube, usually with a snorkel-type mouthpiece, that permits the BC to be inflated orally. The mouth inflator can be used during a long surface swim to a dive site or on the way back to shore or boat. Thus the diver can accomplish the swim in easy stages, since resting with the BC inflated eliminates the need to tread water. To use the mouth inflator under water, the diver simply inhales, takes the regulator out of his mouth with his right hand, exhales into the inflator tube held in his left hand, and then puts the regulator back in his mouth. When a diver is wearing a full wetsuit on a fairly deep dive, say to 100 feet, the loss of buoyancy will require that at least two or three lungfuls of air be exhaled into the vest to compensate for compression and consequent loss of buoyancy of the wetsuit. On ascent, the deep diver must progressively purge the vest, for the amount of air it contained at 100 feet would expand greatly due to lessening pressure, causing the diver to ascend too rapidly.

The BCs suitable for scuba are the large-volume BCs, up to several times the capacity of the small vests available from several manufacturers in a variety of styles. In some large-volume BCs, the diminutive carbon dioxide cartridges of the small-volume vest have been replaced with larger ones or with a metal bottle of compressed air that divers can fill from their scuba tanks. During emergency use, enough air is contained in one of these bottles to inflate the BC effectively down to 200 feet (at greater depths the pressure is too great to allow significant inflation). Other styles of large-volume BCs include a "stabilization jacket" model with air pockets at the sides as well as in front and a design that fastens to the backpack and inflates to form a large inverted U behind the diver's shoulders and head. The latter type has received some criticism for its tendency to float an unconscious diver face down at the surface. Several of the newest buoyancy-compensator designs inflate by directly tapping the regulator's airflow at the first stage. We feel that this mechanical, or auto-, inflator is one of the best features of a modern BC. Compensators with this feature have become extremely popular and seem to be replacing the small, auxiliary air bottles, which must be hydrotested and visually inspected, and carbon dioxide cartridges, which can slowly leak and lose pressure.

The large BCs are made of stronger material than smaller ones, and all models feature a safety valve that automatically purges air above the full inflation pressure. An exhaust (air outlet) hose also incorporates a mouth inflator.

Tanks and Buoyancy Control

Although largely related to the relative compression of the wetsuit at specific depths, a diver's buoyancy is also affected by his tank. When filled, a 72-cubic-foot steel tank is about 5 pounds negatively buoyant (heavier than water) and will sink. When the tank is nearly empty at the end of a dive, it will be nearly neutrally buoyant (weightless in water). The change in buoyancy of a steel tank is usually negligible and is noticed only subliminally by a diver, but the same cannot be said for some of the aluminum tanks still in use. The relative lightness of these tanks poses no problem when the tank is full, but when nearly empty the aluminum tank is very positively buoyant, which in turn causes the swimmer to struggle to stay down. Thus, divers carrying such tanks must compensate by carrying extra weight, which is properly strapped to the tank rather than the belt. Putting extra weight on the belt results in severe orientation problems: swimming on one's side or back, maneuvering in caves or beneath overhangs, or achieving a good camera angle becomes extremely difficult.

By 1975, manufacturers began adding extra weight to aluminum tanks, so newer ones are no lighter than steel tanks but still just float when empty. The older, lightweight aluminum tanks are still seen in bargain sales of used equipment. Divers tempted to buy such tanks should be aware that they do have shortcomings, although with extra weight attached these tanks can perform adequately.

The "Unisuit"

The modern diver's dress has a role in both buoyancy control and body-heat conservation. While the relatively less expensive standard wetsuit, discussed in Chapter 1, is still used by most divers in cool to cold waters, another more advanced underwater garment is taking the fancy of divers who can afford it. This garment is technically known as the *variable-volume dry suit,* or *unisuit.* Unisuit is a trade name of the first manufacturer to offer this kind of suit to the amateur diver. Several companies now make near facsimiles, but in diving jargon unisuit is used for the whole genre.

Externally, the unisuit resembles a one-piece wetsuit. It is made of three-sixteenths-inch-thick or quarter-inch-thick foam neoprene and is lined with abrasion-resistant nylon inside and outside. Hood and boots are part of the one-piece construction; gloves or mittens are separate. Thermal underwear is worn under the unisuit. The suit is donned by means of a frontal zipper, which is the key technological element in the performance of the suit, for the zipper (unlike that in a conventional suit) is both waterproof and pressureproof.

The unisuit can be inflated—that is, air can be injected inside via a connection to the diver's regulator. Also, air within the suit can be purged through a second valve. By using these two valves well, divers can maintain their trim, or state of neutral buoyancy, at any depth. Because they are dry and essentially surrounded by a layer of air that can be maintained against compression, divers remain much warmer in unisuits than wetsuits. U.S. Navy and National Oceanic and Atmospheric Administration (NOAA) divers wearing unisuits in the Arctic and Antarctic have remained reasonably comfortable in the water under ice for up to 8 hours. And, because the wearer stays dry, not only under water but also above-surface, winter conditions are less troublesome than with conventional wetsuits.

Divers wearing unisuits in near-freezing water must take care to prevent the air inlet and exhaust valves from icing. Inflating and deflating the suit with a few short bursts of air rather than a long burst is recommended, as expanding air rushing into the suit automatically cools below its resting temperature. The most serious icing hazard involves the inlet valve freezing in the open position, causing overinflation of the suit.

Overinflation of a unisuit can initiate an uncontrolled ascent, called *blowup*, as expanding air in the suit forces the diver up at an accelerating rate. Once an unintentional ascent begins, it may be impossible to stop. Novice unisuit wearers have unwittingly induced blowup by inflating their suits while in a head-down position. Excess air moving into the foot area may make it impossible for them to recover a horizontal or upright orientation. Fins tend to pop off the inflated feet. As if tied upside down to a rising balloon, the diver will be carried helplessly to the surface.

The chief dangers of uncontrolled ascent are *decompression sickness*, or "the bends," and *air embolism*, in which lung tissue ruptures from being overexpanded and air bubbles enter the bloodstream, eventually lodging in the heart or brain and blocking circulation to those vital organs. (We will return to these topics in some detail in Chapter 4.) Occasionally, the exhaust valve of a unisuit will stick, preventing excess air from being eliminated in the normal manner. An emergency technique for releasing air from a unisuit and thereby avoiding blowup is to partially pull off one of the mittens, thus breaking the wrist seal so air can escape from between the mitten and the sleeve. To perform this maneuver efficiently, you must be upright in the water with your hand held overhead. Reach up under the mitten and loosen the wrist seal with your other hand. Be sure that the partially shed mitten is not pulled away by the escaping air.

Some professionals using unisuits also wear a BC. We agree with the emerging idea that a unisuit should be used for warmth only, not for buoyancy control. Keeping these functions separate and relying on a BC for buoyancy control virtually eliminates the problems of blowup and of sudden loss of air caused by failure of a zipper or seam, or by the accidental perforation of the unisuit. Such a sudden loss of air would result in negative buoyancy, rapid sinking, and chilling of the diver. The combination of a BC and a minimally inflated unisuit is optimum for cold-water diving.

Before venturing into cold water or polar waters, divers should become thoroughly familiar with the unisuit and practice exigent maneuvers under mild underwater conditions.

Important Accessories

Several extra items of equipment are usually worn or carried by divers. Some of these accessories are useful and important in all open-water diving; others are optional or become important in deep water or under special conditions, for example, night diving. The most essential accessory, we believe, is the *submersible pressure gauge*. Connected by a two-foot length of pressure-proof neoprene tubing to the first stage of the regulator, it continuously monitors the air pressure in the tank as air is used during a dive. It is almost incorrect to call this item an accessory, since most divers now consider it an integral part of the regulator. In use, the gauge hangs at the diver's side, providing a readout of tank pressure at a glance.

Depth gauges come in two basic types: oil-filled and capillary models. They normally attach to the diver's

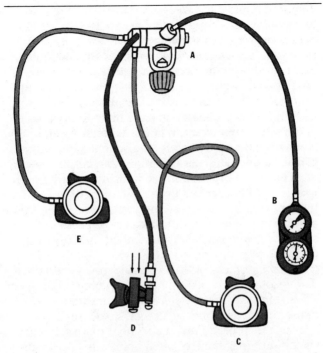

3.4. *An octopus rig, showing accessories incorporated into a modern two-stage regulator. Clockwise from top: A, first stage of regulator. B, gauge console including tank pressure gauge and depth gauge (a compass is sometimes also incorporated in the console). C, extra second stage for buddy breathing in an emergency (note long hose). D, auto inflator device to deliver tank air to BC. (Double arrow indicates attachment for hose to BC, which is not shown. Mouthpiece permits oral inflation of BC in lieu of using tank air.) E, standard second stage of regulator.*

wrist like an oversized watch. The *diving watch* itself is pressure-proof, typically to several hundred feet—deeper than any amateur diver can expect to penetrate. Another accessory is the so-called *octopus rig*, or *octopus regulator*, a safety system that permits more than one diver to breathe simultaneously from the same tank in an emergency. One or more extra second-stage units are attached via pressure tubing to a single first stage, and a submersible pressure gauge completes the rig. The entire assemblage with its dangling hoses and three or more attachments begins to resemble an octopus (see Figure 3.4), hence the name. Depth gauges, watches, and octopus rigs are now widely used and have become essential in deep diving and repetitive diving, subjects that we will take up in Chapter 8.

An *underwater compass* is a very useful item for pathfinding below. We will have more to say about underwater orientation in later chapters. As an option to wearing them separately, the submersible pressure gauge, depth gauge, and compass can be purchased as a combined unit in a single housing, called a *gauge console*. This is attached to the same length of pressure tubing extending from the regulator's first stage that otherwise would hold the submersible pressure gauge alone. A gauge console is illustrated in Figure 3.4, as part of an octopus rig.

A *diving knife* is often a valuable tool, especially if you encounter old fishing line or other entangling obstacles. In selecting a knife, pay special attention to the sheath and how securely it holds the knife. Knives are all pretty much alike, but there are several sheath designs, some of them poor. The knife is the item of diving equipment most frequently lost.

Most scuba divers also carry a *snorkel* as standard equipment. Most often the snorkel is used during a long surface swim to and from a dive site, or during a wait at the surface prior to rendezvous with one's dive partners. Using a snorkel at the surface conserves the air supply in the tank for use below.

A simple but important accessory is a *whistle*; the dime-store variety will do. Preferably it should be a loud one that can be fastened with a nylon cord to any convenient location on one's person, perhaps around the exhaust tube of the BC. We mention nylon cord since it will not rot in sea water as cotton or hemp cord will. A whistle, of course, is only useful at the surface—to get the attention of fellow divers or a boat operator from a distance.

A *diver's slate* allows you to communicate with dive partners below or to record information such as photographic exposure data. The slate is a small square of quickly erasable stiff, white plastic. The writing tool is a soft lead pencil attached by a rubber thong; a wax pencil or crayon also works. A slate allows you to be far more explicit and expressive than is possible using hand signals and pantomime. Most divers carry a slate that will fit into a pocket of their wetsuit or BC.

A variety of *underwater lights* and small flashing *strobe lights* are available for night scuba diving or snorkeling. A bright, steady light is a necessity; the strobe is primarily a safety device in case you become separated from other divers or a boat at the surface. Lights are often carried on fairly deep daytime dives as well, because artificial light makes it possible to distinguish warm colors—reds, orange, yellow—which are not naturally visible in deep water.

The last accessory we will mention here, and an important one, is the *diver's flag*—conventionally red with a white diagonal bar. Flags can be purchased or easily made of nylon cloth or plastic. A diver's flag mounted on your boat, or attached to a small inner tube or other float that can be anchored at your dive site with lightweight line and a small lead weight, warns boaters and fishermen that there are divers below.

Equipment Care

You should begin a cycle of care and maintenance for basic scuba gear before every day of diving. Begin by being attentive when loading your car or boat. Stow the regulator together with small fragile items—pressure gauge, depth gauge, compass, and perhaps your mask—in a safe spot where heavy tanks won't roll or settle on top of them. Don't let rubber or nylon materials come into contact with oil or gasoline, or you will find holes dissolved in your wetsuit, buoyancy compensator, and the like. The best approach is to use a bag for storing and transporting your gear and to make various spare parts, such as rubber "O" rings (valve seals) and perhaps a first-aid kit, a permanent part of the bag's contents.

When you have completed your dive, admired the

catch, stowed the treasure, and compared notes with your buddies on the boat or beach, you should turn your attention to the care of your equipment. Maintaining your gear in good condition is largely an exercise in keeping metallic components from corroding and rubber and fabric components from deteriorating physically and chemically. Be very careful to keep your gear away from sand if you are diving from a beach. It's a good idea to remove the regulator from the tank before you start for home. Also, clean salt from the little cap that seals over the screened first-stage opening by licking it with your tongue and then blowing it dry with a burst of air from the tank. Some divers, however, merely dry the protective cap with a towel or rag.

As soon as possible after an ocean dive, use a hose to rinse all your gear thoroughly in fresh water. Drape or hang each item over a rack or a strong clothesline to keep sand, dirt, and grass from getting where it doesn't belong. We recommend that you immerse small expensive items, such as cameras, gauges, and even regulators, in the ultra-clean warm water of the bathroom sink to eliminate all traces of salt. Warm water will hasten the dissolving of dried salt.

The regulator is the first piece of equipment to consider. Contrary to popular lore about the danger of the regulator corroding internally, depressing the purge button on the second stage as you rinse the regulator is permissible. Some divers do this routinely. If you do so, however, be sure to blow the regulator dry again by connecting it to the tank after each rinse.

You need not rinse your gear after a dive in a lake or freshwater stream unless there is sand or mud on it. However, follow practice or training dives in a chlorinated swimming pool by rinsing unless the tap water is as badly chlorinated. Chlorine in water causes the rubber and fabrics used in scuba equipment to deteriorate. Pay special attention to gear with orifices that allow little pockets of water to be retained inside, often out of sight. We have seen expensive buoyancy compensators used in scuba classes rotted through from the inside after only a few months. The damage was done by a few cc's of chlorinated water that had entered via the mouth inflator and remained in the bottom of the devices while they were hanging up between uses. BCs to be stored for more than a few days should be rinsed with fresh water, then drained, then blown up, and finally left to hang so that water can drain out through an open exhaust orifice.

All diving equipment should be allowed to dry before being put away for an extended period. However, pay attention to manufacturers' recommendations against prolonged exposure of rubber, plastic, or fabric to direct sunlight. This is especially important in the summer nearly anywhere, and at all times in the tropics, where ultraviolet rays, capable of making tough neoprene rubber and nylon as flaky and fragile as tissue paper, are most intense.

Store scuba gear in a cool, dry place. Excessive heat may damage wetsuits, buoyancy compensators, and the like, causing cracking or surface flaking. Freezing temperatures too may be extremely damaging to such equipment as regulators if they have not been carefully drained. Also, prolonged exposure to chemical fumes, as from gasoline and dry-cleaning products, will cause severe deterioration of neoprene and synthetic fabrics. To be safe, don't store your rubber diving goods in a closed-up garage or boathouse where gasoline fumes may be concentrated.

Simple maintenance and repair procedures for equipment quickly become routine. Metal zippers, swivels, snaps, and turnbuckles all require occasional lubrication with a silicone compound. This substance, which is harmless to neoprene, is available in pro dive shops. Tears or split seams in wetsuits are easily repaired with a neoprene cement, also obtainable from any diving store. Many divers cement rubber knee pads onto their suits to protect this area of frequent wear. If your suit has a nylon liner over the rubber inside and out, repairs or extra pads will require skilled work with needle and special thread. Consult a local diver's supplier for your particular needs.

Some divers may be tempted to perform more intricate repairs, for example on the regulator. Be warned, however: scuba repair work is highly complex, requiring special tools and spare parts, and without proper, long-term training, the average diver is well advised to seek professional help, well worth the usual low cost. For diving expeditions heading to remote regions, special courses and seminars in scuba repair and maintenance can be arranged through professional diving organizations and some equipment manufacturers.

A word or two is appropriate here concerning the purchase of used diving equipment, a brisk market for which operates in most parts of the country. Our advice is to be very cautious, especially if you are looking at used regulators, tanks, or BCs. A second-hand wetsuit may just make you cold, but problems with the other items can have more serious consequences. Take the gear you are thinking of buying to a pro dive shop. Have a tank visually inspected, a regulator thoroughly dissected, and a BC gone over for damage to inflation and exhaust features. Make an agreement with the seller that you will pay the inspection fee if the gear passes scrutiny. If it doesn't, he'll be the one that's out, not you when you're down at 100 feet.

Once you have obtained professional instruction and practiced with your equipment, becoming familiar with how it feels and functions, you are ready to explore under water nearly anywhere. Before moving on to the real thing—the experience of open-water diving—we now need to consider the most important equipment of all: the human body and how it functions in the underwater environment.

Chapter 4

The Human
Body Underwater

B ASIC DIVER TRAINING emphasizes protective and
defensive practices that relate to certain immutable and irrefutable natural laws. These laws and their
consequences are vitally important to divers, impos-
ing limits on human performance in the deep and
providing the rationale for many diving procedures
and techniques. Thus in this chapter we are digress-
ing from the narrative on equipment and technique to
describe the laws in question and the physiological
problems they pose to the submerged human body.

Much of what is covered in this chapter involves
certain risks that diving poses to health and safety.
The risks are real, and it is our philosophy that it's
best to approach them in a straightforward manner.
There seems to be a very recent trend in diving instruction to gloss over the potential medical problems
associated with diving, or to touch on them vaguely.
While we do not disagree with the industry's promo-
tional sloganeering for instruction and equipment
sales ("Diving is fun for everyone"), we feel it's important to add that diving is a serious way to have
fun. Still, set in a modern perspective, when one
follows the rules, scuba diving is safer than many
routine daily activities—driving a car, for example, or
crossing a city street in traffic. That said, we turn to
the fundamentals of pressure physics and their application to the snorkeler's and the scuba diver's world.

Matter that goes down is compressed; matter that comes up expands. Matter that becomes warm increases in volume or in the pressure it exerts; matter that becomes cool decreases in volume or pressure. These statements express basic natural laws that operate in all earthly environments and even in some extraterrestrial ones—wherever atmospheres and oceans exist and changes in temperature occur. If you remember your high school physics, you may recall learning the two natural rules that specifically govern the behavior of gases, such as the components of air, in the environment. These two fairly familiar rules are called Charles's Law and Boyle's Law, after the scientists who originally discovered them. Both laws are simple in concept and application.

Pressure Physics

Charles's Law describes the effect of temperature on a gas. A rise or fall in temperature will cause a corresponding change in the pressure or the volume of the gas. (The volume of a gas may be measured in cubic feet; pressure in pounds per square inch). For scuba divers, whose air supply resides in a tank of unchanging volume, in accordance with Charles's Law, only the pressure can change with temperature. A couple of practical examples will demonstrate the relevance of this law to scuba diving.

If you take a tank from a cool shady place and leave it in the hot sun for a while, the air pressure will rise up to several hundred pounds per square inch. If the tank is full, or perhaps a bit overfull, there is a chance that the safety plug on the valve will blow out as described in Chapter 3.

On the other hand, if you start with a warm tank of air at, say, 2500 psi, you will notice that shortly after jumping into cool water—if you breathe through the snorkel alone for a while—the monitoring gauge on the regulator's first stage will read perhaps 2300 psi. In accordance with Charles's Law, the cooling of your tank and the air supply results in a reduction in the pressure, and hence in the amount, of breathable

4.1. *The effect of Boyle's Law on a snorkeler. A descent of 33 feet (10 meters) compresses the chest cavity until the volume of the air-filled lungs is half that at the surface.*

air in the tank, even before you have taken a single breath from the regulator. Tanks usually are filled when cool for this reason. Descending from the surface through the *thermocline,* the boundary between the warm surface water and the cold bottom layer, will reduce the tank pressure by perhaps another 50 psi, again effectively reducing the air supply and curtailing bottom time.

Boyle's Law, which describes the effect of pressure on the volume of a gas, is of even more immediate and vital interest to a diver. This law states that the volume of a gas at any given temperature will vary inversely with a change in pressure. For example, a gas occupying 10 cubic feet at 15 psi would compress to 5 cubic feet at 30 psi. The descending snorkeler experiences the effect of Boyle's Law as middle-ear pain, as pressure squeezes the eardrum inward, and a gradually collapsing chest cavity.

Of practical concern to the underwater explorer is the effect of water pressure, or *hydrostatic pressure,* on gases distributed throughout the body. Purely liquid and solid materials react negligibly to pressure in the range experienced by the diver. However, gases dissolved in blood, spinal fluid, and the protoplasm of every cell are subject to compressional forces as inexorably, though more subtly, as air in the middle ear, facial sinuses, and lungs. The special studies relating to human hyperbaric physiology and diving medicine are largely concerned with the behavior of air and its component gases in the submerged human body.

Unlike a snorkeler, a scuba diver continues to breathe normally as he or she descends. The air supply in the tank is incompressible; its volume remains the same. The diver's lungs and chest, of course, are compressible. However, with each inhalation the regulator delivers air at the proper pressure to inflate the lungs against the collapsing force of the water.

4.2. *Pressure compensation in breathing during a scuba descent. As depth increases, greater air pressure is required to fill the lungs against the opposing pressure of the water. This means that the deeper the descent, the more quickly a given amount of compressed air in the tank will be used.*

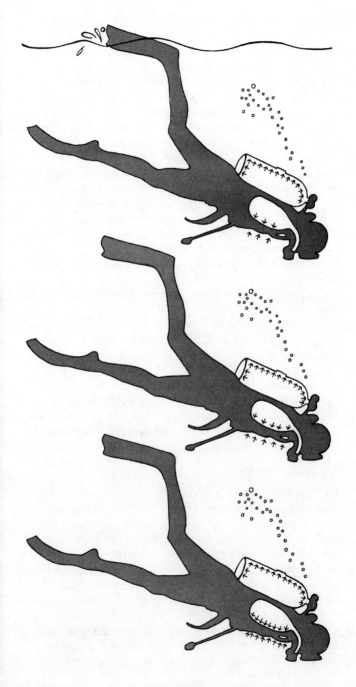

At the surface of the ocean, the pressure is said to be atmospheric, equaling 14.7 pounds per square inch, or 1 *atmosphere*. Under water, pressure increases by 1 atmosphere with each 33 feet of descent. At 33 feet, twice the surface pressure, or nearly 30 psi, is required to fill the lungs. It is somewhat startling to realize that a mere 33 feet of water exerts the same force as the entire atmosphere, which extends for more than 100 miles overhead. It follows that at 66 feet, air at three times the surface pressure is required for breathing; at 99 feet, four times, and so on. It is easy to see from this progression that pressure controls the rate at which divers use their air supply—at 33 feet, air is used twice as quickly as at the surface; at 66 feet, three times as quickly, and so on. According to Boyle's Law, a diver uses an extra lungful of air (as measured at the surface) with each breath taken under water to offset the pressure gained in every 33 feet of descent.

Keeping Healthy Underwater: An Introduction to Diving Medicine

Boyle's Law, which should become intuitive knowledge in every diver's mind, forms the basis for much of diving medicine. For the diver, Boyle's Law translates into the expansion or compression of air spaces in the body.

Ear and Sinus Problems

In Chapter 1, we mentioned the effect of pressure imbalances on the air-filled middle ear and sinus cavities in the head. If unrelieved, the common diver's malady known as ear squeeze may cause bleeding into the nose and throat from swollen membranes and ruptured capillaries. A person who manages to tolerate the pain of ear squeeze may even rupture his or her eardrums, allowing water to enter the middle ear. Such a rupture will relieve the pain, but can cause temporary hearing loss, dizziness, and loss of bodily orientation (vertigo). Cold water rushing into the middle ear tends to disrupt the delicate mechanism of equilibrium housed there, and a badly afflicted diver may have to watch his or her bubbles to distinguish up from down. The symptoms of severe vertigo, caused by cold water impacting the middle ear organs of balance are usually relieved rapidly as the intruding water warms up.

As bad as it sounds, a pressure-ruptured eardrum will usually repair itself naturally without resulting in a permanent hearing impairment. The torn tissue begins to knit together in a couple of days, but it should be protected from pressure changes for two months. If you suspect that you have suffered a ruptured eardrum, see a physician—if possible, one who is also a diver and will have had experience with this malady, will be aware of up-to-date treatments, and so on. The most severe consequences of a perforated eardrum, including permanent loss of hearing, result when infection develops in the middle ear. This can happen if the diver was in polluted water at the time of the injury. In such a case, a diver would be wise to consult a doctor as soon after sustaining the injury as possible, and perhaps be treated with an antibiotic prophylaxis at the doctor's discretion.

The facial sinuses are rigidly constructed spaces in the skull that are connected with the nasal passage by small ducts. Normally, air exchanges take place freely within the sinuses, and compensation for pressure change occurs automatically. However, allergy reactions or head colds can cause mucous membranes surrounding sinus ducts to swell and obstruct the flow of air. Diving with blocked sinuses is painful; frequently, bleeding results, becoming apparent later as blood trickles into the nose or back of the throat. Unlike the middle ear (which can be cleared by blowing against the pinched nose), sinuses are difficult to clear voluntarily, although blowing the nose hard may be temporarily effective. Also, as noted earlier, in case of a very mild cold or allergy, a nasal decongestant used just before a dive may help to prevent sinus pain under pressure. Diving with a bad cold or serious bout of allergy is never wise: it is always uncomfortable and may cause serious injury.

The Eustachian tubes and sinus ducts generally purge their respective air spaces readily and without the diver's conscious effort as he rises through lessening pressure. However, at depths of 10 feet or more the trapping of high-pressure air in sinuses or middle-ear spaces, known as *reverse block*, can cause pain, possible membrane injury, and bleeding on ascent. This condition is much less common than the difficulties associated with descent. Generally, cases of reverse block come with bad head colds or allergies, but are often associated with the use of decongestants before a dive. Sometimes the decongestant effect insidiously wears off while a diver is down; then, on ascent, the sinus passages are swollen closed and unable to purge the expanding air easily.

Like head colds, the pressure-induced maladies affecting the middle ear and sinuses are mild compared with the life-threatening effects that can occur in the chest if a diver is careless, panicky, or ignorant. Here, we are speaking of scuba divers only. The air in a snorkeler's lungs will never achieve the overpressure that causes delicate tissues to tear and air to escape and expand in the upper portions of the body and bloodstream.

Don't Hold Your Breath: Overpressure and the Lungs

Like the middle ear and facial sinuses, the air-filled lungs are subject to Boyle's Law. *Overpressurization* of the lungs is the cause of some of the most serious medical problems in diving, involving not only the lungs but secondarily the brain and heart as well. The whole problem can be avoided by observing the cardinal rule of divers: *Don't hold your breath.* In reality, conscious breath holding is sometimes practiced with great caution by advanced divers under highly special circumstances, for example by stationary underwater photographers to steady themselves or to avoid frightening their subject with a flood of bubbles. Nevertheless, the effects of Boyle's Law over a vertical range of only a few feet are a life and death matter for scuba divers. Ironically, the greatest precautions must be taken near the surface.

For a mental picture of the consequences of breath holding, imagine a scuba diver 66 feet down, blowing up a balloon. Assume that the balloon is highly flexible, and that the diver seals it after it contains 6 quarts of air. He then lets it go and we are able to watch it as it rises to the surface. From Boyle's Law, we can calculate that as the pressure surrounding the balloon lessens, the balloon will expand. At 33 feet it has expanded to 9 quarts, and at the surface its volume has reached 18 quarts.

Sixty-six feet down, an average diver fills his lungs with about 6 quarts of air; if he held his breath, this air, like the air in the balloon, would expand inexorably with ascent, reaching 9 quarts at a depth of 33 feet, and then doubling to 18 quarts in an ascent to the surface. Obviously, this condition would put an impossible strain on the lungs. Note that in an emergency ascent from 66 feet, a diver must exhale at least 12 quarts of air on the way to the surface. An important point to remember is that the closer one is to the surface, the greater is the percent change in pressure or volume upon ascent.

Physicians experienced in hyperbaric medicine agree that individuals vary considerably in their sensitivity to overpressure in the lungs, but there is no safe way to test one's tolerance. Deceptively mild ailments such as a chest cold or asthma may place even normally robust and experienced divers at risk. The danger comes from mucus plugs in some of the myriads of small air ducts, or bronchioles, within the lungs. A bronchiole may become blocked after inflation of the small portion of lung it serves. Overpressure of the trapped air and tissue rupture may occur without the person's awareness during a normal ascent. Persons whose lungs have been damaged or operated upon, or contain scar tissue due to heavy smoking, emphysema, or pneumonia should consult a knowledgeable physician before taking up scuba diving. Further, Dr. C. V. Brown, diving medicine consultant for *Skin Diver Magazine*, recommends that people with slight lung conditions, even though cleared for diving by a doctor, refrain from using scuba for ten days following recovery from a chest cold.

Occasionally, extreme environmental conditions are responsible for overpressure accidents. A case in point, involving ocean diving during the occurrence of large surface swells, took place in 1975. An experienced East German diver participating in an international-fisheries research project was ascending from 110 feet off Gloucester, Massachusetts, when he stopped to perform a maintenance task on a fixed tower several feet below the surface, which was very rough. Suddenly, a swell much larger than average, estimated at 15 feet from trough to crest, swept through the area. The depth of water over the diver must have dropped nearly instantaneously from perhaps 20 feet to 5 feet as the wave passed. The resulting drop in external pressure triggered an overpressurization of the lungs that later proved fatal. Needless to say, you should exercise great caution beneath a rough surface. At shallow depths you can often feel the pressure changing in the middle ear due to even moderate swells passing overhead. In this situation, ascend slowly; exhale fully with each breath, but avoid full inhalation.

Air in the lungs is contained in microscopic sacs called alveoli (singular, alveolus). An adult human's pair of lungs contains about 300 million alveoli packed in small clusters within a bulky webbing of blood vessels and air tubes. If laid out in a flat, contiguous sheet, the alveolar membranes that form the air-sac walls, thinner than the finest cellophane, would cover an astonishing 750 square feet. The alveoli receive and discharge air via tiny bronchioles, which lead to larger tubes in a vast network that ultimately connects with the trachea, or windpipe.

Surrounding the alveolar clusters and completely permeating the substance of the lungs are hundreds of miles of capillaries. Throughout the lungs, they lie a fractional hair-breadth away from the several quarts of air contained in the alveoli. Blood and air, separated by the scantiest membranes, easily, vitally exchange gases: oxygen diffuses inward; carbon dioxide outward.

An overpressure accident occurs when air pressure in the lungs substantially exceeds the pressure surrounding the body, causing alveolar membranes to burst. The rupturing of alveoli in an overpressure accident is usually undetected by a diver. In many cases, only small amounts of air burst through the membranes, often in numerous parts of the lungs. Escaping air in the form of frothy bubbles seeps through the folded membranous structure of the lungs, passes into the chest cavity, or enters the bloodstream through torn capillaries adjoining the burst alveoli. As the diver continues toward the surface and external pressure diminishes, the froth and bubbles begin to expand.

Complications Involving Lung Ruptures

Ruptures of lung tissue may lead to the development, either singly or in combination, of a variety of extremely serious medical conditions. *Mediastinal emphysema* is the result of expanding air moving outward, often seeping along the external surfaces of blood vessels and airways of the lung into the mediastinum, the middle chest cavity containing the heart, major blood vessels, and trachea. Symptoms include pain beneath the sternum, or breastbone, and shortness of breath due to a compression of the lungs and respiratory passages. In especially severe cases, the trapped air interferes with circulation due to distorting pressures on the vena cava, the vein that returns most of the body's blood to the heart.

Subcutaneous emphysema is caused by air in the mediastinum being forced upward beneath the skin of the neck. The skin becomes puffy and tight, and the sound of the victim's voice may change as the larynx is compressed. A large amount of air under the victim's skin causes a crackling sensation when the neck is touched or stretched by movement of the head.

Pneumothorax is the term used to describe the trapping of air between the lungs and the wall of the chest cavity. Expansion of this air may cause partial or total collapse of the lungs. The heart may shift in position toward the collapsing lung. Symptoms of pneumothorax include uncontrollable coughing and shortness of breath, chest pain, and uneven chest expansion during breathing.

The remaining pathway for escaping air, and the most dangerous one, is directly into the circulatory system via torn blood vessels lying immediately next to the burst alveoli. In this situation, air bubbles are sucked into the venous system of the lungs, pulled toward the heart, and pumped into the aorta, which distributes blood to arteries all over the body.

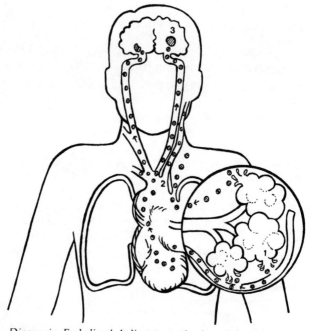

4.3. *Diagnosis: Embolism! A diagrammatic view of the sequence of events in a severe overpressure accident.* 1) *Tiny alveolar sacs in the lung burst, allowing minute air bubbles to escape into the surrounding area. Some of the air bubbles enter adjacent torn capillaries.* 2) *Air bubbles enter the general circulation and move through the carotid arteries of the neck toward the brain.* 3) *As ambient pressure lessens due to the affected diver's ascent, bubbles expand in blood vessels of the brain, restricting vital circulation.*

The presence of air in the circulatory system is known as *air embolism*. Untreated, it is frequently fatal.

Air bubbles reaching the heart may first enter the coronary arteries, interfering with the heart's own blood supply and triggering *myocardial infarction*, a sudden form of heart attack. Air that moves through the heart into the arterial system tends to move upward. The bubbles float in the blood and rise through major arteries toward the brain. There the bubbles lodge at random in capillaries and obstruct blood flow, bringing on varying combinations of dizziness, lack of coordination, convulsions, paralysis, and unconsciousness. Other warning signs of air embolism are air bubbles in the vessels of the eye, a noticeable pallor on the tongue, and areas of pallor or marbling on the skin. In a severe case, death may follow.

Treatment for the complications following lung rupture always extends beyond first aid. If oxygen is available, it should be administered immediately. It will be of direct aid to a person exhibiting shallow or labored breathing, and it will prolong tissue life in areas where bubbles are causing partial circulatory blockage. Victims of mediastinal emphysema, subcutaneous emphysema, and pneumothorax should be examined by a physician without delay. In pneumothorax, the trapped air is often removed by thoracentesis, the insertion of a hollow needle through the chest wall. This procedure must be performed prior to recompression in severe cases.

The only hope for saving a person suffering from air embolism is immediate treatment in a recompression chamber. Naturally, if a person's heart has stopped, or if he or she is not breathing, resuscitation should be attempted first of all. Administering pure oxygen on the way to the chamber is recommended by the experts. Also, the victim's feet should be kept elevated above his head. Keeping the victim in this position can prevent bubbles still in the general circulation from entering the brain, though this precaution will not dislodge bubbles that have already reached the cerebral arteries and capillaries.

The embolism patient must be recompressed in a

special chamber to the depth equivalent of 165 feet (6 atmospheres pressure). A recompression chamber is a small room, often cylindrical in shape and sometimes portable via truck or ship, reinforced with a sealing door and capable of sustaining high internal air pressures. Chambers are found in many coastal cities, large hospitals, naval and Coast Guard bases, private professional diving facilities, and major scuba resort centers. They are controlled and operated by trained persons certified by state, federal, or military agencies. The operator controls pressure in the air-filled chamber from the outside; however, some chambers are large enough to permit a physician inside to treat one or more patients. Recompression physically reduces the size of the air bubbles blocking blood vessels, and as the excess gas inside the bubbles dissolves, they gradually shrink further, eventually restoring effective circulation. Six atmospheres is the established recompression limit, since greater pressure has little effect in further reducing bubble size and also necessitates a longer period of treatment. Once the patient's circulation is restored, the chamber pressure is reduced very gradually, and after a period of several hours, according to standard decompression procedures, the victim is returned safely to atmospheric pressure. Normally, hospitalization for more care and observation follows.

It is the unanimous opinion of hyperbaric physicians that do-it-yourself treatment of embolism by returning the afflicted person under water, no matter how many helping hands are present, is tantamount to a death sentence for the victim. Together with first-aid in transit, all rescue efforts must be directed toward reaching a recompression chamber as soon as possible. All divers should know the location of the nearest chamber. Even more important is knowing telephone numbers of emergency rescue services in every diving area one visits. Where distances of more than a few miles separate the diving site and the nearest chamber, air evacuation of an overpressure-accident victim is generally best. Barring availability of Coast Guard or other helicopters, professional ambu-

lance services or local rescue squads are usually vastly
superior in driving and paramedical skills than one's
diving buddies.

People do survive overpressure accidents, provided their diving partners recognize the symptoms
immediately and then act promptly. Nonfatal cases
involve the risk of brain damage, heart damage, and
permanent paralysis if recompression therapy is delayed.

Decompression Sickness

Probably the most famous diving illness, sometimes
confused with air embolism, is *decompression sickness*,
or "the bends." Though generally less serious than
the complications of lung rupture, decompression
sickness has occasionally been fatal or severely crip-
pling. The ailment often brings excruciating pain.
Repetitive bouts of the bends, even if not severe,
tend to progressively damage many parts of the body,
including the brain, heart, bones, and nerves. Decompression sickness is the most common serious
malady afflicting scuba divers.

Basically, the condition results from gas, chiefly
nitrogen, entering the bodily tissues and bloodstream,
and coming out of solution as small bubbles in response to reduced pressure. The process is identical
to the bubbling or foaming that occurs when a bottle
of beer or carbonated soft drink is opened. The drink
was originally bottled under pressure, which caused
an excess of gas (carbon dioxide, in this case) to dissolve. Opening the drink suddenly releases the pressure, and the excess gas can no longer be held in solution.

As a scuba diver descends, the surrounding pressure causes a gradually increasing amount of air, predominantly nitrogen (78 percent) and oxygen (20
percent), to dissolve in the blood and other fluids
throughout his or her body. The air is thus steadily
being "bottled" under pressure. Oxygen is not a contributing factor in decompression sickness because the
excess is used in bodily functions before it can cause

any harm. Nitrogen, however, is not used, and if a diver breathes compressed air for long enough in the depths, the amount of nitrogen dissolved in his or her body will be considerable. If the diver then goes quickly to the surface, the gas will begin to fizz in the blood and elsewhere in the body.

Symptoms of decompression sickness vary according to the portions of the body in which bubbles form. Under the skin, bubbles produce merely a localized skin rash and itching or prickly sensations. Bubbles forming in the brain and spinal cord can be life-threatening after initially causing combinations of dizziness, deafness, numbness, speech defects, personality changes, loss of bowel and bladder control, paralysis, and unconsciousness. Another prominent symptom of nervous system involvement is loss of coordination, known as "the staggers" among old-time helmet divers, since victims have difficulty in walking.

Respiratory symptoms, sometimes called "the chokes," are less common and appear later than signs of neurological damage. In severe cases, however, bubbles may block the flow of blood within the lungs. Initially, respiratory involvement brings a burning sensation in the chest accompanying a deep inhalation. Coughing and rapid shallow breathing are also common symptoms.

By far the most common symptom of decompression sickness is pain in the arms and/or legs, mainly in the joints. This effect is the source of the descriptive term "bends," for the pain may be so great that an untreated victim is bent double in agony. Pain in the limbs nearly always appears in decompression sickness (in 92 to 95 percent of cases). In more than 66 percent of cases it is the only symptom.

The time for onset of symptoms varies. Between 50 and 85 percent of cases become apparent within the first hour after a dive; 95 percent are evident within three hours. However, medical records show a few cases in which symptoms were delayed as long as twenty-four hours. Neurological symptoms, if they appear, usually precede pain in the joints. The worst cases of decompression sickness resemble air embolism, but according to the NOAA *Diving Manual*, a lapse of fifteen minutes before signs of illness generally rules out embolism.

Any symptom of decompression sickness, even skin rash and itchiness (if other causes can be eliminated) is serious and demands prompt recompression therapy in a chamber. As in embolism cases, treatment acts to shrink the bubbles, restore circulation, and allow the body to eliminate excess gas during slow decompression. Returning a bent diver to the water for decompression is almost never a viable alternative. Even if symptoms appear minor, they may suddenly grow worse. Administering pure oxygen on the way to the treatment center provides some relief of pain and even accelerates the body's elimination of excess nitrogen.

Fortunately, simple and reliable methods exist for preventing decompression sickness, which, like other diving maladies, should fall into the realm of preventive medicine. First, it is theoretically impossible to develop the bends following dives that do not exceed 33 feet. After returning to the surface, the body should be able to tolerate all the excess nitrogen forced into solution at this depth. In reality, a few rare cases of decompression sickness, with delayed and mild symptoms, have been recorded after very long submergences at close to 33 feet. Average divers ascending from this depth after average dives will never be troubled by the bends. The excess nitrogen will not form bubbles, but will slowly return to the normal bodily concentration by elimination via the lungs.

On deeper dives, a sliding time scale of "non-decompression limits" exists, which the diver must observe if he or she wants to return directly to the surface at the end of a dive. The deeper one goes, the shorter the dive's duration must be. Table 1 shows the nondecompression limits associated with given depths.

Contrary to popular belief, it is possible to get the bends after a dive using a single 72-cubic-foot tank of air. The risk begins operating in dives reaching ap-

Table 1: Nondecompression Limits: Depths and Times

Depth (feet)	Single Dive Nondecompression Limit (minutes)
10	—
15	—
20	—
25	—
30	—
35	310
40	200
50	100
60	60
70	50
80	40
90	30
100	25
110	20
120	15
130	10
140	10
150	5
160	5
170	5
180	5
190	5

proximately 90 feet and becomes greater with increasing depth. Individuals who can "stretch" a tank of air by skip-breathing (missing a breath at frequent intervals), whether automatically or consciously, should be aware of this fact. Divers who do little to exert themselves—for example, still photographers and biologists observing fairly sedentary creatures—will use air slowly, prolonging bottom time and perhaps exceeding the limits shown. No matter what your breathing rate, the time spent at depth is the crucial factor governing the accumulation of excess nitrogen in your body. Novice divers should *always* observe the nondecompression limits given in Table 1.

After gaining experience and confidence in yourself and your diving partners, and after taking some special advanced diving courses, you too may decide to try some decompression diving, which opens up the deep range for visits longer than a few hurried minutes. Safe deep diving, in which the painful and sometimes permanent injuries of the bends are avoided, requires careful planning and record keeping. A diver who exceeds the nondecompression limit passes a point of no return—direct return to the surface, that is. This diver is making a decompression dive. To avoid the bends, he or she must ascend in stages, making intermediate stops and waiting to allow excess nitrogen to flow out of the body safely in the lighter pressure layers, and ascending to the surface only after the concentration returns to a level that can be tolerated there. Chapter 8 covers decompression diving in more detail.

Another way of exceeding nondecompression limits is to make repetitive but fairly shallow dives on the same day. For example, after returning from a 60-foot dive, you want to use another tank of air to explore close to the 50-foot level. The problem is that you have absorbed some excess nitrogen at 60 feet; if you went immediately back down to 50 feet with a fresh tank, you would soon exceed the nondecompression limit. But if you relax at the surface between dives for a specified amount of time, you will eliminate enough of your residual nitrogen to permit a second dive without decompression worries. In Chapter 8 we discuss repetitive diving more fully, describing the special equipment available for estimating the body's burden of nitrogen during a dive and citing examples and calculations from U.S. Navy repetitive- and decompression-diving tables.

A special and very serious situation regarding the bends pertains to pregnant women who dive. Studies done at Texas A and M University in 1977 and 1978 indicate that a mammalian fetus is considerably more susceptible to decompression sickness than an adult.[*]

---

[*]As reported in "Human fetus susceptible to bends," *Sea Grant Newsletter*, (University of Hawaii Sea Grant College Program, August 1978), p. 6.

The actual studies were done with pregnant sheep during simulated dives with pressurized air in hyperbaric chambers. After "surfacing" from the deepest simulated, nondecompression dive—100 feet for 25 minutes—sheep fetuses were stricken with such massive cases of the bends that they would have died without immediate treatment. The mothers showed no sign of the bends.

According to the Texas A and M researcher Clifford Simmag, sheep in general are more resistant to the bends than humans. Thus, pregnant women should interpret their depth and time limits conservatively. Until more is known about the specific sensitivity of the human fetus to pressure changes, we would recommend that women who are pregnant, or who suspect pregnancy, avoid scuba diving at all but the shallowest depths (less than 20 feet). Repetitive dives on the same day should also be ruled out. We also advise that you check with a diving physician for the latest information on this subject.

Drowning: Causes, Prevention, and Rescue

Drowning—filling of the lungs with water—completes the roster of dangerous diving mishaps. In fact, drowning is responsible for more scuba diving fatalities than any other condition. It results directly from the physical inability to hold the breath beyond a certain point. The victim who reaches this point gasps automatically. Water is drawn into the lungs, replacing air, and the victim passes out from insufficient oxygen (anoxia). Usually within five minutes, anoxia stops the heart, and the spontaneous breathing mechanism ceases to function at about the same time. With a few more minutes, permanent brain damage is likely, closely followed by death.

Drowning results from many diverse causes, all of which can be easily prevented or avoided with proper diver training and a knowledge of the underwater environment. Panic, exhaustion due to fighting currents

and surge, an unexpected exhausting of the air supply, an inability to cope with routine problems such
as a flooded mask—one or more of these factors are
commonly discovered to have preceded a drowning.
A person's respect for the risks involved in underwater exploration is always a major safety factor. U.S.
Navy professionals have a saying: "There are old divers and bold divers, but no old, bold divers."

Causes of Drowning

Research on diving accidents published by the National Association of Underwater Instructors (NAUI)
surprisingly reveals that a large proportion of diver
drownings occurs near the very end of the dive, after
the divers have surfaced safely and normally. Trouble
on the surface has its roots in the psychology of diving. Surfacing can give false confidence. Panic can
begin suddenly and totally unexpectedly with a breaking wave, a lost mask, a flooded snorkel, a strong current, or strong surge. The first impulse is to struggle,
an ancient holdover in human behavior that has become inappropriate in the age of inner and outer
space.

Despite training, many divers who find themselves at the surface choking on water or fighting
against a current to reach boat or beach forget to inflate their BCs. Drowned divers most often still have
their weight belts on. Typically in diving, as little time
as possible is spent at the surface. The urge is to
get below fast at the start and to get out fast at the
end—away from the toss and turbulence. Perhaps
diver training should place more emphasis on surface
training, permitting divers to get used to choppy
water or to relax in a current while a boat maneuvers
to pick them up. Some may even learn to enjoy the
rough and tumble rhythms of the sea.

In certain circumstances, even advanced divers
face the threat of drowning. Among the most serious
of these are nitrogen narcosis, carbon monoxide
poisoning, and entanglement in lines, cables, or nets.

Nitrogen narcosis, also called "the narcs," "the
drunks," or "rapture of the deep," usually begins at

depths a little greater than 100 feet. Early symptoms are lightheadedness and a mild high, virtually identical to the feeling one experiences after consuming a modest amount of alcohol. Even at its onset, however, rapture of the deep has been shown to impair judgment and lengthen reaction time in an emergency. With increasing depth, the diver commonly becomes mellow, giddy, or euphoric. According to some divers, feelings of grandeur can develop between 150 and 200 feet. A diver tends to feel very sure of himself; he is the ruler of all he surveys. Below 200 feet derangement can become severe. A helmet diver at 270 feet is on record as attempting to unbolt his helmet's faceplate, the man having whimsically decided to escape from his suit. Most professional divers and diving doctors agree that at 250 feet the average diver is disabled to an extent that jeopardizes his own safety. The chance of drowning quite happily, but nonetheless permanently, is a fact of life at this depth. (See Chapter 8 for more about nitrogen narcosis during deep dives.)

A few individuals never develop the euphoria and sense of well-being associated with nitrogen narcosis. Instead, below 100 feet they become increasingly nervous, frightened, or depressed, conditions that tend to be self-correcting as soon as the diver ascends to lesser depths. This inverse rapture seems to occur in dark, cold waters rather than the clear, warm conditions of the tropics. Interestingly, one of us (JLC) has experienced these depressing symptoms at 125 feet, amid a ghostly school of silver hake on a dark bottom off Boston, where lights are often necessary to see clearly at high noon. In Hawaii, however, at comparable depths, the feelings of gloom and doom were replaced by the onset of true rapture. Fortunately, nitrogen narcosis yields to the simplest remedy. Recovery is usually immediate upon returning to shallower depths.

Commercial divers and divers in the U.S. Navy, NOAA, and other organizations safely perform deep-water work by substituting the less intoxicating gas helium for nitrogen. Oxygen also poses a problem in deep diving. Ironically, oxygen at high pressure can be poisonous, and at great depths a breathable atmosphere must contain less oxygen than is present in normal air. Using air mixed in nonconventional proportions is called *mixed-gas diving*. It is usually beyond the financial means of amateur divers, and requires precise scientific understanding and exhaustive training. We leave it to the professionals.

Carbon monoxide poisoning is a rare but insidious problem in scuba diving. Usually, it is associated with the use of small, amateur-operated compressors to fill scuba tanks. For example, with a gasoline-powered compressor, exhaust fumes can be drawn into the intake hose unless one is careful to place the hose as far away from the compressor as possible—preferably, directly upwind. Even with an electrically driven compressor, at high operating temperatures some types of lubricating oils may burn partially or flash, producing carbon monoxide. Only special heat-resistant oils should be used on compressors, and older compressors should be inspected to guard against overheating. In commercial, certified air stations, intakes are on the roof or in other locations to ensure that only the purest air available is delivered to customers' scuba tanks. At times, in certain big cities, the air may not be exactly fresh, but a diver breathing city air is no worse off than a person on the street, perhaps jogging, bicycling, or running to catch a bus. We recommend having tanks filled professionally. A person who fills scuba tanks for himself or others should have some formal training in this diving support activity. Needless to say, all amateur airfills should be accomplished out in the open, not in garages or next to idling automobiles.

Carbon monoxide acts to displace oxygen in the bloodstream. Hemoglobin, the special substance in the blood that normally carries most of the oxygen, will preferentially accumulate carbon monoxide in place of oxygen. The affinity of hemoglobin for carbon monoxide is two hundred to three hundred times stronger than its affinity for oxygen. Thus, a very small amount of carbon monoxide in respired air can be dangerous. A few hundredths of 1 percent in the air will build up to startling levels in the body and cause collapse within an hour. When 30 percent of the blood's hemoglobin has combined with carbon monoxide (possible when a mere .07 percent of the air supply is carbon monoxide), unconsciousness ensues and the victim may die.

Early warning symptoms of carbon monoxide poisoning are most commonly a headache (a sensation of having a tight band around the head), feelings of dizziness, drowsiness, weakness, and nausea. In some cases, unconsciousness occurs before such noticeable symptoms are experienced. Onlookers can identify a case of carbon monoxide poisoning by the unusual color—described as cherry red—of the lips, tongue, and other parts of the body where blood is close to the surface. This effect is due to the abnormally brilliant red color of blood containing carboxyhemoglobin. First aid consists of exposing the victim to fresh air. Administering pure oxygen is even better. As soon as possible, the person should be examined by a physician for possible complications. In extreme cases transfusion may be needed.

One other cause of drowning among experienced divers as well as novices is entanglement by ropy obstacles in the depths. This hazard is often prevalent around wrecks and dumping grounds, where a careless diver may run afoul of tangled cables and wire. On rare occasions certain kinds of kelp may snag a diver. Concentrations of crab and lobster traps should signal caution. Their buoy lines to the surface form ignominious but sometimes deadly snares. Divers in such environs should carry sharp knives. The possibility of becoming entangled underwater presents a powerful supporting argument for diving with one or more partners and remaining with them during the dive. We will have more to say about such hazards and precautions against them.

Rescue and Resuscitation

Immediate efforts to resuscitate a drowned person

(restore heartbeat and breathing) are essential. A rescuer should begin mouth-to-mouth rescue breathing in the water as soon as the victim is brought to the surface. After inflating both his own and the victim's buoyancy compensators, the rescuer can perform rescue breathing, with effort, even in deep water while moving toward shore or waiting to be picked up by a boat. Water-safety experts estimate that many drowned persons have been lost merely because resuscitation was delayed until they were brought ashore. Thirty seconds could be the margin between life and death.

Rescue breathing is easy to learn, and should be practiced by all divers. The important points are these:

1. Tilt the victim's head back to open the airway to the lungs.
2. Clear the victim's mouth and throat of any obvious foreign matter (occasionally solid vomited material is pulled into the trachea).
3. Pinch the victim's nose closed.
4. Blow into the victim as hard as you can; watch for chest inflation and then deflation when you remove your mouth. Repeat twelve to fifteen times per minute for adults, twenty to twenty-five per minute for children.

Upon reaching the beach or boat, the victim first should be checked for a pulse. If the heart has stopped it may be necessary to try external cardiac massage, although rescue breathing alone may stimulate the heart to resume beating on its own. External cardiac massage consists of depressing the victim's breastbone, or sternum, two inches with a quick, smooth motion followed by release. One push per second is necessary to give a pulse close to 60. Considerable force is needed to depress the sternum, but too much pressure may damage the liver and lungs or break ribs. Ideally, cardiac and respiratory resuscitation is performed simultaneously by two or more rescuers. With heroic effort, one person can manage both operations, following each lungful of air delivered mouth-to-mouth with four or five depressions of the chest. These efforts should be continued until breathing begins or the victim is declared dead by a doctor. Rescuers should never leave a non-breathing victim to seek help. Resuscitative measures lasting nearly an hour have occasionally proved successful. To achieve competence in external cardiac massage and rescue breathing, now known collectively as *cardiopulmonary resuscitation,* or CPR, divers can take a short course in the subject offered by the Red Cross. An alternative, or perhaps a refresher for some, might take the form of a hands-on demonstration of CPR by a physician or paramedic at the next meeting of your dive club. Water rescue courses and CPR training should be high on the list of extracurricular activities of anyone who dives frequently.

In certain baffling cases of drowning in cold water, the victims have survived without such complications as brain damage after submersions of up to a half hour. The theory that has emerged to explain these cases is that the victims' bodies and, most importantly, the brains, had cooled to the point of dramatically reducing the need for oxygen. Long after fatal anoxia should have set in, the cooled vital tissues were still alive, able to function on the small amount of oxygen left in the blood. These fortunate victims, however, were not scuba divers wearing insulating suits that served to keep the body's temperature at its normal level. The drowning of an insulated person in cold water will typically prove fatal in a very few minutes.

Eating, Drinking, and Smoking

A lot of divers undoubtedly remember being ordered as kids not to go into the water for an hour after eating. We were convinced that if we broke the cardinal rule we were sure to suffer the unspeakable fate of "stomach cramps" and perhaps drowning too. The whole gruesome course of events was never fully explained. For some of us this meant an agonizing wait on the sand, sometimes after nothing more than an unguarded munch on a cookie or handful of peanuts. Unflatteringly for our parents, this old wives' tale once was totally accepted as truth nationwide.

The truth is, the one-hour rule is totally unfounded in fact. A diver who overeats just before going under water may suffer a very uncomfortable volume of stomach gas (especially upon surfacing) and a horrible case of indigestion, but not true stomach cramps. Theoretically, stomach cramps could occur if one went naked for a while in Antarctic waters, but fatal hypothermia would probably ensue first.

Sensible eating before diving consists of a nutritious meal of average volume consumed about an hour or two before the diver enters the water. Drinking a moderate amount of fluids, preferably not a diuretic (caffeine-containing) type, is also good. Diuretic drinks promote the loss of water in urine and sweat, not desirable, since dry, pressurized air in a scuba tank and the small amounts of sea water invariably swallowed by the diver also tend to cause dehydration. A thermos or canteen of water or fruit juice is as much appreciated after as before the dive.

Alcohol in any form or concentration should be left for the end of the diving day. The effects of an alcoholic drink, even a single beer, can be greatly magnified under pressure. Anything that makes a diver high or, conversely, sluggish and dulled is dangerous, since one's reaction time under water can be a matter of life or death.

Aside from its effects on general health, smoking is specifically known to increase the risk of embolism in divers. This increase is due to the accumulations of tar and mucus in the small air passages within a smoker's lungs. The special case of marijuana smoking by divers has been studied by medical researchers at the University of Hawaii, prompted by reports in *Skin Diver* magazine that some divers feel colder under water after smoking pot. Their studies, published in 1976, indicate that users of marijuana experience a higher than normal rate of heat loss in water. The scientists suggested that in extreme conditions the use of marijuana just before a dive could lead to a rapid onset of hypothermia in some individuals. The studies were carried out in cold air as well as water. The volunteers were all frequent pot users, but were screened so that biased opinion did not skew the results of the experiment. Those tested did not know what the researchers were measuring, and control tests were conducted after periods of no smoking.

Prerequisites for Safety

Safety in diving, as in any adventurous activity, begins with a state of mind. The awareness of one's personal limits, and the reliability and state of repair of one's equipment, as well as the ability to identify risky situations before one becomes a captive of them are examples of *knowledge*. This is the first of two essential principles for a long and happy career as an underwater explorer, amateur or professional. The second principle is *practice*. The only way to be sure that you will not panic, choke and drown, or embolize in an emergency which might be as simple as losing your mask or weight belt, is to go through the motions of saving yourself before the situation arises. The precautions and first-aid skills that make up the greater content of diving medicine should be practiced in a diving course held in a quiet place conducive to learning. Later these techniques will have to be adapted and applied to the extremely variable environments encountered on different dives. Diving is fun, exciting, challenging, and extremely rewarding. The underwater world is majestic, peaceful, and beautiful, but, like any wilderness, it can also be unforgiving.

Chapter 5

Open Water

F OR MOST DIVERS and might-have-been divers, the first open-water plunge in full scuba gear is an unforgettable experience. This dive is probably the most critical phase in the whole learning process. Unfortunately, bad experiences on the first time out of the pool are common and are related to the high dropout rate of scuba students at this point in their training.

By the time you are ready to assimilate the material in this chapter and compare its precepts and descriptions with your own experience, you will have become familiar with basic scuba gear and its use in an introductory diving course. The instructor will have gone into aspects of hyperbaric physiology and underwater safety. You will be in pretty good physical shape and will have practiced the techniques and simple emergency measures outlined in Chapter 2, such as clearing your mask; buddy breathing; removing and replacing your weight belt, regulator, and tank on the bottom of the pool; and perhaps an emergency ascent from the deep end, a few feet below the diving board. In this chapter, we will cover these basic skills as they would be performed in open water. But assume, for now, that you are ready for your initial open-water checkout. Arriving to meet the instructor and the rest of the class early in the morning at the coastal site, you may be embarrassingly nervous. Although some of them may be hiding it well, most of your classmates are undoubtedly feeling the same way.

On a more positive note, a visitor to the underwater wilderness should be prepared to experience sights, sounds, and modes of travel no backpacker ever dreamed of. Often a diver will move through terrain that recalls a mysterious, fog-shrouded landscape. The strangeness and wonder of exploring the depths are conveyed in part by the unique bodily sensations divers feel. Everything happens in slow motion. Most beginning divers recall classical dreams of flying without support or encumbrance, and feel as if these fantasies were being realized. They find that they are virtually weightless and can stand on one finger on the bottom of the sea.

In time, the state of nervousness so common before those first few dives will evolve into a positive attitude embodying careful but relaxed preparation and a rational respect for the environment you are about to enter. Perhaps the first principle for worry-free diving is to take your time getting ready. Talk through your plans for the dive with your buddies before donning any equipment. After you have carried your gear to the beach or jumping-off place, rest for at least a minute or two until you are breathing normally again. Entering the water already winded and fatigued is a bad way to start.

The Checkout Dive

It is usually a good idea to get dressed as close to your entry point as possible. Put on your gear at your own pace, making sure that you zip all the zippers, snap all the snaps, turn all the turnbuckles. Keep your larger buckles and fasteners clear of one another.

Be sure that your regulator is securely mated to the tank valve, and that the valve is turned on. Putting on your tank, you are well advised to do it the easiest way. Have someone assist you by holding the tank with its backpack at shoulder level as you slip your arms through the straps. Your assistant can still support most of the tank's weight as you secure and snug the straps. If you have to don a tank by yourself on dry land, often on rocks with precarious footing, there are hard ways and an easy way. Have your instructor demonstrate the easy way—the over-the-head method that allows you to remain perfectly centered and balanced. After practice you will be able to toss your tank on your back in seconds. We apologize for not explaining the method here, but it would take a page of complicated prose and is nearly impossible to illustrate on paper.

Carefully secure your knife, gauges, compass, and other accessories. Everyone has his or her own style and order of dressing for a dive. Just don't hurry to keep up with others; haste could result in lost equipment or the slipping of a strap under water. When you are ready, make sure that your weight belt and its buckle are clear of everything else around your middle, in particular, the waist strap and buckle of the backpack.

Many student divers newly out of the pool find that the familiar fussing with the gear absorbs their nervousness, and that, with the instructor in the water, they are able to function as usual. However, if you are still a bit apprehensive after entering the water, don't try to hide your feelings. Tell the instructor or your buddy, and, while you are close to shore, try to relax, floating with your BC inflated. Naturally, we are assuming that your first few encounters with the underwater wilderness will occur in fairly quiet water with decent visibility, not along some exposed rocky coast with difficult access on a day when six-foot swells are lifting gravel off the bottom.

If your nervousness remains intractable, even after a few minutes in the shallows (this is extremely rare), try being a surface observer for a while. Usually, the instructor will work with one or two students at a time in the first open-water dive, and the dive will be no deeper than 20 or 30 feet. Give your place to the next person in line and follow the divers out on the surface. After watching them explore the bottom below you, their streamers of bubbles rising, shimmering, and expanding in the soft light, you may feel tempted, curious, and angry enough at your own timidity to brave the mysteries of the deep, not really very deep here at all.

During your open-water checkout, the instructor will probably signal you to start a short round of buddy breathing. Typically, he will confront you and dramatically toss his second stage over his shoulder, perhaps making exaggerated hand signals to symbolize loss of air. Since you've already practiced this exercise in the pool, it shouldn't be any different in the ocean, or wherever, 30 feet down. Let's go over the procedure.

Buddy Breathing: How It's Done

Step 1. Remember, since the instructor is in the role of the person needing air, you are in control of the regulator.

Step 2. You inhale, remove the second stage from your mouth, and guide it to the instructor's mouth. Your hand stays on the second stage, since you are in control of this simulated emergency. (A fine point: keeping the mouthpiece turned down will help keep water out of the second stage, though some flooding is inevitable.) Meanwhile, you slowly begin to exhale the last breath you took.

Step 3. The recipient of your air must clear the water from the mouthpiece. This can be done with a forcible exhalation, but if one has no air left to exhale, it can be done just as quickly by punching the purge button located on the front of the second-stage unit (see Figure 3.2), first placing the tongue in the opening of the mouthpiece, so that the water is forced outward, not back into the mouth. This opens the valve to the medium-pressure air in the regulator's hose and sends a blast of air through the second stage, blowing water out the exhaust openings.

Step 4. The standard procedure is for each person sharing the regulator to inhale, exhale, then inhale again before passing the second stage back to the buddy. Your recipient, therefore, releases the breathing unit after his second inhalation. Your hand should still be holding the second stage; his should let go as you return the unit to your mouth. Meanwhile, your buddy begins his slow exhalation as you take the prescribed one and a half breaths before the cycle is repeated.

The Anatomy of a Dive

At this point we will assume you have completed your basic scuba certification, and that you and your buddy or buddies are ready to dive in open water without the presence of an instructor. In our description of a typical open-water dive, we will skip over the fine points of entering, since these differ in shore- and boat-based diving; we will describe each type of entry in Chapters 6 and 7 respectively. Once the diver is in the water, a typical open-water dive consists of four separate phases: snorkeling out to the site, the descent, exploring the bottom, and surfacing. What follows is a description of each phase in turn.

Snorkeling Out

Divers snorkel out from shore to a planned dive site to avoid wasting time in an underwater search and consuming air from the tank before they reach the area of interest. Snorkeling out is often the most fatiguing part of a dive. Traveling along the surface, especially if there is much turbulence, is far less efficient and more energy-consuming than swimming below. The bulky gear, with a great deal of fluid drag, resists being moved through choppy water. Some kinds of buoyancy compensators present a wide front to the water when inflated. Inflation in these models should be adjusted to minimize swimming resistance. In choppy conditions, try swimming on your back for a change of pace, thus placing the tank below the zone of impact of the little breaking waves. If you are carrying a spear, keep it aimed in the direction of travel. One of us often carries a large mesh bag containing small plastic containers for storing aquarium specimens. Bunching the bag as tightly as possible around its contents and trailing the package just behind the buttocks seems to conserve energy on a long surface swim. A large camera case and strobe create a very considerable drag. There is little one can do about this except to hope the pictures will be worth the effort.

If necessary, stop and relax during the swim, but be wary of a surface current that could carry you away from the projected path of your swim. As long as you can see the bottom, you can observe and correct any drift due to a slight current. If you lose sight of the bottom while you are snorkeling out, you will have to rely solely on shore reference points to check for drift, not as precise a technique as hovering motionless and watching the bottom.

All divers, and especially beginners, should be cautious in the presence of currents. Currents due to tides can change drastically in direction and strength within a few minutes. Often, a given current at the surface will be weaker at the bottom and, in an emergency, a submerged diver may be able to use rocks or other handholds to pull himself against a strong flow of water. We will return to the subject of currents in Chapter 6. For now, suffice it to say that they can be an aid to diving and a lot of fun to play in; however, they can also sweep divers offshore and drown those who are unprepared.

The Descent

Once you arrive over the intended diving location, you rendezvous with your buddy and go over your equipment (check to see that your weight belt and other straps are secure, your tank valve is on, and your regulator is functioning normally). Some instructors recommend opening the tank valve all the way and then reversing it one-half turn so that the valve turns freely in both directions. Later, below the surface, if something is disrupting your air supply, your buddy can immediately ascertain from the free play of the valve that air is being supplied to the first stage.

5.1. *Diver's view of a neutrally buoyant, properly weighted partner at the surface. This diver has just inhaled a normal breath. With an exhalation, he will slowly sink.*

Disturbingly, in an underwater emergency one can become befuddled to the point of confusing the direction of a valve's opening and closing.

Usually, the equipment check only takes a few seconds. Next, you and your buddy exchange your final verbal communications—changes in the dive plan, and so on—and you place the regulator mouthpiece in your mouth, secure your snorkel, and, remaining upright in the water, begin to purge your BC. Properly weighted, you will sink very slowly until your eyes are at the surface as the BC becomes exhausted. At this point, a full exhalation should get you started below the surface. If you seem to be sinking too rapidly, leave some air in the vest as your head clears the surface. If you seem too buoyant, with your head remaining well above the surface after the BC has deflated, try removing any trapped air by sucking gently on the mouth inflator. Lastly, exhale deeply into the regulator; this should get you started downward. If you are still too buoyant, you will have to start with a surface dive and kick your way down until compression of the wetsuit renders you trim. In most advanced diving circles, having to muscle yourself below the surface is taken as a lack of finesse. You risk gaining a reputation as an old-time aquatic gorilla. Also, in struggling to descend, you may have difficulty clearing your ears.

We find that when visibility is good, a slow passive free fall through fluid space is one of the finer pleasures of diving. You drop gently down along a canyon wall that is sprouting exotic life forms, dazzled by the riotous colors showing in the beam of an underwater light. Or you descend toward a distant bottom of sand channels and patch reefs, the coral heads and tiny fish in spiraling clouds growing larger as you drift down among them.

Descending slowly and at ease allows you to clear your ears in stages, preventing the sensation of pressure from building into pain. If you are wearing a wetsuit, you will find yourself falling faster the deeper you go due to the suit's compression and loss of buoyancy. Of course, you can slow your descent by making upward-swimming motions with your fins. This is every new diver's natural tendency, but the buoyancy compensator will do the job effortlessly. You can make yourself as weightless as an astronaut, take a leisurely look around your landing zone, and then, emitting a tiny burst of exhaust, you can touch down more lightly than any NASA engineer's dream of planetfall.

In conditions of relatively poor visibility, an open-water descent is not as much fun. Often along many temperate coasts, divers in as little as 20 feet of water will be unable to see bottom from the surface. This is also true for a majority of lakes in the United States and Canada. In descents of 40 feet or more outside of clear oceanic (chiefly tropical) waters, divers will often temporarily be out of sight of both surface and bottom. Passing through this "blind" midwater zone of variable depth, which we call the *nether layer*, is not especialy pleasurable to anyone. To some divers it may even be a little frightening.

One usually experiences the nether layer as empty and silent space, tinged a monotonous greenish gray. It seems devoid of life; almost never does one encounter a fish here. Normal environmental referents are lacking. If you are descending slowly, perhaps nursing your ears, you may not even feel yourself moving in the water. Only your bubbles will remind you which way is up, although often the view appears brighter toward the surface. If you are descending along an anchor line from your boat, this too provides a directional cue, but for a time the line has no beginning or end; it trails into obscurity in both directions. If your buddy is not in sight, either above or below you, the nether layer can be the loneliest place on earth.

Depending on the season and locality of your dive, you may pass through zones of differing temperature as you descend. For most divers in the temperate zone, water will be colder in the depths, and summer divers in many northern coastal areas and lakes will meet, with a shiver, the often sharply defined thermocline between warm surface water and frigid deeper water. The thermocline separates a relatively warm and light surface layer from denser and deeper water whose temperature remains about what it was during the past winter. The thermocline may lie at any depth between about 5 and 50 feet. It only reaches the deeper end of the range toward the end of the summer.

Often, visibility is considerably better below the thermocline than above. The warmer, brighter surface water promotes a more luxuriant growth of plankton than can be sustained in the dim frigid depths. Occasionally divers will discover that the sea exhibits an even more complex pattern of layering, especially in the proximity of rivers and offshore currents. Diving in late spring off the North Carolina Outer Banks, near Cape Lookout, we discovered a distinct triple-layered system. We were over a shipwreck in 55 feet of water about 4 miles from shore, and the surface was warm and relatively clear. These conditions prevailed until we had gone down about 30 feet; at that point we suddenly entered a strikingly cooler and very turbid layer. After the surface water, it felt almost cold and, with arms fully extended, we could barely see beyond our hands. Just as suddenly, we passed downward out of the chilly turbid zone into dimly lit but very clear warm water about 10 feet above a sandy bottom. We noticed that our passage into the clear bottom layer left blurry, streaky, swirling eddies, suggesting the mixing of water masses having different salinities.

We later collected samples of water from all three layers and confirmed our expectations, and those of oceanographers at nearby Duke University Marine Laboratory, that the strange, cool, turbid layer consisted of distinctly brackish water sandwiched between two marine layers. Judging from its cooler temperature and dense load of suspended sediment, we deduced that the middle layer probably derived from a strong local estuarine discharge after heavy rains; it apparently remained stable for a time and undercut the warm (hence lighter) nearshore ocean water. The densest layer along the bottom most likely came from a shoreward drift of clear and very salty (hence heavy) Gulf Stream water.

Generally, on blind descents through the nether layer, the approach to the bottom brings mysterious, other-worldly feelings. Trying to visually pierce the murk below, one is not quite sure what to expect to see down there. The feeling is a kind of monotonous anxiety, like that felt by a passenger peering through the window of a descending fogbound plane. At last one sees shadowy patterns and forms; then, usually quickly, the seascape reveals itself and the diver settles on firm ground, perhaps with a slight feeling of relief.

Diving in the proximity of surf or beneath an

ocean swell, a diver will encounter *surge*, a rhythmic, back-and-forth movement of the water that sometimes reaches as deep as 50 or 60 feet. If you descend in surge, you will tend to move in its influence, as if dangling from a swinging pendulum. You may not notice this motion in midwater; you may imagine your downward progress as essentially a straight line. But as you approach or hover above the bottom, you will have the disconcerting impression that the rocks, sand, seaweed, and the rest of the terrain are sweeping rapidly in wide arcs beneath you, and this sometimes brings on sensations of dizziness or nausea. The remedy: descend and touch bottom firmly with your hand. Your brain will instantly perceive that the oscillating motion belongs only to the water.

On the Bottom

Once on the bottom, you become intimately aware of and involved with your new surroundings. Even if the visibility is only fair, usually you will quickly find recognizable forms of aquatic life resting on or swimming near the bottom, fixed to rocks or hiding under them, or occupying burrows in the sediment. In many temperate coastal areas, and especially in the tropics, you will immediately be able to hear some of the creatures of the deep. These sounds can often be detected from the surface, or as you descend, but they always seem to intensify near the bottom. Crackling, crunching, beeping, burping, and squeaking sounds are the most common. The sounds are loudest and most varied in coral-reef environments. We will identify some of the undersea noisemakers in Chapter 11.

Once on the bottom, it is a standard practice to recheck your gear, especially buckles and straps, which will have loosened due to compression of the wetsuit. Adjust straps until they are comfortably snug but still loose enough to allow you to take a deep breath easily. If the straps resist your efforts to inhale, you will tend to breathe rapidly and laboriously and will use your air considerably faster than if you allow for normal ease of inhalation. Other factors such as exertion, becoming chilled, and even nervousness cause you to consume air rapidly. Generally, as you become a more experienced diver, your rate of air consumption will drop and you will enjoy longer visits under water.

Once again make sure that your weight belt is free of all other straps and encumbrances. We recommend that you always arrange the quick-release buckle of the weight belt in the same way so it is always operated, say, by a right-hand pull, while the backpack's waist strap is released by the left hand. Upon reaching bottom, too, it is essential to trim your buoyancy.

On the bottom, you will begin traveling in largely a horizontal mode. The beginning underwater explorer may be surprised to find that his or her greatest

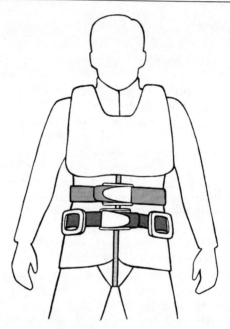

5.2. *Arrangement of weight-belt buckle opposite to that of a BC or backpack. The weight-belt buckle should always be positioned in the same way and should always open in the same direction: an important safety habit. A cutaway view of the BC is shown to illustrate the buckles clearly. Divers rely on the sense of touch to locate specific straps and buckles.*

effort will be spent not in moving up or down, but on level traverses. The physical exertion of underwater travel is greatest where a current is flowing against the diver. Furthermore, following preplanned routes or finding specific sites on the bottom usually requires first-class orienteering skills. In contrast, ascending and descending can be accomplished passively, in total ease. Learn to use your head and save your muscles when you dive. Relax in the water and plan your diving to let the natural forces, such as buoyancy, current, and surge, work for you.

Currents and surge, if present, now come into play as aids or hindrances to the diver. Of course, caution is the rule where these water movements are significant. If you encounter a bottom current against which you can barely make headway, or surge that threatens to sweep you about uncontrollably, it is wise to abort the dive and return to shore or your boat immediately. Having to brace yourself with a limpet's grip on rocky bottom while torrents of water swirl past you does not constitute enjoyable and safe diving. A word to the uninitiated: strong surge and currents can readily tear off your mask and may even relieve you of your fins. In areas of strong tides, the flow of a surface current may be reversed along the bottom. If you are exploring off an unfamiliar coast, check the tide tables and seek competent local information before you dive.

In a moderate current, usually no greater than one-half knot (a knot is equal to 1 nautical mile per hour), prudent divers begin their exploration by moving into the flow. This way they are exerting themselves most during the first part of the dive when they are fresh. Then, a return to near the starting point, if desired, can be accomplished with an easy swim down current toward the end of the dive.

In moderate surge, it is advisable to be very cautious around rocks, coral, sea urchins, and other bruising, abrasive, or piercing objects. Even very light surge often shows a cyclic increase in intensity. Be especially careful of caves, narrow canyons, and arches, where, as in the case of wind in an alley, compression or funneling effects may increase the water's velocity severalfold. If you should find yourself clinging to a boulder, always face into surge or current, or you risk a flooded mask. The best way to travel in surge is to remain in the open. During the backsurge, when water is moving against you, kick only as hard as you have to in order to stay in place. Do not fight to move ahead against the water. As soon as you feel the flow starting to move in your direction, take off and zoom as far ahead as you can until the resistance again begins to take over. A lot of new divers exhaust themselves trying to force their way against backsurge. Instead, learn to adapt and enjoy this exhilarating swooping motion in the sea.

The bottom you are exploring may rise or drop away to greater depth. If the changes are substantial, you should adjust your trim. As a courtesy to your fellow divers, avoid stirring up silt storms, especially if someone is trying to photograph. Most important, be aware of the elapsed time and the nondecompression limit at your deepest level.

Sometimes a diving objective, say a wreck, cannot be seen when you first reach the bottom. If you and your diving partner (or partners) are carrying underwater compasses, you can make a systematic search. First choose a prominent landmark, perhaps a nearby rock, as a starting point. Then choose different compass bearings and go in those directions. At intervals, depending on the visibility, make a trail to follow back by drawing a finger or the edge of your hand through the sand (if there's no sand, turn over stones—due to encrusting marine life on their tops, they nearly always look strikingly different when overturned; just remember to turn them back again, as a conservation measure, on your way back). If you do not find your objective within a reasonable distance, return to the starting point, rendezvous with your buddy, and try a new direction. If you do find what you are after, return nevertheless—making sure your trail is well marked—pick up your buddy, and go back together to the site of interest. You can hurry your partner's return to the starting point by using a predetermined signal, such as tapping on your tank with a knife or stone.

If your dive has taken you a good distance from shore or from your boat, and if you are secure in your bottom orientation, you may want to swim back as far as possible along the bottom. This is usually easier and more fun than snorkeling at the surface, and following the bottom into shore generally assures a very gradual rate of ascent. But returning along the bottom requires prior planning; you must have saved a substantial amount of air for this phase of the dive.

Surfacing

Your excursion on the bottom usually ends when your air supply becomes low, although chilling or other reasons may intervene to end the dive prematurely. The procedure for ascent recommended by most diver-instruction organizations begins when your submersible pressure gauge indicates 500 psi remaining in your tank. Strictly speaking, ascent should start when the first member of a diving pair or team reaches the 500 psi mark. Leaving a significant air reserve in the tank assures you of easy breathing on the surface for an extended period should you require it, for example, due to a lost snorkel or a high degree of turbulence. Persons relying on a manual air-reserve mechanism should begin ascending immediately after tripping their J-valve lever. Remember too that you should keep at least 100 psi in the tank between airfills to avoid water seepage and internal corrosion.

As you leave the bottom, put your mind on the action at hand. Stop sightseeing, scanning for lobsters, and so on. Put a little air in your BC or simply start swimming toward the surface. Concentrate your awareness on your buoyancy and upward movement.

Having been in trim at the bottom, you will automatically become progressively more buoyant as you rise, due to the expansion of air in your BC and wetsuit. Your main concern is to watch and control your rate of rise. Your left hand should be over your head manipulating the exhaust valve on the BC hose. Your glance should be continuously upward as you watch the exhaled bubbles from your regulator. The bubbles should not stream below the hand holding the hose. If they begin to gather lower, close to your elbow or face, slow down by letting some air out of your BC quickly. The normal rate of ascent should not exceed 60 feet per minute: watching your bubbles, as outlined above, will allow you to approximate this rate closely.

Try to take consciously shallow breaths (sipping on the air), and exhale fully. Looking up not only allows you to gauge your rate of ascent relative to your bubbles; it also opens the back of your throat to the maximum extent. Exhaling fully is easier with a wide-open throat.

Even in the nether layer, ascent toward the growing brightness is usually pleasant. During your rise, you will hear a nearly continuous gurgling and growling in your head as your middle ear and sinus cavities automatically exhaust their expanding air.

On any ascent, it is a good practice to make a short stop about 10 feet down—15 to 30 seconds is enough—to give your lungs a chance to loosen any pressurized air still held back in remote lobes and recesses and to get it moving outward. At shallow depth, be especially conscious of your breathing. If you see or feel turbulence from significant swells overhead, try to take no more than half breaths, and exhale fully. This will protect you from a sudden drop in external pressure. Resist the urge to breathe deeply. You can inhale a deep, satisfying lungful as soon as you break through to the atmosphere.

As you approach the surface, listen for sounds of boat motors. Even if you are ascending beside your boat or dive flag, do not surface if you hear a loud or approaching motor noise. Wait it out. Go up only as the sound starts to recede, or proceed very cautiously if the sound is near but unchanging.

Sooner or later, every diver loses track of a buddy under water. Usually this occurs in fairly shallow water, and it can happen embarrassingly easily if the water is murky. What to do? The recommended practice is for both partners to ascend normally to the surface, rendezvous, and go back down to finish the dive. If you lose your buddy in conditions where visibility is only 10 feet or so, it can be a real surprise to surface and find him or her as close as 15 or 20 feet away, searching the horizon for you. Losing track of your buddy on a deep dive is a far more serious matter. This simply should not happen. See Chapter 8 for a discussion of the vital importance of the buddy relationship in deep diving.

Emergency Conditions and Emergency Ascents

In open water, whether the sea or a lake, such problems as a lost mask or an accidentally dropped weight belt often seem much more serious than they did during training sessions in a swimming pool. In reality, they are usually easy to deal with if you keep your head, but they may be a bit more complicated due to such environmental variables as current and surge. Most minor emergencies can be handled without the need to return to the surface, but on rare occasions, an ascent must be made unexpectedly or under emergency conditions.

If you ever have to make such an ascent, your success will depend on the thoroughness of your prior training, your physical fitness, your presence of mind, and your ease in the water. Different situations and types of equipment call for variations in technique. All relevant procedures should be thoroughly discussed, safely practiced, and irrevocably committed to memory by students during scuba class and pool sessions.

The type of ascent indicated varies according to the nature of the emergency, the depth at which it occurs, and whether or not one's buddy is close by at the time. There are basically four kinds of ascents that can be made in response to situations ranging from minor mishaps to grave emergencies; we will discuss them beginning with the least serious case.

Normal Ascent in a Minor Emergency

A lost mask may or may not be cause for an ascent, depending on whether or not you can retrieve it. A close encounter with your buddy's flippers or with an unexpected corner of reef are the most common causes of a lost or dislodged mask. The worst thing about it is the sudden surprise and distress at water (often cold) impacting your previously dry and warm eyes. The naked view is blurry, but you will still be able to see your mask if it hasn't drifted away or fallen behind a rock. It is to be hoped that your buddy will notice your plight and render aid if necessary. Signal by tapping on your tank with your knife or a stone. If your mask cannot be found, you should abort the dive and make a normal ascent, breathing as usual. Put a little air in your BC to get started and follow your bubbles; they will be out of focus but plainly visible.

If the mask can be retrieved, merely pick it up, put it back on, and clear it. You will recall from your basic scuba course that there is more than one way to clear the mask. We feel that the easiest way is to look up toward the surface, tilt the lower rim of the water-filled mask (the part around the nose) slightly away from your face, and exhale through your nose. The exhaled air rises into the mask, displacing water in the same manner that air would fill an inverted glass tumbler under water. Still looking straight up, you re-seat the mask with its trapped air gently on your face. Figure 5.3 illustrates this procedure.

The Uncontrolled Ascent from Shallow Water

An accidentally lost weight belt is a little more serious than a dropped mask, particularly if you are in relatively shallow water (less than 50 feet) and wearing a full wetsuit. With loss of compensating weight, perhaps 20 pounds, your suit's buoyancy will take over and you will be pulled upward. If you are a very strong swimmer and react instantly, you may be able to remain head down within reach of the bottom by kicking at an Olympian pace. Grab a large rock, kelp,

5.3. *Simple technique for clearing a flooded mask. Facing upward allows air exhaled through the nose to be caught in the mask. Water is forced out under the lower edges of the mask.*

coral head, or anything else in reach to keep yourself down until you locate your belt.

If you have started upward, and there is no convenient kelp, rocky cliff, or anchor line to swim to and cling to, prepare to make an uncontrolled ascent. It will be fairly rapid, but you can slow yourself down somewhat by letting as much air as possible out of your BC immediately. Above all, remember to exhale slowly but continuously, if possible. If you must inhale on the way up, a short and *very* shallow breath will be enough, followed by immediate continued exhalation.

An uncontrolled ascent under these circumstances is, of course, an involuntary one. Ditching the weight belt deliberately to cause an uncontrolled ascent should never be done except in certain deep-water emergencies; we will return to this a little farther on.

Air-Loss Emergencies and the Controlled Ascent

Sudden equipment failure affecting one's air supply on the bottom is very rare, though obviously very serious. Faulty valves can cause the regulator to free flow (continuously discharge air) or to shut off the air supply. A ruptured diaphragm in the second stage can cause flooding of the mouthpiece. Often, divers can overcome even fairly drastic problems without resorting to an emergency ascent. An experienced diver can still breathe from a freeflowing regulator, and the human mouth is highly efficient at separating air and water, rejecting the latter and retaining the former.

The most urgent occasion for an ascent is when the air supply is restricted or exhausted, or when the air delivery system fails totally. Fortunately, all of these circumstances are very rare, the last extremely so. If the occasion should arise, however, the normal reaction at relatively shallow depths (again, less than 50 feet) should be to make a controlled emergency ascent. As defined in Chapter 2, this means coming to the surface with all equipment in place as you slowly release a single breath of air. As in a normal ascent, try to match your rate of rise to that of your bubbles, controlling it with your BC.

Cases of restricted air flow, air leakage, or water entering the second stage can range from barely detectable to severe. Slight air leakage is commonly caused by the presence of a grain or two of coarse sand in the valve which admits air to the low-pressure chamber of the second stage. Such a problem rarely crops up in the middle of a dive. It can be prevented altogether by proper equipment maintenance, with special attention to keeping the regulator away from sand.

Running out of air happens most to users of the outmoded J valve. The cause is simple accident or human error—forgetting to set the air-reserve lever before the dive or accidentally tripping it to the reserve position during the dive. In either of these situations, when breathing resistance begins to increase, the diver reaches around for the pull rod to depress the lever and finds that it is already down. If the diver doesn't panic and starts immediately for the surface, he or she will be able to obtain at least several more breaths from the tank, if inhaling becomes absolutely necessary. This is because an "empty" tank at, say, 100 feet still contains air at approximately 4 atmospheres pressure. Naturally, the diver cannot draw much more air into lungs opposed by an equal pressure. But during ascent, the surrounding pressure lessens steadily and the air in the tank will flow freely from the tank on demand from the lungs.

Many instructors now discourage trying to inhale from an "empty" tank on ascent. They rightly point out that fixation on inhaling in such an emergency is dangerous; the diver should be concentrating on *exhaling* whether the ascent is controlled or uncontrolled. In water less than 50 feet deep, our recommendation is to forget about obtaining more air from your tank and make a controlled emergency ascent.

Emergency Ascents from Deep Water

If an air-loss emergency occurs in deep water (below 50 feet), the preferred option is to share the air supply in a buddy's tank—either by using an octopus unit or by buddy breathing—and both divers should immediately make a controlled ascent. Both methods involve considerable difficulty and risk, and are discussed in detail in Chapter 8, "Going Deep." If, however, your buddy is too far away to reach, you may have to risk an uncontrolled ascent.

On paper, the basics of an emergency solo ascent from deep water are simple enough. You first remove and drop your weight belt as quickly as you can, even as you are starting up from the bottom. Unanimously, instructors advise pulling the belt completely clear of the body and dropping it at arm's length, not merely tearing the buckle open and letting the belt slide down—with the possibility of catching on the knife strapped to the leg or snagging on a dangling lobster bag. The snagging of a shed weight belt on a knife sheath has been implicated in a number of drownings. Hence, as an added precaution, divers are now advised to mount their knives on the inside of the calf.

After the few seconds it takes to remove your belt, you should be already heading up and inflating your BC, if possible, with the emergency air bottle or carbon dioxide supply. The big BCs will bring you up at speeds of more than 200 feet per minute, but due to the possibility of air embolism this can be dangerous in itself. We don't know of any diving organization that recommends free ascents from deeper than 50 feet. Below this range, the interdependence of a pair or team of divers becomes absolute. In Chapter 8, we will cover the significance of partners in deep diving.

To counteract some confusing statements made in recent popular diving literature, we repeat for emphasis one point made earlier: a person making any emergency ascent should be looking straight up toward the surface, a posture that should be instinctive. Looking up has both psychological and physiological value, since it affords you the most optimistic view possible under the circumstances and opens your airway automatically, promoting ease of exhalation and preventing overpressurization in your lungs.

The Buddy System and an Alternative

To a very great degree, safety and security under water involves the relationship between diving partners. This fact has led to an emphasis—we believe it to be an overemphasis—on the buddy system in diver training. The conventional wisdom is that a diver is not safe and should not feel secure unless he knows exactly where his buddy is in the water. In this section we present our own appraisal of the buddy system as it exists in contemporary diving. We hope to initiate a polemic in the diving community on underwater safety, especially in relation to the much overrated buddy system.

Early in the history of recreational scuba— throughout the 1950s and early 1960s—the buddy system was little more than a friendly gesture. Diving alone was a routine practice for many enthusiasts. Surprisingly, the scanty records that exist for that period indicate that the relative number of injuries and fatalities in the underwater population did not exceed—and may actually have been smaller than— that on record for the present period, in which intensive and extensive instruction are practiced, certification is required, and superior equipment is used almost universally.

The buddy system seems to have originated in a dimly perceived concept of safety in numbers. Now, after a decade or more of fanatical devotion to the buddy system, serious questions as to its effectiveness are being raised. An increase in double drownings, even at very shallow depths (less than 35 feet), seems to bear witness to the existence of some fatal deficiencies in the buddy concept as it is now practiced.

Our proposal is simple. First, we suggest that, as a means of developing their self-reliance, new divers be trained as Self-contained Underwater Persons (SCUPs) as they learn the basics of scuba. The bottom limit for SCUP training would be no more than 50 feet, and nondecompression limits would be observed. Basic certification of new divers would be as usual, but, as SCUPs in training, students would be required to make an underwater horizontal swim—without breathing tank air—of 50 feet in a pool while neutrally weighted in full scuba gear. In training for the swim, divers would learn to exhale slowly a single lungful of air over the distance. Also, SCUP training would train students in the theory and mental preparedness necessary for making a controlled ascent from 50 feet or less in the event of an air-loss emergency. We are not recommending here that beginning diving students be trained to make free ascents in open-water conditions. Rather, the 50-foot underwater swim would serve to ensure that students seeking certification as scuba divers were sufficiently fit and had the confidence to ascend properly, with an excellent chance of reaching safety by themselves in an emergency.

We are not abandoning the buddy concept with this proposal, merely refocusing it. Buddies would still help each other in many ways short of the ultimate risky practice of sharing a regulator. The mutual-aid function of a buddy pair would continue to be vital in cases of entanglement with lines or kelp, underwater injuries, the slippage or loss of equipment, and so on. And there's no disputing that a buddy always helps to dispel the loneliness and spookiness frequently felt amid strange watery surroundings. But the point to be emphasized here—and that we hope will be stressed in diver-training courses worldwide—is that, at least in water less than 50 feet deep, divers can and should learn to be self-reliant in an emergency. The buddy system can break down—it does so the moment a diver loses sight of his or her partner. Our intention is to convince divers that when this happens they can still handle an emergency situation successfully as individuals.

Diving Psychology and Self-Reliance

Imagine yourself 50 feet down in a cold, green world. Visibility hasn't been very good—so far, it's only 12 to 15 feet, and it seems to be decreasing as you move across dark sand patches broken by clusters of huge boulders. Disturbingly, you have just lost track of your buddy. He is somewhere out there—perhaps within 20 feet—but he and his bubbles are nowhere to be seen in the surrounding murk. You debate with yourself as to what to do: should you surface (the prearranged plan in case of separation), or should you continue to search for a minute or so?

A subliminal uneasiness quickly enters your consciousness. The dimness and silence and alien landscape begin to seem a little threatening. You feel exposed, very lonely and vulnerable . . . but to what? Then, quite suddenly, something touches your shoulder from behind; you nearly jump out of your wetsuit as you whirl around to confront your lost and found buddy.

Many a diver will recognize himself or herself in this scenario. It is meant to dramatize some psychological stimuli and reactions common among divers, especially beginners.

Humans are visual animals. More than 90 percent of our information about our surroundings—where we are in relation to other objects and obstacles, and what we can expect to meet as we move through a variable environment—comes through the eyes. When visual perception is severely restricted, as at night or in turbid water, a person becomes apprehensive about possible encounters with dangerous situations—real ones that involve potential bodily injury or imagined ones too vague to describe or inspired by superstition.

Being alone in alien surroundings is another source of fear. The intensity of an imagined threat (no specific danger in sight) and perhaps even a perceived threat (a shark is seen) is inversely proportional to the number of one's companions present. This relationship does not follow a straight line; nor does it account for the special kind of panic that affects crowds in a disastrous fire or earthquake. But it is safe to say that each of a group, or pair of divers (where, after all, there is a 50 percent chance that the other guy will be bitten), faces a lone shark with far less anxiety than does the average diver by himself.

Jumpiness to touch is very common among divers. Even the lightest unexpected contact with things that go bump in the deep—unseen marine life, overhead obstructions, fellow divers—can be extremely upsetting. Reactions typically range from violent recoil to momentary paralysis.

Diving psychology is an extremely important topic, but it has received little attention in the fields of diver instruction and underwater medicine. Most of the emphasis in preparing new underwater explorers, both recreational and commercial, has involved the physical and technical aspects of diving. This emphasis is understandable, since the technology is developing and changing rapidly. However, despite the appearance of fantastic new equipment and push-button refinements, human limitations and frailties in the underwater wilderness remain. The physiological responses of the human body are now well known and are being taught effectively. Psychological parameters, for the most part, are neither well understood nor treated by instructors. To us, the high dropout rate of new divers seems largely due to mental and emotional factors rather than true physical ones. And, while anxiety and lack of confidence plague beginners, overconfidence can become the nemesis of veterans.

We feel that the human factor in diving safety must be approached from two directions. One approach, explored in the preceding section, involves the relationship between diving partners. The other path leads inward toward a self-knowledge that yields self-confidence, physical fitness, and mental preparedness.

"Know thyself as an underwater person" should be the first psychological commandment for any diver. Being honest about your physical abilities and mental apprehensions is your first line of protection against a situation you cannot control. If you suspect you will have trouble making a 300-yard swim through surge to a dive site, or if you are not mentally ready to cope with a night dive, don't go. Your decision will be respected by your fellow divers, who, it is to be hoped, are in tune with their own abilities and the underwater environment. Every diver does have physical and mental limits, and collectively these extend over a considerable range; but from time to time the elemental sea vastly overpowers all human ability, and at that point only the fish should be down there.

Outwardly, diving offers satisfaction through mastery of a specialized technology, competency in an alien environment, development of individual capacities for planning, and close vital cooperation with others in a recreational setting. In these ways, diving resembles technical mountaineering, although the former seems accessible to more people and usually proceeds at a more relaxed, fluid, and less saltatory pace. Divers, like hang gliders, experience a three-dimensional freedom that acts as a counterpoise, perhaps even as a form of therapy, in the face of the progressively more restrictive and depersonalizing influences that are slowly pervading modern life. We think that the inward adventure of diving, the opportunities it offers for self-discovery and personal development, are at least as important as the thrill of outward exploration.

It is our belief that future advances in underwater safety will grow primarily out of a more complete understanding and effective instructional approach to diving psychology. Improved equipment and technique alone are unlikely to bring about a significant reduction in the diving-accident rate. To us this seems a reasonable prediction. The finest, most expensive buoyancy system available will not save a panicked individual who forgets to inflate it. And a partner's octopus unit is only as useful as it is close at hand in a deep emergency.

Every individual must approach diving with an honest appraisal of his or her physical abilities and behavioral tendencies under a variety of diving conditions. Ideally, a new diver's mastery of psychological problems under water should not lag behind his physical and technical training. However, in practice this lag seems to occur frequently, and novices are coaxed or cajoled into rough open water or into making a 100-foot descent before they are truly at home 30 feet beneath a calm surface. We would like to see this style of instruction change. We want to see the plunge rate and the accident rate slowed down and, gradually and progressively, the threshold for panic raised as divers discover at their own pace the wonder of spending a small part of their lives under water.

A beginner should place the greatest emphasis on learning and knowing, on flowing with the sea, not forcing his or her way beneath it. Divers are explorers in the best tradition, self-powered and in direct bodily contact with the wilderness. They should be well prepared to appreciate the unique physical and biological properties of the aquatic realm and to anticipate its idyllic and fearsome moods, its dreamlike enchantments and subtle dangers, and, ironically, its great vulnerability.

Chapter 6

Starting from the Shore

F OR A MAJORITY of divers, the invitation "Let's go diving" usually means a shore dive. The advantages of shore diving include some flexibility in scheduling and the relatively low cost. If the weather and water conditions are poor, or if someone has a cold, the planned dive can be postponed without the loss of the deposit money on a charter boat. Furthermore, shore diving is no less interesting, less serious, or less demanding of careful planning than boat diving. Most divers would agree, however, that shore divers work harder at having their particular brand of fun. The extra work of a shore dive involves the actual entry, the potentially long swim out to the exploration site, and the return and exit from the water.

Shore Entries

The most serious problem a diver faces in getting into the water from the shore is turbulence—surf or shore surge—sometimes coupled with rough terrain. Hence, rule number one for shore diving is, Look for the calmest entry spot available. You don't have to find a sandy beach to begin your dive. In fact, most experienced divers like to avoid sand in churning shallow water whenever possible. Sand has a way of causing insidious problems with finely tuned regulators and promoting leaky masks and BCs, stuck zippers, and so forth.

The Deep-Water Entry

The simplest kind of entry is the deep-water type, where the entry point is a rock ledge, a pier, a sea wall, or the equivalent, which allows you to drop no more than a few feet directly into a comfortable depth of water. Even the best entry point at such a shore site is seldom ideal, however. For example, there may be rocks directly below the jump-off point. In such a case, watch for the depth to change over your projected point of impact; it may be safe to step off into a swell that briefly adds 2 or 3 feet of water to the spot and then sweeps past, carrying you smoothly into deeper water. Note, however, that while a rocky step-off or jump-off point can make for a fine start to a dive, it will usually not be the place to attempt to leave the water. Exits will be covered more thoroughly later in this chapter.

The main steps in a deep-water entry are these. First, secure all equipment. Inflate your BC to about one-third capacity and place the regulator in your mouth. Hold your mask against your face with one hand, and hold your gauges, console, speargun, camera, and so on away from your body with the other hand. Then, take one giant step into the water. If you are carrying a diver's flag, it's a good idea to mount it on a small collapsible float. The float can be rigged on shore and tossed into the water ahead of the divers. Or it can be carried into the water in the furled/collapsed state, and rigged and deployed in the water just before descent.

The Beach Entry

Probably the most common entry point in shore diving is a sandy beach. The big (and important) advantage here is the lack of obstacles, chiefly rocks. A beach entry in calm water holds no mysteries and presents no difficulties. Simply wade into the water with your BC partially inflated. To prevent sand in your booties from chafing your feet, you may choose to wait to don your footgear until you begin to float free. This little nicety is not possible on all beach entries, however.

If the surf is high, before you even start to get dressed take a few minutes to relax and study the water. Large and small waves usually come in alternate sets, sometimes with as many as seven to ten waves to a set. The pattern is not always regular, but by watching the sea for a while you will get an idea of how long is the relative lull (your entry "window") between sets of big incoming swells. Due to variations in bottom topography, one part of a beach may consistently draw higher surf than another. Also, local surf conditions alter dramatically with changes in wind strength and direction, tidal currents, and so on.

Watch for signs of a rip current heading seaward. Rips develop most strongly where a beach bows deeply into the land to form a horseshoe-shaped cove. Incoming water is deflected and focused toward the head of the cove, where it piles up consistently and forms a continuous "headwater" supplying the outward flow through the center of the cove. A rip is often indicated by the presence of turbid grayish or brownish water extending out to sea in a tongue from the beach. The coloration is due to suspended sand in the current. Rips generally are not a hazard to the person who is at ease in the water, though the surf that frequently accompanies them can be dangerous for the unprepared. Experienced divers sometimes use a moderate rip to get started off shore, but they don't try to return the same way.

To penetrate moderate to high surf, make sure that all equipment is securely in place on your body before you enter the water. Some divers protect octopus rigs or cameras by encasing them in a tightly closed plastic bag during entry through the churning sand. Put your fins on in the shallows well before you are in a position to be bowled over by surf. You should be neutrally weighted, with no air in your BC. Naturally, you are advised to approach surf rationally. Very experienced divers on familiar shores can enter and return safely through 10- to 12-foot breakers. Beginners should not even think of diving in such conditions.

A surf entry is nearly always a solo effort. Buddies are generally unable to help each other in surf, so you must be an expert swimmer to attempt a surf entry. Experienced divers stop when they are knee-deep in white water and wait for a backwash heading seaward. Of course, their timing ought also to coincide with the beginning of the lull. To follow this example, get prone, place the regulator in your mouth, and push off with the backwash, or suction. You should be precisely aligned, heading straight into the oncoming breaker or the white water closer to shore. Use only your fins for propulsion; hold your gauge console and any other dangling paraphernalia close to your body. If you are carrying a spear or speargun, pull rather than push it through the water; be sure it is not cocked in any way and that the business end is capped or corked.

You may have to go through several increasingly powerful surges of white water before you reach the breaker zone itself. Stay on the surface to keep yourself heading outward. You won't be able to see anything below in the foam anyway. Don't exhaust yourself by forcing your way through the incoming surge; just concentrate on staying aligned. You may even lose a little ground, but you will more than make up for it when the suction starts. Farther out, as a breaker looms ahead of and above you, dive to the bottom and slip beneath it. You may return to the surface after the wave passes over you; if so, head for the next. If you do stay under, take a compass bearing and keep on moving outward along the bottom. Remember that the higher the waves, the longer is the distance between crests and the farther you have to swim to get beyond the breakers. At the breaker zone, the bottom usually begins to slope down more rapidly and the water will be steadily clearing. Usually, you will encounter two or three waves at their peaks of power in the breaker zone. Slide beneath them, and you will be home free in the more gentle surroundings of deep water. Most beach divers rendezvous with their partners at the surface a comfortable distance outside the breakers.

When you have reached the intended dive site, pause for a minute or two at the surface to adjust and tighten straps, check all functioning equipment, and make any last-minute modifications in plans. Check equipment again when you reach bottom. After a few dives, this little ritual of securing straps, keeping your weight belt clear of other gear, and trimming buoyancy will become automatic.

Returning to Shore

If you chose your diving site wisely and with your exit in mind, returning to shore need be no more difficult than entering the water. Frequently, the exit point of a shore dive is not the same as the entry point. The best exit is usually via the sandy beach with the calmest water in the vicinity.

If you have to come back through heavy surf, the landing procedure is essentially the reverse of the entry. First, be sure to save enough air in your tank to come in through the surf while breathing from your regulator (500 psi should be plenty). Stay at the surface, but with your BC nearly deflated in case you have to dive under an especially large breaker. Approach the surf zone slowly, watching for the start of a set of smaller-than-average waves. Let the insurge carry you, and resist the backwash vigorously but not to the point of fatigue. Be sure you are not fighting in against a rip. If you find yourself entering a rip, swim parallel to shore outside the breakers until you encounter relatively clear water again. Don't try to stand up until you can touch bottom with your hands from the surface. Actual body surfing on the crest or in the curl of a breaking wave with a scuba tank on your back is not recommended; a wipe-out could result in serious injury. If you are caught in front of a big breaker on the way in, turn around, dive back under it, and make your shoreward move again. At some point while you're working through the set of smaller waves, the larger ones will reappear; but now you will find yourself well inside the breaker zone, able to ride with the white water toward shore. Remember, when you are going through the surf in either direction, your diving flag should be rolled and held securely and its accompanying float should be collapsed, with the line coiled or wadded, and tucked away in your catch bag or a pouch in your BC.

Two Shore-Dive Scenarios

In this section, to illustrate some basic practical problems of shore diving we present two very different diving sites and diving objectives, illustrated with sections of coastal navigation charts (U.S. Coast and Geodetic Survey and the National Ocean Survey). Given the information provided on tides and wind conditions for the two sites, you will be able to exercise in your imagination your shore-diving acumen, and we will comment on major points to assure safe and enjoyable diving in each of the examples.

If you have never seen a nautical chart, you will find it to be an underwater map, showing depths and bottom characteristics as well as surface objects such as buoys, shore configurations, and landmarks useful in navigation and position-finding. Of greatest significance to the shore-based diver are the features along the shoreline immediately opposite a dive site, representing points of access to the water; the nature of the bottom; and depths that will be encountered. Charted depths close to shore are usually shown in feet below *Mean Low Water* (or the average low tide level); farther offshore, charts may show depths in meters or fathoms. The depth unit used will be listed on the chart. Look for the smallest scale chart available depicting the area of the dive. Such a blowup will provide the most detail.

Often, bottom characteristics are expressly noted on a chart—for example, by the words "mud" and "coral," or by such abbreviations as *Rk* (rock), *hrd* (hard bottom of undetermined character), *S* (sand), *Sh* (shelly bottom), *Co* (coral). Also shown are natural surface features such as zones of breakers. The positions of large, numbered navigation buoys are indicated prominently by terse abbreviations next to a buoy symbol. These abbreviations refer to light signals visible on the buoy at night; for example, "Fl R 4 sec." means: "flashes red every 4 seconds." A complete index to symbols and abbreviations used in nautical charts can be obtained from the U.S. Government Printing Office. It is usually also available, along with the charts themselves, at larger nautical and boating supply stores.

The exact geographical locations of the diving sites illustrated here are not important. The examples are intended as composites representing a variety of areas and shore-diving situations confronting North American divers. The main idea here is that you gain practice in planning a shore dive. Assume that the areas are brand new to you. How would you approach each of these diving problems?

Area A

The average tidal range—the difference between high and low tide—here is less than 2 feet. In summer, the winds are nearly always very gentle and rainfall is nearly nonexistent. Winter conditions, however, can include high winds, generally from the south, and gully-washer tropical rains. The coast is exposed to the open sea on the south, and large ocean swells, producing surf on the coral reef up to 10 feet high, appear occasionally throughout the year.

As you might expect, diving here is most interesting outside the coral reef, just beyond the mouth of the harbor on the eastern side. You have heard that there are some extremely photogenic fishes and coral landscapes out there. But you and your buddy have no boat. What should you consider in making your dive plan?

The dominant topographic feature on the chart is the enormous shallow reef flat—the area between the shore and the reef crest, or edge, defined by the

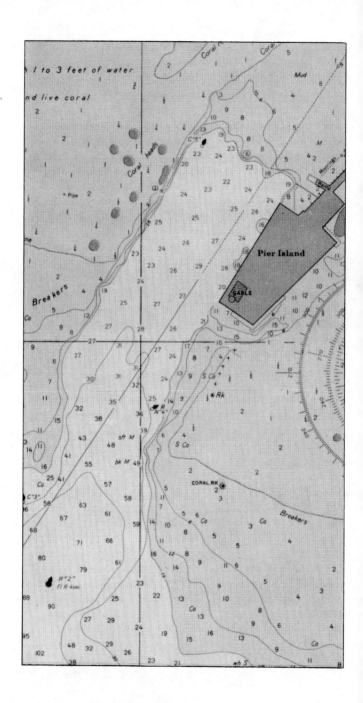

breaker zone and extending half a mile or more. Because of its shallowness and obstacles of mud and coral heads, much of this terrain looks unswimmable, especially by divers carrying cameras and strobes, and the only obvious entry is from the large pier facility. You should make friendly inquiries to determine the legalities and niceties of using the pier to stage your dive. Check with the dockmaster or harbormaster to find out if any large ships will be entering or leaving the area during the time you plan to dive, and make your plan coincide with the period of the least traffic. It's uncomfortable to be on the bottom at 40 feet as a 35-foot-draft vessel passes overhead. Also, check the pier for an easy-exit ladder or ramp as well as an entry point. Chances are that the easiest access will be on the back or eastern edge of the pier island, where small boats probably dock.

It would also be wise to swim out and back along the edge of the shallow reef, well inside of the red marker buoy (N "4") and away from ship traffic. If a large ship does come into the harbor unexpectedly during your swim, even though it will be moving slowly it will make waves as it passes, so you should make sure you don't get caught where the water is too shallow. Keeping 8 or 10 feet of water beneath you provides security from unforeseen swells and breakers.

Ships maneuvering inside the harbor may further affect diving conditions adversely by stirring up soft bottom sediments. Judging from the shape of the inner harbor, extensive dredging has been done, and the basin created is probably uniformly floored with fine silt and muddy debris. But the contours around the harbor mouth and outside suggest that the big cut into the reef originated as a natural feature—probably an old, drowned river gorge cut when sea level was lower. (This gorge is the obvious passageway to the area outside the reef.) Outside the harbor, the bottom terrain is probably firm, with living coral and limestone interspersed with sandy patches and channels.

6.1. Area A: *Coastal chart section, based on a nautical chart published by the National Ocean Survey of NOAA, United States Department of Commerce.* Scale: 1 *inch = approximately* 140 *yards.*

Nevertheless, it is possible that with an ebbing tide, or, with certain wind conditions, an outflow of turbid water from the inner harbor will considerably muck up the good visibility you might be hoping for along the reef on the outside. A heavy rainstorm with consequent discharge into the harbor from a sizeable stream nearby would have the same effect.

The normal tidal difference here is so small and the coast so open—there are no major estuaries or funnel-like bays—that tidal currents are unlikely to be a hazard to divers. This is not to say that dangerous currents do not occur at this site, however. They do. And the two key factors determining current strength, as you may have guessed, are the wide shallow flats and the strength and direction of the wind. A larger-scale chart of this coast would show that the wide flats extend for miles in either direction. On the relatively few days of the year when the wind blows strongly from a southerly direction, it piles up high breakers and drives masses of sea water in over the reef. Especially when its direction is off-perpendicular, or oblique, to the trend of the reef front (either from the southeast or southwest), the wind sets in motion nearly the whole wide sheet of shallow water between the reef edge and the shore. Over the shallows, the water motion is parallel to the shore and may be so powerful in narrow channels between coral heads that a person has difficulty standing against it in 3 feet of water. Swimming against the mass movement may be impossible over much of the shallows.

This wind-driven current may also pour into deeper holes and channels in the reef flat with a force that could hold a diver or snorkeler under the surface or pinned under coral or a rock ledge. This phenomenon was implicated in the drowning deaths of three reef fisherman in Hawaii in 1978.

When such a mass flow suddenly reaches a major channel transecting the shallows and leading back to the outer ocean, powerful rip currents can be set up. In extreme cases, such currents extend a mile or more out to sea. In the case of a channel rip driven by the wind, the current tends to be strongest on the downwind side of the channel. Thus, in the seascape shown in Figure 6.1, a southwest wind would tend to develop a strong seaward flow along the eastern side of the harbor entrance. There would be much less outward movement, and perhaps, as in a river channel, a return eddy would exist along the opposite, or western, edge.

It's about a 300-yard swim from the end of the pier out to the approximately 50-foot bottom along the fairly steeply contoured reef. Our advice for this dive is that you choose a nice calm day (common enough at this tropical site, on a southern coast away from the Northeast Trade Winds), confer with and get permission from harbor officials to use the pier, carry a dive flag and collapsible float to alert small boating traffic, and, after descending, stay oriented to the rising edge of the reef. If you follow this plan, you ought to have a fine and memorable dive.

Area B

The second diving site features a very rough, rocky coast near the mouth of a small bay and estuary. The prevailing winds in summer (the normal diving season here) are light to strong sea breezes (breezes toward the land) from the southeast. The tidal range averages 9 feet; this indicates that a lot of water moves along this coast every 6 hours. Your diving objective is to explore the buoyed wreck (designated "WR") that lies just inside the 60-foot contour west of Brimstone Island. How would you plan this dive?

First, you have probably already noticed that this diving environment, even when conditions are good, is a potentially severe one—not only in terms of physical effort, but also, almost certainly, because of rapid changes in such variables as current strength and direction and water clarity. Only excellent swimmers in fine physical condition should attempt a shore dive here. Although the swim out to the wreck buoy appears to be little more than half the distance to the reef site in the previous example, this dive demands more precautions and much greater precision. Assuming that you are new to the area, the best approach is

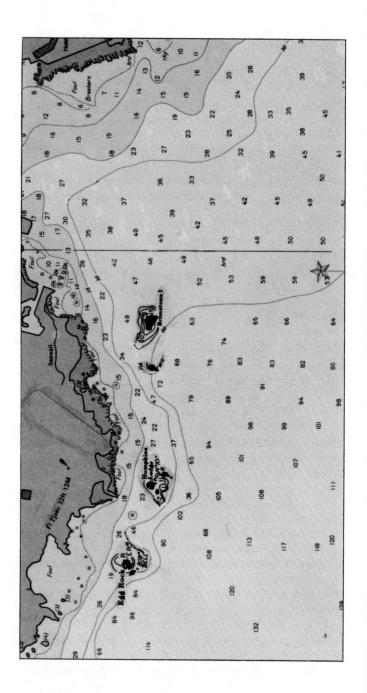

to take your chart into a local pro dive shop and make up your dive plan with the assistance of people who have been there before. After studying the chart, however, you should have several specific points to raise, and you may impress your new acquaintances regarding your sea sense.

First, consider possible entry and exit points. This is an exposed coast, and a south to southeast wind and/or remotely generated swell could throw up some impossible breakers along much of the obviously rocky shoreline. Incidentally, the areas near the shore designated "foul" do not harbor sewage outfalls, dumps, or evil-smelling muck. Here, foul means extremely rough, rocky, shallow bottom, often beneath turbulent water, that will damage boat propellers and snag anchors, anchor lines, nets, and the like. This ground is unsafe for navigating, fishing, and perhaps swimming. But the outline of the coast does indicate the presence of tiny protected coves that may offer safe entry and, in particular, exit points.

The chart section does not show roads down to the shore, but these are almost sure to exist, and you will probably be able to drive around the area or else check a local road or topographic map to determine the accessibility of potential entry-exit points. Helpful advice from the dive shop may be the quickest way to decide where to start and end your dive. But before you start, be sure to get permission to cross shore property from private landowners or residents if state rights of way to the shore do not exist or are inconvenient. Sad to say, good will toward divers on the part of seaside residents is rapidly diminishing. Some choice coastal areas are being closed off because a careless, boorish few among divers do not ask permission and then compound the insult by leaving picnic trash and other refuse strewn around a beautiful coastal site.

You will already have realized that the timing of

6.2. Area B: *Coastal chart section, based on a nautical chart published by the National Ocean Survey of NOAA, United States Department of Commerce.* Scale: 1 *inch* = *approximately* 140 *yards.*

this dive is going to be critical. The key elements here are tidal currents, wind, and underwater visibility. All three factors are more or less predictable, with forecasts of tidal current strength and direction being the most reliable and those of wind conditions the least.

In nearly every coastal area, you can pick up a tide table or chart, giving the times and heights of high and low tides. Tidal heights are still most commonly expressed in feet relative to Mean Low Water, or the average low tide, for the area, which is set at 0.0 feet. Local tide tables, obtainable at dive shops, fishing and boating supply stores, many gas stations, and so on, are based on exhaustive official tide tables published for several thousand coastal sites all around the North and South American continents. These tables, published by the Coast and Geodetic Survey (U.S. Department of Commerce) and equivalent agencies in Canada, are fairly accurate for the localities named, but interpolations to determine the tidal cycle at unlisted sites, such as offshore islands, are only of approximate value. And these tables do not include information on current velocity. In a few areas, tidal current velocities have been measured over lengthy periods and predictive tables are available, again published by the Department of Commerce. Both kinds of tide-information tables are issued every January for the calendar year and may be obtained at very low cost from local yachting suppliers, or by writing directly to the U.S. Superintendent of Documents.

In most areas, high and low tides occur roughly six hours apart, but tidal heights and their times of occurrence are not the same every day. The greatest range in water level between high and low tides usually occurs twice a month, at the times of full and new moon. The smallest ranges occur at first-quarter and third-quarter phases of the moon. In most areas, a given stage of the tide—say the daytime high—will come about fifty minutes later on each successive day. Wherever you dive you should seek local information on the length of slack-water periods or, in a remote area, observe the tidal changes the day before you dive.

Given the information that the average tidal range in the area of this dive is 9 feet, you can expect tidal currents to be swift and possibly dangerous. Therefore, you must plan your entry for slack water—no tidal current running—usually approximately a half-hour period at high or low tide. Actually, you should have considerably more time than this, for tidal currents are often feeble for as much as an hour before and after the time nominally designated as slack water.

Will the diving in Area B be equivalent at slack low and high tides? The answer is that slack high tide, when clear ocean water has flooded into the entire area, will probably offer the best visibility at this site. By low tide, a lot of estuarine water, which may be quite turbid, will probably cover the site. Also, low tide on such a rugged coast can present a hazardous steeplechase to divers stumbling their way over slippery boulders and algal mats to reach swimmable water. At high tide, the slight extra swim out and back over the obstacles to the high and dry beach is a pleasure.

Look at the depth contours in the area of the wreck compared with those in the rest of the chart section. The bottom slopes down much more steeply along the western edge of the bay. It appears that the estuarine channel may be continuous with the deeper water lying along this side. Together with the three islands forming a chain just off the coast, the steepness (with possible ledges and caves) makes for more exciting diving than the gentle shelving on the eastern side of the bay. But the steep contours and islands probably also make for much swifter currents when the tide is running.

The very worst conditions here would coincide with an ebbing tide and a brisk southeast wind. The wind would tend to deflect much of the outgoing tidal flow toward the western shore. Water piling up here would flow faster than usual, especially in the natural sluiceways between the islands. Backed by such a tidal "pressure head" of 9 or 10 feet, which would inexorably leave the estuary within 6 hours, and enhanced by the sea wind, currents along this shore could easily reach 4 or 5 knots, an impossible swimming obstacle for anyone. A diver on the bottom in the lee of Brimstone Island might not notice anything but a fractional increase in the current, but would surface into an unswimmable situation. The safest choice in this case would be to swim for Humpkins Ledge and wait for slack low tide before trying to reach shore.

Winds along some coasts can shift direction or change greatly in strength in as little time as fifteen minutes. Based on our given average summer wind conditions here, the ideal time for this shore dive would be early morning. The sea breeze, which typically comes up strongly later in the day, would thus be avoided. A summer sunrise on the coast is a beautiful send-off for a dive, and the often glass-smooth water at this time of day is another treat.

Naturally, even though this should not be a decompression dive, you should be wearing a watch so you can coordinate the dive with the tide schedule (be sure to check the tide chart for a daylight-saving correction, if one applies to your area). A compass will also probably prove useful. Depending on your dive plan and the local boating traffic, a marker flag may or may not be useful here. It could prove to be a big drag if you run into some current.

At the end of the dive, it may be a good idea to swim back inshore along the bottom. Often, tidal movement begins at the surface and gradually entrains deeper water. Thus, as the tide turns, the current will usually be noticeably less forceful along the bottom.

One final consideration: unless you can see bottom 60 feet down, you should make your descent along the anchor chain of the wreck buoy. However, your objective may not lie right beside the buoy's anchor (usually a massive concrete slab). Thus, if visibility is average, you may not see any sign of the wreck when you reach bottom. It probably lies within 30 or 40 yards, however, and a search will be greatly aided by a compass. Therefore, when planning this dive, you should anticipate utilizing a well-coordinated search pattern, such as the one we described earlier, which involved drawing or marking a return path. Also, the buoy and its anchor chain will prove useful if you choose to surface over the site. Ascend along the anchor chain and come up next to the buoy. This is at least as effective in avoiding boats as using a dive flag. Just don't come up under a big buoy when the surface is rough.

With care, skill, and knowledge, shore divers seeking the wreck at this site can have a safe and extremely rewarding underwater adventure.

Chapter 7

Diving from a Boat

H APPY ARE THE DIVERS who have access to a good
boat. For one who loves the water, nothing can
match the anticipation that comes with loading the
last of the gear aboard an inflatable just off a quiet
beach at dawn; heading cleanly outward from a busy
launching ramp; or cruising into some isolated cove,
with its smooth, clear water and an undisturbed wild
shoreline, to drop anchor and prepare for the dive.
And in the mind's eye, the unique, untrammeled
horizons and secluded places below the water's surface are even more alluring than those above.

What Makes a Good Dive Boat?

Almost any boat, down to and including a modified
kayak, can be used as a base for scuba diving. However, several design features and pieces of equipment
are normally associated with safe, efficient, and enjoyable boat diving.

The first two features, which usually occur together, are roominess and stability. For warm-season
day trips in most areas, a wide, open boat, whether of
rigid or inflatable construction, is hard to improve
upon. Savvy dive boaters nearly always remove the
seats from their craft, thus greatly increasing stowage
space and making retrieval of gear easier, while si-

multaneously reducing the risk that encumbered divers will stumble and hurt themselves. For similar reasons, some diving-boat owners even remove the windshields. A boat need not resemble a sportscar. A windshield can be an aggravating and sometimes dangerous barrier to the free exchange of people and gear fore and aft, for example during anchoring or when equipment is being stowed in or retrieved from a forward well.

For winter trips or cold-country trips at any time of year, an open boat is not recommended. Nor does a canvas or similar enclosure usually provide sufficient protection from the topside elements in winter to assure a healthful, comfortable experience. Even wearers of full winter wetsuits exposed to subzero chill factors delivered by icy sea winds will sooner or later become uncomfortable and even dangerously chilled in an open or poorly enclosed boat. Unisuits, on the other hand, will keep you warm in an Arctic gale (so it is said), but, where possible in cold weather, it is much more fun and relaxing to dive from a larger boat having a closed cabin and a source of heat. The cozy rewarming of your body and topside reunion with your fellow divers over hot drinks will provide one of the finer memories of the trip.

The power of a boat's propulsive equipment should be commensurate with the load, distance, and water conditions estimated for the diving trip. U.S. Coast Guard regulations specify the maximum and minimum power allowable for any given type of boat. This information may be obtained from any boat dealer, or from the Coast Guard itself. On trips far from shore, one is well advised to carry a small auxiliary outboard motor for use in case the boat's main power source fails.

A sailing dive boat? Why not—as long as the boat is comfortably broad-beamed and no one is in a hurry? But be wary of the boom when you straighten up after donning a tank; lines, cleats, capstans, and other hazards to divers lurching about with heavy tanks abound on a sailboat. Also, be ready at the dive site to rely on auxiliary power while selecting the anchorage, maneuvering to pick up drifting divers, and other such tasks.

A recent development in scuba support vessels is the diver's kayak, invented in California and, at this writing, appearing on parts of the East Coast as well. This fiberglass craft looks like a somewhat flattened racing shell. Special wells for the tank and other gear are located fore and aft of the paddler's compartment. Weighing about 35 pounds, the kayak can be carried by one person fairly easily (unless there is a breeze, which will twist and tug the lightweight shell mercilessly). The only drawback to the diving kayak is that it only serves one diver, and the 35-pound craft added to the rest of your gear necessitates an extra trip back to your car and down to the beach at both ends of the dive. Strictly speaking, the kayak is most useful as an aid to shore diving rather than as a dive boat. The kayak makes for a much swifter, less laborious trip to a dive site than swimming. However, once on site, the diver, who must be already partly dressed, has to don his or her tank in the water, since the kayak is not stable enough to support this operation.

Design features that aid a diver in entering and leaving the water complete the list of major structural factors to look for in a dive boat. Low-built boats, of course, are easy to leave and only a little more difficult to board over the side or transom. Jumping or rolling into the water from higher boats can be thrilling (shades of James Bond), but if you're carrying camera and strobe, an expensive new speargun, an underwater light, and so on, you may opt for a gentler entrance. In such a case, a boarding ladder or a diving platform solves the problem. The former is cheap and simple to install; it's a lightweight ladder whose lowest rung dips a foot or two below the surface of the water and the tops of whose uprights curve broadly to hook over the boat's gunwale.

The diving platform represents a more deluxe approach to entering and leaving the water. Usually of slatted construction and attached outboard of the boat by basal hinges and guylines, the platform is lowered

7.1. *Dive platform in use at the stern of a boat.*

for use and lies flat at the water's surface. Platforms are easiest to rig on transoms of boats with inboard drives. They may also be fitted around outboards, and are sometimes operated from the sides or the bow of a dive boat. A platform permits the easiest of entries and exits and is very useful when one is carrying heavy or delicate equipment such as cameras, collecting gear, or specimen containers. Dive platforms are generally most useful on larger boats (more than 25 feet in length); they are apt to be unwieldy and unnecessary on smaller craft.

Equipping the Boat

A few pieces of essential equipment and some recommended gear remain to be mentioned in this section. The essential items are an anchor (with chain) of the proper type and size for your boat, an anchor line measuring at least three times the depth at which you will be operating, a marine or CB radio if you intend to go outside coastal bays and harbors, a good first-aid kit, and, last, all accessories for boats of your type required by Coast Guard regulations—topping the list are a fire extinguisher and flotation devices for everyone aboard. A 100-foot length of line with a buoy or life-ring attached to one end, which can be thrown to a tired diver on the surface, is an important safety measure. Also essential are nautical charts for the areas in which you will be boating.

For details on the appropriate anchor, chain, and line for your boat, consult a book on boating or your local nautical store. If you are new to boating, it's a very good idea to take one of the courses in small-boat handling and water safety offered by the Coast Guard, Red Cross, or local power squadrons in all parts of the country.

If you will be taking your boat into potentially rough and remote waters, a radio on board will contribute mightily to the peace of mind of everyone concerned—both the seafarers themselves and those who wait at home. A fairly good corrosion-resistant CB radio with antenna specially designed for marine use will transmit reliably up to 10 miles. Since the summer of 1978, the Coast Guard has monitored CB Channel 9 (the emergency channel) in all coastal areas. But the CB should be considered an absolute minimum for emergency communications. Channel 9 is sometimes pre-empted by individuals for routine conversation, and in your hour of need you may find yourself in contact with a local pizza delivery truck —definitely not the most efficient way to obtain help. A second and better option is to buy a more expensive marine radio (the Coast Guard-approved VHF model with the traditional FM emergency band). On board an open boat, keep your radio in a waterproof box to minimize damage from salt spray. Another safety device that is rapidly becoming popular is the Emergency Position Indicating Radio Beacon, or EPIRB, which floats and uses battery power to put out an automatic signal detectable at great distances by rescue aircraft.

A good first-aid kit will include the standard remedies and patch-up aids for abrasion- and contusion-type injuries, stings, sprains, strains, and so forth, as well as seasick pills (a good idea to take these if needed well before leaving the dock), and antihistamine nasal spray (for occasional use as an aid to clearing the ears and sinuses). Oxygen-breathing equipment (for surface use in decompression sickness) is often considered a deluxe extra, but we recommend that it be carried in *any* boat used for fairly deep and frequent diving.

We strongly recommend that you cover the bottom inside of your boat with rubber mats to protect the floor of the boat from contact with heavy, abrasive equipment and to keep your gear from sliding about when the boat is underway and rolling in swells. Also, extra lengths of light line are always useful, for example in fastening tanks and weight belts to the boat prior to reboarding at the end of a dive.

Once you have participated in a few boat dives, you will no doubt form your own opinions concerning the construction and outfitting of an ideal dive boat. Divers' opinions, like those of sports-car drivers and hang gliders, tend to vary widely regarding the preferred craft serving their sport. Somewhat wider agreement seems to exist in the dynamic aspects of diving from a boat.

Planning the Boat Dive

Most of what we will say in this section pertains to a self-guided day trip in a small to medium-sized boat. On larger boats, skippers, charter operators, or diving instructors often have operations so firmly programmed that the diver is guided into, under, and out of the water, and constantly offered food, drink, and entertainment above the surface.

The first stage of a boat dive is primarily a mental exercise. Think critically about your equipment and leave unnecessary items behind. Street clothes, shoes, purses, wallets, unhoused cameras, and the like usually end up wet, crumpled, or at least in the way before the trip is half over. Unneeded gasoline cans, picnic baskets, buckets, nets, and fishing tackle should also remain behind. The point is to leave as much space for the divers and essential gear as possible. Packing the gear and stowing it aboard is a matter for experimentation and personal preference. However, a good guiding principle is for everyone on the trip to be responsible for keeping his or her own lightweight equipment together and out of the way of others. The skipper or boat owner on the trip should have jurisdiction over the stowage of tanks and weight belts. The passenger-carrying capacity of a given boat is usually stated by the manufacturer, and in many areas is regulated by state laws. On a diving trip, it is wise to reduce the maximum safe number aboard by one-third to one-half. If every inch of the deck is hidden under gear—while people form a second layer—only a boatload of saints will truly enjoy the trip, no matter how good the diving. When you find yourself shoulder to shoulder with your companions in a Boston Whaler, merely keeping your gear together and getting it properly attached to your body require the combined skills of a military honor guard and a chorus line dancer.

If you are going to a new area to dive, everyone on the trip should go over the nautical charts of the dive site before leaving the dock. As you saw in the preceding chapter, the charts give clues as to the types of bottom and water conditions the divers will find. Also try to obtain local information. Be sure to leave a float plan with responsible friends or family members. This is especially critical if you are going well offshore. Stick to the float plan and leave with the understanding that if you are not home within a certain time (allow some leeway for unavoidable delays) someone will call the Coast Guard or Harbor Patrol.

Good housekeeping is essential aboard a dive boat. Keep diving gear together and out of the way of others, especially the boat operator. Be extremely careful with gasoline. *No smoking* is an ironclad rule on a small boat. Keep the boat clean and free of even small gas spills. Gasoline will eat holes in expensive neoprene goods before your eyes; even a greasy gas tank can damage a wetsuit or a BC draped over it. Gasoline also dissolves synthetic foam products, such as beer coolers. It's a good idea to avoid styrofoam-type equipment wherever possible. In the ocean, synthetic foam breaks down into microscopic particles, insidious pollutants that are eaten by plankton organisms and other tiny creatures, including baby fishes. These organisms are often killed by the indigestible particles blocking their intestines.

Take plenty of water or other nonalcoholic potables on your trip. In tropical areas or during the temperate summer, remember to bring some effective form of sunburn protection. In an open boat, you may be exposed to ultraviolet radiation for hours. If you are not careful you can receive extremely serious burns that may require medical treatment.

As with shore dives, in many areas it is extremely important to plan your boat dives with tidal currents in mind. Intervals of slack high and low tides vary from a few minutes to an hour, and may even change at the same location with the cycle of stronger and weaker tides throughout the month. Slack high tides generally offer better visibility than slack low tides in most nearshore locations. Offshore, however, differences in visibility between the tides may be undetectable. In some areas, you may be able to extend the dive at either end of the slack period.

At the Site

A simple aid in selecting an anchorage at the dive site is a light sounding line with a lead weight attached. The line should be marked in fathoms for a quick read. You can use a two-pound diving belt weight for a sinker. If you are exploring a new area and want a preview of the type of sediment on the bottom, try looping a strip of electrical tape into a circle and pressing the circle of tape on the bottom of your sounding lead. When the sticky piece of tape touches the bottom it will bring up some of the sand, mud, dead seaweed, or even pebbles, and reveal in general what sort of bottom conditions—whether silty or clear—you will find on your dive.

In clear water, divers often select the anchoring spot by donning a mask and leaning over the side. A more comfortable option, if you have room in the boat, is a *look box*—an open box or bucket with a bottom of glass or clear plastic. In ideal conditions you can preview bottom features through a look box in 80 to 100 feet of water.

If there is a current at the site, or if a tidal current is expected to materialize, the boat will usually, but not always, be pulling against the anchor in the direction of the current. Wind is a complicating factor and can reinforce the drift caused by a current, or else oppose it to varying degrees depending on the relative directions of movement of air and water. Therefore, before you anchor, check the drift of the boat and plan the anchoring and diving operations accordingly.

Anchoring technique and success generally improve with practice. The recommended procedure is to keep the engine idling and to release the anchor at the bow when you are directly over the chosen spot. There is no need to dislocate your shoulder by flinging the anchor. Simply hold the anchor and its attached chain clear of the boat and let it go straight down (keeping the chain free of kinks and tangles). As the line begins to pay out, the boat operator should begin to back the boat up slowly so that the line streams ahead of the bow. Usually, only a slight amount of back momentum is necessary. If there is a noticeable drift, the boat should be backed in the same direction. The engine should be idled again well before the line tightens and the anchor begins to bite into the bottom. Adjust the length of the line paid out to measure about three times the depth. Cleat the line securely, but be sure that it can be cast off quickly if the need should arise (more about this later).

Once the anchor is holding securely in a sedimentary bottom, it will rarely become dislodged by itself.

Even if the direction of drift changes, the anchor will usually maintain its grip in the bottom as it is turned, perhaps as much as 180 degrees. Rocky bottom, however, sometimes provides an exception to this statement. A boat swinging around a rocky anchor point may pull loose and drift a short distance before the anchor reaches a new hold. The most problematical of rocky anchorages occur where fairly shallow ledges lie adjacent to deep water. In such a location, a drifting boat can pull the loose anchor over the deep, thus continuing to drift with a uselessly dangling anchor. On every dive, no matter what the type of bottom, the first divers down should inspect the anchor and, if necessary, reinforce its hold on the bottom.

Once you have anchored, it's a good idea to relax a little; talk over the dive plan again with your partners; and have an orange, candy bar, or cup of something refreshing. Now is the time to rig the short lines over the side for later use. Also deploy the long line—100 feet or so—with its safety buoy off the stern. You may find it convenient to have your lines end with snap links. The short lines, as mentioned earlier, will permit surfacing divers to "tie off' tanks and weight belts prior to reboarding the boat. This is especially important if no one is left in the boat at the end of the dive to help lift heavy gear out of the water. Of course, muscular individuals can board a boat in full gear, but they risk injury from falls, pulled muscles, and possibly even hernia in doing so.

The long line at the surface is especially important if a significant current is running. Divers who surface away from the boat in a current may still be able to reach the trailing line and pull themselves in hand over hand.

One of the unsung challenges in sport diving involves the donning of one's gear in a small boat that seems to be rolling, pitching, and yawing all at once. First, of course, you have to put on the wetsuit (if you are not already wearing it). The pants, or farmer-john unit, occasions the most contortion and risk to life and limb, since you have to stand up in the boat to get a comfortable fit. After the suit, the BC should be donned, and then the weight belt. A good technique for securing a heavy belt is to kneel on the boat's bottom and bend forward from the waist. Let your back take the weight as you position the belt and fasten the buckle. The tank is the last heavy item, but before you put it on, be sure your regulator is working perfectly, and that all your accessory gauges and your compass, knife, and so on, are in place on your person. Also at this time, place your mask, snorkel, fins, and goody bag within easy reach, so you or your buddies won't have to fumble and stumble about searching for them after donning a heavy tank. It's also a good idea to give your mask the saliva treatment and rinse just before putting on your tank.

In donning a tank aboard a small boat, we recommend that you enlist your buddy's help rather than using the solo, overhead technique. In tossing on your own tank in a crowded, unstable boat you risk falling, even from a kneeling position, and injuring yourself and others. Once the tank is on, don your mask, snorkel, and fins. Obviously, you should not try to move around the boat with fins on.

The simplest way to enter the water from a small boat is by back rolling over the side. Basically, the back-roll entry proceeds as follows: First, check all your equipment (secure all buckles, make sure the weight belt is clear of all other straps, see that the regulator is functioning). Inflate the BC to about one-third to one-half full. Hold your fins clear of all gear and obstructions on the floor of the boat. Put the regulator in your mouth. Look behind you in the water for people or other obstacles. Hold your mask in place with one hand; hold the hoses for the octopus, your gauges, and all other appendages with the other. Then, place your fanny outboard as far as possible, take a breath, and fall gently back. You will barely have time to register the sensations of a splash and the surrounding coolness and wetness before you are bobbing at the surface beside the boat. An alternative to the back-roll entry is the side roll. With this technique, begin by straddling, rather than sitting on, the boat's gunwale.

Before you make your exit, gauge the stability of your boat in response to weighted divers going over the side. Small, rounded-hulled boats can capsize if excessive weight is applied to one side. Ideally, two divers should roll off opposite sides simultaneously, or, if a single diver is entering the water, someone should serve as a counterweight by placing himself on the opposite side of the boat. At least, be sure to warn people remaining aboard to brace themselves just before you roll out of the boat.

Once you are in the water, the usual procedure is to pick up any accessory gear—such as spear, camera, and light—from people in the boat and then rendezvous with your diving partners around the anchor line just ahead of the boat. If the sea surface is rough, or if there is an appreciable current, you may opt to skip the surface rendezvous and meet at the anchor itself. Naturally, you will have to purge your BC to get started below.

During the Dive

The obvious way down is to follow the anchor line. This procedure is mandatory whenever you can't see the position of the anchor from the surface. If you don't follow the anchor line down and visibility is poor, you may have difficulty locating the anchor and your buddies even if you use a compass. At the very least you will have wasted time and air in the search.

Before doing anything else on the bottom, put yourself through a little drill—the same one used on a shore-based dive. Readjust your weight belt, keeping it clear of all other gear and keeping the buckle where you can find it. Trim your buoyancy by putting some air into the BC. Check the compass bearing to the boat by sighting along the anchor line if you cannot see the boat on the surface. Check the direction of the current, if any. Decide which way you and your partner will travel, and determine the compass bearing back to the anchor. If the water is fairly murky, you may want to plan your return swim so that you come up between the anchor and the boat. The two compass bearings are then integrated with an estimate of distance traveled. A compass functions the same way under water as in air, and while underwater orienteering is certainly not as accurate as that practiced on land, some divers learn to navigate very well in the depths.

As an alternative to anchoring the boat during the dive, some underwater explorers prefer to have the boat moving freely and following the progress of the divers. In this case, the trick is for the boat operator to keep track of the people below. He or she should not try to follow bubbles, for these are often impossible to keep in view, especially if there is a light chop. Instead, the divers should tow a small buoy or a diver's flag attached to a light line.

The boat operator should not keep the boat's engine running continuously. The preferred practice is to maneuver near the diver's marker and then to turn off the engine and drift for a while. This procedure is more important for the divers' safety than for conserving gasoline. One reason for turning off the engine is that exhaust fumes tend to spread across the water surface. A concentrated whiff of these noxious gases is unpleasant for any surfacing diver, and some susceptible individuals become severely nauseated from them. The other reason, less likely but with greater consequence, is that the shift lever of an idling engine may be inadvertently engaged while a diver is in the water beside the engine; divers have sustained severe lacerations and have even died as a result of this particular set of circumstances.

Drift Diving

Perhaps the most exciting yet straightforward kind of nonanchored boat diving involves a one-way trip in the grip of an ocean current. This sport, called *drift diving,* is practiced fairly commonly in such places as the Bahama Islands and southeast Florida. In the latter area, divers ride the edge of the most powerful oceanic current of all, the Gulf Stream.

During a drift dive, as the term implies, both the boat at the surface and the divers below are traveling with and at essentially the same speed as the current, which may be as fast as three or four knots. But with virtually no relative motion, the boat and divers remain close together, and the divers tow a surface marker for insurance.

We do not recommend drift diving for newly certified individuals, and a drift dive should not be approached simply as a joy ride—although, in truth, that phrase does capture the spirit and sensations of the experience. Careful planning and coordination with the boat operator are required, however. The following precautions and prearrangements are the minimum required to ensure a safe drift dive:

1. Do not enter a strong current in murky water (that is, where visibility is less than 30 feet).
2. Do not drift dive at night.

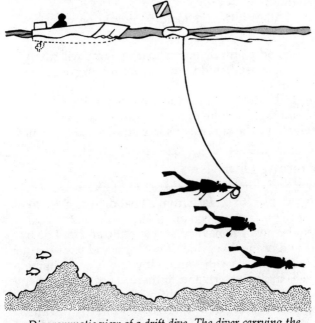

7.2. *Diagrammatic view of a drift dive. The diver carrying the buoy line may opt for a spool or reel to regulate the length of the line as depth increases or decreases.*

3. Make sure that the surface current and the current at diving depth are moving in the same direction. If this is not obvious, the most experienced diver in the group should descend briefly at the end of a line fastened to the drifting boat and determine the current direction at the bottom, where the divers will be.

4. All divers in the party should stay together. No more than six divers, teamed up in three buddy pairs, should constitute a drift-diving party, and only one party per boat, please.

5. Each party of divers should tow a surface float.

6. Prearrange a surfacing time and synchronize the watches of the divers and boat operator. Be sure that the planned diving time is well within the air-reserve capacity of the hardest-breathing diver in the group. This implies that each diver is advanced enough to know his or her approximate time limit for consuming a tank of air at the maximum depth anticipated. Be conservative!

7. All drift dives should be nondecompression dives.

Ideally, on a drift dive, the boat's engine will rarely have to be used, and then only for minor course corrections to stay near the float tethered to the divers below. Under water, the aquanauts will be able to cover a mile or more of terrain effortlessly, as if in orbit above the surface of some strange exotic planet.

After the Dive

Always plan to surface from a boat dive as close to the boat as possible. If you are able to relocate the boat from below or to navigate back to the anchor line by the end of the dive, fine. If not, you and your partner should surface (with caution if you can hear engine noises in the water), and, if there is boat traffic in the area, resubmerge after sighting the boat, taking a compass bearing that will lead you directly toward it.

Where the current is strong, surfacing on the downstream side of the boat may present difficulties, especially if you have missed the safety line trailing off the stern. This is the time to signal the boat operator, assuming that someone aboard is competent at running the boat. Inflate your BC fully, and use your whistle instead of yelling yourself hoarse. Relax and wait.

From the boat operator's standpoint, a situation involving tired or weak swimmers caught in a current and unable to return to the boat calls for fairly simple actions. But a couple of tricks can save time. First, it is a fine idea to have the bitter end of your anchor line tied to a float which, after the line is uncleated, can be cast cleanly into the water. Thus, the boat is freed entirely from the anchor and the anchor is marked for retrieval. The boat then approaches the drifting divers, but should stay slightly (15 to 20 feet) to one side of them. The operator should throttle down and maneuver until the boat's speed in the water matches the drifters' and then cut the engine. He or she should warn the divers not to approach the boat until the engine is off and, after the pickup, remember to go back for the anchor.

When a number of divers are returning to the boat together, the short lengths of line with the snap links that were placed over the side before the dive are really well appreciated. Having to cling to the side of the boat, the motor, or even a ladder for a few minutes waiting your turn to climb back on board can be tiring and sometimes hazardous, particularly in rough water. But holding onto a 6-foot line, comfortably buoyed and away from the crush, can be a pleasure.

It is never wise to try to board a rocking boat with all your scuba gear still attached to your body. When there is a crowd at the boarding ladder or platform, relax and take your time. The coldest or tiredest people should be permitted to get out of the water first. Remove your heavy gear—your tank and weight belt—in the water. The lines will come in handy at this point too—especially if your boat operator is on the small side and not eager to haul in several heavy tanks and weight belts. You can tie off the tank and belt, climb on board, and then pull them in yourself.

After you hand up or tie off your tank and belt, be

sure to keep your mask, fins, and snorkel. Take off your fins to avoid stumbling and perhaps damaging them only when it is your turn on the boarding ladder. If you are exiting the water via a diving platform, or boarding an inflatable, keep your fins on until you are out of the water.

If you are one of those helping to bring gear into the boat, avoid dropping or throwing weights, banging equipment on the sides of the boat, and so on. Careless treatment can shorten the life of both equipment and boat. Once the gear is all together in the boat again, organizing it becomes a struggle against human nature. Somehow at the end of a dive disorder tends to prevail with greater force than before, and extra effort and care are needed to prevent the crushing of compasses, the breaking of cameras, and the chipping of gunwales.

It is true that boat-based excursions demand more discipline and cooperation before and after the actual diving than shore-based diving, but we believe that the extra preparation and precision are worth it. The ease of access to places of interest under water is a pleasure greatly envied by embattled shore divers weary of sand-slogging, rock-hopping, and surf-ducking. Another positive note is that boat divers do not take home a load of sand imbedded in their wetsuit zippers, regulators, mask linings, camera housings, and the like. A casual poll is likely to reveal that nine out of ten divers find it easiest to appreciate a sunset from a comfortable corner of a dive boat heading shoreward after a successful dive.

Chapter 8

Going Deep

I T IS NATURAL for divers in love with the sea to
want to dive deeper and longer, to extend their
personal frontiers of underwater experience and to
discover what it is like far down there in the immense
twilight and silence of the ocean wilderness. In this
chapter, we cover the practicalities involved in deep
diving, which we define as diving below 50 feet.

Amateur deep diving has had a fairly short history, and the attitude among leaders in the industry
has changed sharply—or perhaps evolved is a more
accurate word. Before about the mid-1960s, deep diving by sport divers was virtually unknown. It seems
that marine scientists, who were not professional divers, led the way in the mid- and late sixties. Among
the pioneers were biologists and geologists from
Scripps Institution of Oceanography in California.
They explored the head of La Jolla Submarine Canyon, which begins a short distance off the beach and
drops sharply toward the deep sea. The late Dr.
Thomas Goreau will probably always be best remembered for his research in coral physiology and ecology
on the deep reefs of Jamaica. Goreau discovered that
the growth forms of certain species of coral change
with increasing depth, that massive, rounded coral
heads near the surface gradually give way to extremely flattened table forms of the same species 150

to 200 feet down. These scientific explorers, motivated by their curiosity, sometimes went well below 200 feet while using what today would be considered extremely primitive equipment.

A fairly liberal outlook toward deep diving prevailed for a time in the early seventies as more and more divers discovered the profoundly spectacular walls and hanging reefs of the Cayman Islands, Andros, Roatan, and other Caribbean sites. But it appears that a rising diver-accident rate (peaking in 1974 in the United States) prompted diver-training organizations, dive-boat operators, and diving-resort managers to take an increasingly conservative stand and to exercise a policy of constraint regarding deep diving. Although the statistics on diver accidents for 1970–74 do not support the idea that deep diving contributed significantly to the increase in fatalities (most serious accidents then occurred, and now continue to occur, in the upper 30 feet of the water column),* deep diving has become one of the biggest bugaboos in the industry.

At present, unless one has access to a private boat, it is difficult, even for expert divers, to make a truly deep dive. Universally at resorts and aboard charter boats, regulations enforced by hard-eyed divemasters forbid descent below 130 feet. Some organizations are reducing the depth limit to 100 feet and enforcing a 15-minute rule, which allows divers to stay at 100 feet for no more than 15 minutes. (The maximum interval for a nondecompression dive at this depth is 25 minutes.) Because of the startlingly rapid recent growth of the amateur diver population, and a concomitant lack of deep-water experience on the part of most divers, we largely agree with the new conservative approach to deep diving.

Endangering the novice, and many experienced divers too, are a lack of familiarity with nitrogen narcosis and rates of air consumption at great depth as well as the lure of clear, tropical waters where it feels

---

*U.S. Department of Commerce (NOAA) *et al. United States Underwater Fatality Statistics 1975* (March 1977).

so pleasant to keep on going down. Nevertheless, some amateur divers will make their way into very deep water—for scientific purposes perhaps, or to satisfy the human urge to explore, to face the challenge posed by the unknown, or for other, more obscure personal motives related to those that draw mountaineers toward high and difficult summits.

Although we hope that some useful information on deep diving will be provided by this chapter, we by no means certify its sufficiency for diver preparation. In our opinion, anyone who ventures below even 50 feet should take a course in deep diving taught by a professional instructor. Our philosophy of deep diving is simply that it should be taken very seriously. Diving anywhere is not an activity for fools and children, and this rule applies in double or triple measure for deep diving. A serious purpose and a serious, detailed plan for the dive should go hand in hand. Deep inner space is strange—beautiful in some ways, not so beautiful in others. The deep-diving range is demanding of immense respect by human visitors. There are lessons to be learned here in self-discipline, vital cooperation with others, and the precariousness of the human condition in the face of uncontrolled environmental forces. However, when performed by cautious, mature, knowledgeable people, who understand their own limitations and those imposed by the environment, the logistics of deep diving should hold no mysteries and no threats.

Nondecompression versus Decompression Dives

As we noted in Chapter 4, the absorption of nitrogen in the body takes time. Therefore, the duration of a dive is a key factor in the buildup of body nitrogen toward the *nondecompression limit*, or critical nitrogen load—that is, the pressure of dissolved nitrogen in the body that cannot be exceeded if the diver is to return directly to the surface. This maximum safe bodily load of nitrogen accumulated at any depth is the equivalent to the full load (or saturation level) that would be absorbed by a very long or indefinite stay at 26 feet. If the diver absorbs any more nitrogen at any greater depth, he or she risks the bends in rising directly to the surface without stopping for decompression.

The rapidity with which a diver accumulates nitrogen depends on the depth, or, more accurately, the ambient pressure that forces the nitrogen into the body. Refer back to the table of nondecompression limits in Chapter 4. Note, for example, that at 35 feet the critical loading time—at which nitrogen in the body begins to exceed the nondecompression level—is 310 minutes, while at 135 feet, the same amount of nitrogen is stored in the body in 10 minutes. Beyond these time limits at these depths, too much gas has been bottled up in the body to allow a sudden "removal of the cork," or total release of the outside pressure. The pressure must be released in stages, through decompression. We will cover the use of diving tables in detail later in this chapter.

Most of our discussion and recommendations in this chapter are limited to nondecompression or nonsaturation diving. In excursions to very deep water, this method is also called *bounce diving*, since, at the target depth, divers will just about have time to look around the immediate area before starting upward again in order to prevent an accumulation of nitrogen in the body that demands decompression. Still, due to unforeseen delays that exceed the nondecompression time limit at a given depth, a bounce dive can turn into a decompression dive, and the diving party must be prepared for this eventuality.

Equipment for Deep Dives

For the deep diver the first commandment regarding equipment is, Get the best! In a regulator, this means a top-of-the-line unit with a balanced first stage and adjustable breathing resistance at the second stage that will deliver air at the slightest demand. The inhalation forces needed to trigger the flow of air in a regulator can be measured at a pro dive shop. The breathing resistance of a regulator used in a deep dive should not exceed 1 inch of water. Any regulator used for deep diving should have been recently cleaned and calibrated. This piece of equipment ought to be in perfect mechanical condition, like the apparatus making up an astronaut's life-support system.

Naturally, your regulator must include a recently calibrated submersible pressure gauge, and at least one member of each diving pair, or two out of three, must carry an octopus unit.

A good-quality, oil-filled depth gauge is also a must for deep diving, along with a diving watch. With careful planning, one watch per buddy pair is permissible, as long as the designated timekeeper is meticulous about the task. Divers staying down past the nondecompression limit may also choose to carry a capillary depth gauge. While the oil-filled gauge is accurate in the deep range, the capillary gauge, which operates on the principle of air compression in a narrow tube, is considerably more accurate in shallow water than the oil-filled unit. Thus, it permits the divers to precisely stage decompression stops at 10-foot intervals as they approach the surface. However, capillary gauges are prone to malfunction, since the narrow air tubes, open to the environment, can be clogged by particles of sand and other foreign material. To be sure of depths near the surface for decompression stops, most divers prefer to suspend a weighted line below the boat marked at precisely 10, 20, 30, and 40 feet. With this option a good oil-filled depth gauge is the only one needed.

A high-capacity BC or stabilization jacket, with 35 to 50 pounds of lifting capacity is also essential for the deep diver. We recommend an autoinflator capability, which delivers tank air directly to the BC. As we noted earlier, high-pressure air bottles incorporated into the BC are preferred by some divers, but the little bottles entail extra maintenance. They must be hydrotested and visually inspected on the same schedule as the regular scuba tank. Also, without the diver's special vigilance, all the pressurized air can easily bleed out of a BC bottle, allowing moisture to enter and hasten corrosion. Strictly speaking, a deep diver should save bottled compressed air for a potential emergency and not use it for trimming buoyancy.

Single 72-cubic-foot or 80-cubic-foot tanks are sufficient for bounce diving, but if you use them you must pay scrupulous attention to your air supply. For deep diving, we recommend a larger tank (94-cubic-foot steel tank) or a double-tank combination, both of which will provide extra air for emergencies and delays in deep water. Also, extra tanks must be suspended on a line at specific depths below the boat to be available for ascending divers in case decompression is required. Typically, one tank and regulator is provided at 10 or 20 feet for each diver down. However, use of an octopus rig will make a single tank available to two people during decompression.

We also recommend that you go deep only with your own equipment or an exact facsimile that you know to be in perfect working condition. Avoid diving deep with rented equipment unless you know the renter very well, and, above all, avoid going deep with unfamiliar equipment. Deep water is not the place to experiment with life-support technology.

Usually, a deep-diving team should not include more than three divers. Larger groups should be broken up into self-reliant pairs or triplets. A loosely knit group without well-delineated partnerships does not belong in deep water. A false sense of security brings the likelihood of someone being left alone or a lack of coordinated response in an emergency.

Naturally, a person who is knowledgeable about diving as well as boat operation should be aboard the boat throughout the dive. This person should be fully aware of the dive plan and should time the dive from the start. In the event that decompression becomes necessary for the divers, the boat operator should be prepared to lower spare tanks and regulators attached to a line to the divers if, for some reason, equipment was not placed in the water at the start.

The Bounce Dive

The Stop-and-Go Descent

For deep diving, it is imperative that weather and water conditions be very good to excellent. Large swells, bad chop, and all but the slightest current should rule out a deep dive. So should turbid water; we recommend visibility of not less than 25 to 30 feet.

A deep dive begins almost like any boat-based dive. However, you should always descend along a weighted diveline, hanging straight down below the boat, not an anchor line. It's a good idea to descend slowly, no faster than 50 to 75 feet per minute. There is a strange physiological malady dubbed "the uglies" by some divers, which can be triggered by too rapid a descent into fairly deep water. The symptoms include dizziness, disorientation, and blurred vision. A leisurely drop is easier on your body and usually more enjoyable as well.

You should plan two stop-and-rendezvous intervals. The first should be around 50 feet. Here check all systems, cinch up your weight belts, and give special attention to your octopus units. At this stop, someone should also take several breaths from each extra second-stage unit the dive party is carrying. Anyone experiencing equipment difficulties or second thoughts about the deep dive should abort at this point and return to the boat. If a person aborts from a party of three or more and this does not affect the original dive plan, the remaining divers can continue descending. Otherwise, all should return to the surface and replan the dive.

The second stop and rendezvous should occur at around 120 feet. It's a good idea to check the octopus regulators again at this point. Also, spend a quiet moment trying to determine if nitrogen dissolving in your body fluids is beginning to exert its mysterious effects. It is interesting and worthwhile on a deep dive to carefully explore your susceptibility to nitrogen, trying in particular to pinpoint your personal threshold, or minimal depth, for the onset of "the narcs."

Some people will not feel anything unusual at 120 feet. But at 150 feet down, most divers are very definitely aware that they are becoming narced. As we noted in Chapter 4, the feelings vary. One of us may experience a very calm, pleasant personal drunkenness, with a buzzing sensation or a very light vibration behind the eyes. Others may experience, to varying degrees, a slowed reaction time, an exaggerated sense of self-confidence, mild to extreme euphoria ("rapture of the deep"), and a false sense of warmth. As one goes deeper, he or she might notice a bitter or metallic taste in the mouth, a ringing in the ears, tunnel vision, and increasing dizziness and disorientation. Nearly any one of the symptoms listed is a powerful reason why you should not descend below a point where you know you are feeling the nitrogen. Be especially wary if you have recently taken any sort of medication. Mention to the doctor who wrote your particular prescription that you dive, and ask him if there are any known or predictable side effects of the medicine under high pressure. In particular, physicians should be concerned about hyperbaric effects of drugs on the human nervous system. If you or the doctor have any doubts, do not dive while you are under treatment.

Bottom Time

On the bottom, divers should remain in easy view of the vertical dive line. In cases of exceptional visibility, when the boat can be seen from the bottom, experienced divers may opt to leave the immediate vicinity of the down line, but only if they will still be able to locate it again for possible later decompression.

In most deep-diving areas, the abundance and diversity of marine wildlife diminish greatly below about 75 to 100 feet. The marine biology spectacles featured in movies and on TV are usually found close to the surface. Some undersea landscapes, for example in Hawaii, are almost barren-looking below about 75 feet. Encounters of exceptional interest do occur in the deep, however. The hopes of sighting some large fish, black coral, or rare shells are offered by some divers as motives for going deep. Scientists are intrigued by special aspects of biology, geology, and chemistry at depth, and direct sightings and personal experience in these areas are often both necessary and rewarding. The Manned Undersea Science and Technology (MUST) office of NOAA, itself an agency of the U.S. Department of Commerce, is a clearinghouse of information and lends support to scientific researchers who consistently become involved in deep diving.

If your party is involved in a scientific dive, one partner should be designated as being on watch. He or she must pay total attention to time, depth, air supply, and distance traveled from the diveline, while others are preoccupied with the objectives of the dive. He or she is responsible for assuring that the others adhere rigidly to the dive plan, especially with regard to bottom time.

Very clear water can be a liability, particularly on a deep dive. Ironically, clear water presents a real threat to divers at any depth for it conceals one of the chief psychological dangers in diving. There is a false sense of security in being able to see your diving partner at a considerable distance. The same is true for being able to see your boat at the surface from a long way down. Divers from murky northern continental waters, slipping for the first time into an astonishingly clear tropical sea, find that diving seems almost too easy. However, at such a time, you should remind yourself that your top swimming speed toward your partner, the pressure at, say, 100 feet, and the vertical distance home are the same anywhere—whether or not you can see the whole route. Therefore, safety demands that diving partners stay virtually within the range of physical touch. Naturally, when in close proximity to others, you should move slowly and carefully. Sudden kicking and flailing of the arms may forcibly remove your buddy's mask or regulator—no fun anywhere, and even less at 200 feet, where lots of precious air will be lost in corrective maneuvers.

On a deep dive, your air supply will dwindle very rapidly, especially if you exert yourself unnecessarily. Again, be sure to trim buoyancy and economize on movement. Practice inhaling and exhaling slowly and fully, with your regulator's breathing resistance adjusted for minimal effort of inhalation. The various straps girding your body should be snugly comfortable, not tight, so they don't interfere with your breathing. Even so, an average diver at rest 200 feet down using a single 72-cubic-foot tank will draw down the tank pressure by about 10 to 15 psi with each breath. He or she will actually be able to see the needle of the submersible tank-pressure gauge falling with every two or three breaths at that depth. Since pressurized nitrogen in your brain can play tricks with your reaction time—sometimes it can take 30 seconds for a narced individual just to read the gauge console—you should be extremely conservative about bottom time. At 200 feet, a 30-second delay will lower the pressure in a 72-cubic-foot tank by roughly 50 to 75 psi, depending upon your breathing rate. This air will, of course, be unavailable for later breathing on the way up or during a decompression stop.

Ascent

On a deep bounce dive, it is wise to leave the bottom with a good deal more air than you absolutely need to reach the surface. While we do not recommend that anyone go below about 130 feet, it is not unheard of for amateur divers to approach 200 feet. At such depths, with single 72-cubic-foot tanks, it is folly to start up with less than 1000 psi showing on the gauge. If for some reason a pair of divers has to use an octopus, they might not make it to the surface if they begin at 200 feet with the single functional tank holding less than 1000 psi.

When ascending from great depth, go straight up, preferably along the vertical diveline. Never come up along an anchor line or any other guideline that deviates from the vertical. Ascending at an angle will waste air, and the delay in reaching shallow water will increase the burden of compressed nitrogen in your body. Let your BC take you by the shortest route (but slowly, please); practice controlling your ascent relative to that of your bubbles, as described in Chapter 5. Again, even on ascent, all the members of your party should remain practically within touching distance of one another.

After a vertical ascent to a depth of 10 feet below the surface, trim off and, even though yours was a nondecompression dive, take 5 minutes or so at 10 feet just as a safety precaution to get rid of some of your bottled-up nitrogen before surfacing. As we mentioned earlier, even in the case of a bounce dive, extra tanks and regulators should have been secured on the diveline, usually at 10 feet. Each diver must know the nondecompression limits for the maximum depth reached and the decompression requirements if, due to unforeseen circumstances, the planned time-depth limits have been exceeded.

Decompression and Repetitive Diving

Though we are firm in our recommendation that sport divers not exceed nondecompression limits in the depth and duration of their dives, we feel that it is necessary to identify the conditions that require decompression so that readers will be able to avoid them. A diver is faced with the problem of decompression in two situations: a dive that exceeds the decompression limits for its depth and duration; and the *repetitive dive*, in which the time spent on the surface between dives has been too short to allow the residual nitrogen that accumulated under pressure to be eliminated. For the second of two successive dives to be considered nonrepetitive (so that the diver is carrying no residual nitrogen on the second dive), the surface interval between dives must be at least 12 hours.

Remember that after returning to the surface, a diver's body can tolerate indefinitely the nitrogen absorbed from air at nearly 2 atmospheres pressure. In theory and practice, this degree of tolerance to nitrogen under pressure is treated as an overly optimistic estimate, and a safe return to the surface after a dive of very long duration (or indefinite period spent in an underwater habitat) is only guaranteed from 26 feet (not 33 feet, or exactly 2 atmospheres pressure). Interestingly, the same magnitude of tolerance holds with respect to comparable pressure changes at deeper depths. Thus, professional divers whose bodies have become saturated with nitrogen at 3 atmospheres by spending time in a habitat at 66 feet could rise directly to 40 feet and work safely there, where the pressure approaches 2 atmospheres, but could not ascend immediately above this ceiling without risking the bends.

Let us turn now to the practical application of the information in the diving tables relating to nitrogen absorption and decompression. Above all, remember that the nondecompression table and other diving tables are meant to be used conservatively. Therefore, if the deepest point of your dive was just a little more than 60 feet, you should use the entry in the nondecompression table for 70 feet. With respect to repetitive diving, to find the nondecompression limit of a second dive to be made within 12 hours of a previous one, enter Table 2 at Part 1. First, find the depth of your first dive in the left-hand column; then move horizontally to find your bottom interval. In using these tables, consider bottom time to start when the diver leaves the surface and to end when he or she begins the direct ascent. If your bottom time does not coincide exactly with the numbers given in the table, choose the next greater time. In the following sections, we work through the particulars of some sample dives to demonstrate the use of the tables.

Example 1

Let's consider repetitive diving first. Say you made an initial dive to 65 feet for 37 minutes. Enter Part 1 of Table 2 and go down the depth column to 70 feet; then search horizontally for the time, choosing 40 minutes as your bottom interval. Your dive falls into a particular category, repetitive group H, as indicated by the row of letters below the array of bottom times. Note that each vertical column of bottom times represents equivalent dives in terms of nitrogen loading. Thus, a dive to 20 feet for 325 minutes, or 30 feet for 145 minutes, or 90 feet for 30 minutes will all be designated "H."

Now you return to the surface, and perhaps eat lunch on the boat. You stay on board for an hour and 30 minutes (1:30) before descending again, to 50 feet this time. How long can you stay at 50 feet on the second dive without having to worry about decompression? To find out, start at row H on the diagonal

Table 2: Repetitive Diving Table

Part 1: Depth and Time of the First Dive

Depth
(feet)   First Dive Bottom Times (minutes)

	A	B	C	D	E	F	G	H	I	J	K	L	M	N	O	Z
10	60	120	210	300												
15	35	70	110	160	225	350										
20	25	50	75	100	135	180	240	325								
25	20	35	55	75	100	125	160	195	245	315						
30	15	30	45	60	75	95	120	145	170	205	250	310				
35	5	15	25	40	50	60	80	100	120	140	160	190	220	270	310	
40	5	15	25	30	40	50	70	80	100	110	130	150	170	200		
50		10	15	25	30	40	50	60	70	80	90	100				
60		10	15	20	25	30	40	50	55	60						
70		5	10	15	20	30	35	40	45	50						
80		5	10	15	20	25	30	35	40							
90		5	10	12	15	20	25	30								
100		5	7	10	15	20	22	25								
110			5	10	13	15	20									
120			5	10	12	15										
130			5	8	10											
140			5	7	10											
150			5													
160				5												
170				5												
180				5												
190				5											Repetitive	
	A	B	C	D	E	F	G	H	I	J	K	L	M	N	O	Z

Groups

Table 2: (continued)

Part 2: Surface Interval Minimum Allowable Times (Hours: minutes)

Letters on diagonal designate initial repetitive groups. Read across to find minimum time at surface; then read down to find new repetitive group.

```
12:00  0:10   A
12:00  2:11  0:10   B
12:00  2:50  1:40  0:10   C
12:00  5:49  2:39  1:10  0:10   D
12:00  6:33  3:23  1:58  0:55  0:10   E
12:00  7:06  3:58  2:29  1:30  0:46  0:10   F
12:00  7:36  4:26  2:59  2:00  1:16  0:41  0:10   G
12:00  8:00  4:50  3:21  2:24  1:42  1:07  0:37  0:10   H
12:00  8:22  5:13  3:44  2:45  2:03  1:30  1:00  0:34  0:10   I
12:00  8:41  5:41  4:03  3:05  2:21  1:48  1:20  0:55  0:32  0:10   J
12:00  8:59  5:49  4:20  3:22  2:39  2:04  1:36  1:12  0:50  0:29  0:10   K
12:00  9:13  6:03  4:36  3:37  2:54  2:20  1:50  1:26  1:05  0:46  0:27  0:10   L
12:00  9:29  6:19  4:50  3:53  3:09  2:35  2:06  1:40  1:19  1:00  0:43  0:26  0:10   M
12:00  9:44  6:33  5:04  4:05  3:23  2:48  2:19  1:54  1:31  1:12  0:55  0:40  0:25  0:10   N
12:00  9:55  6:45  5:17  4:18  3:34  3:00  2:30  2:05  1:44  1:25  1:08  0:52  0:37  0:24  0:10   O
12:00 10:06  6:57  5:28  4:30  3:46  3:11  2:43  2:18  1:56  1:37  1:19  1:03  0:49  0:35  0:23  0:10   Z
```

A B C D E F G H I J K L M N O Z
New Repetitive Group Designations

Part 3: Second or Repetitive Dive, RNT*/Non-decompression limit (minutes)

Depth (feet)	NR**	A	B	C	D	E	F	G	H	I	J	K	L	M	N	O	Z
40	/200	7/193	17/183	25/175	37/163	49/151	61/139	73/127	87/113	101/99	116/84	138/62	161/39	187/13	213/	241/	257/
50	/100	6/94	13/87	21/79	29/71	38/62	47/53	56/44	66/34	76/24	87/13	99/1	111/	124/	142/	160/	169/
60	/60	5/55	11/49	17/43	24/36	30/30	36/24	44/16	52/8	61/	70/	79/	88/	97/	107/	117/	122/
70	/50	4/46	9/41	15/35	20/30	26/24	31/19	37/13	43/7	50/	57/	64/	72/	80/	87/	96/	100/
80	/40	4/36	8/32	13/27	18/22	23/17	28/12	32/8	38/2	43/	48/	54/	61/	68/	73/	80/	84/
90	/30	3/27	7/23	11/19	16/14	20/10	24/6	29/1	33/	38/	43/	47/	53/	58/	64/	70/	73/
100	/25	3/22	7/18	10/15	14/11	18/7	22/3	26/	30/	34/	38/	43/	48/	52/	57/	62/	64/
110	/20	3/17	6/14	10/10	13/7	16/4	20/	24/	27/	31/	34/	38/	42/	47/	51/	55/	57/
120	/15	3/12	6/9	9/6	12/3	15/	18/	21/	25/	28/	32/	35/	39/	43/	46/	50/	52/
130	/10	3/7	6/4	8/2	11/	13/	16/	19/	22/	25/	28/	31/	35/	38/	40/	44/	46/
140	/10	2/8	5/5	7/3	10/	12/	15/	18/	20/	23/	26/	29/	32/	35/	38/	40/	42/
150	/5	2/3	5/	7/	9/	12/	14/	17/	19/	22/	24/	27/	30/	32/	35/	38/	40/
160	/5	2/3	4/1	6/	9/	11/	13/	16/	18/	20/	23/	26/	28/	31/	33/	36/	37/
170	/5	2/3	4/1	6/	8/	10/	13/	15/	17/	19/	22/	24/	26/	29/	31/	34/	35/
180	/5	2/3	4/1	6/	8/	10/	12/	14/	16/	18/	20/	22/	25/	27/	29/	31/	32/
190	/5	2/3	4/1	6/	8/	10/	11/	13/	15/	17/	19/	21/	24/	26/	28/	30/	31/

*RNT = Residual Nitrogen Time

**NR = Non-Repetitive (no previous dive within 12 hours)

of Table 2, Part 2, the Surface Interval table. Go left along the horizontal row of figures to find your surface time. It lies in the third interval (between 1:07 and 1:42). Now, follow this column down to the row of letters between Parts 2 and 3, and you will arrive at a new category, repetitive group F. A so-called F diver is carrying less nitrogen than an H diver.

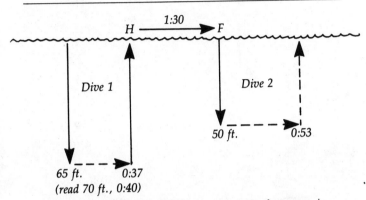

8.1. Example 1: *Summary of first repetitive, nondecompression dive scenario (see text for details).*

Next, enter Part 3 by continuing down the vertical column headed F. Find where column F intersects the row of figures headed by 50 feet on the depth scale. Your nondecompression (allowable) bottom time at 50 feet on the second dive is 53 minutes.

Example 2
Table 2, the repetitive nondecompression chart, can be used as well in calculating the time limit for a third dive or more. Say you only spent 15 minutes at 50 feet on the second dive. Half an hour after surfacing you learn from some surfacing divers about a fantastic school of fish in a cave at 90 feet, just beyond the boat's anchor. You want to photograph the fish. How much time do you have for taking pictures at 90 feet if you want to avoid decompression?

Start in Part 3, where you left off in planning the second dive to 50 feet. But now use the residual-nitrogen time (RNT, the top figure in each pair) listed

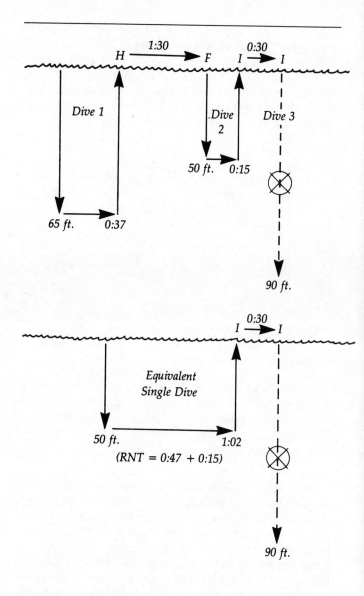

8.2. Example 2: *Summary of second repetitive, nondecompression dive scenario (see text).*

in minutes. In this case, the residual-nitrogen time is a measure of your nitrogen load at the start of the *second* dive. In computing the time limit for your third dive, treat this amount of time as if it were already spent on the bottom at the given depth (here, 50 feet). That is, add the residual-nitrogen time to the actual bottom time of the second dive to get a new "up-to-date" bottom time (or equivalent nitrogen load). Enter the chart again at Part 1 to determine your bottom time for the third dive. Your previous dives have been effectively integrated, so it's as if you made one prolonged dive to 50 feet.

In this particular example, then, you started at 50 feet with 15 actual minutes spent there. Adding 47 minutes of RNT, you get 62 minutes (remember, read this as 70 minutes when using the table). Thus, you find yourself in repetitive group I. The time spent on the surface, while you're readying your camera and gear to go down to the fish cave, is 30 minutes. Checking row I in Part 2, you find you remain in group I as you enter Part 3 of the table. Checking down to the 90-foot entry in Part 3, you discover you are out of time. There is no way you can go to 90 feet now, even for a minute, and return without decompression.

Example 3

How long do you have to wait at the surface, then, to lose enough nitrogen to make a short excursion to 90 feet for some photos? Enter Part 3 at 90 feet and go across the row of numbers. Note that the nondecompression bottom time rapidly dwindles and disappears beyond column G. You feel that 10 minutes would be enough time to shoot the pictures. Ten minutes at 90 feet is okay for an E diver. Now remember that you entered the Surface Interval table, Part 2, as an I diver. Go back to Part 2 and follow row I horizontally from right to left until it intersects vertical column E. You find you must wait at the surface for a minimum of 2 hours and 3 minutes before going down to get your pictures. Such is the discipline of nondecompression diving.

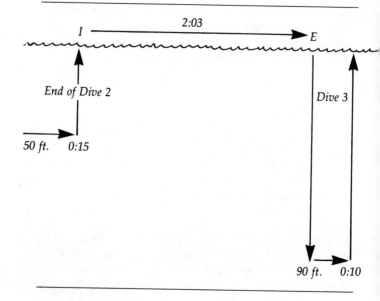

Example 4

Suppose, however, that you are fully prepared for decompression diving and that environmental conditions are benign (calm surface, essentially no current). What sacrifice must you make to Neptune (in the form of depths and times of decompression stops on your return) if you head right down for 10 minutes of photography at 90 feet?

Remember that you are an I diver at the moment. In Part 3, follow the column of figures below I down to the 90-foot depth and observe that your residual-nitrogen time is 38 minutes. Therefore, you are already over the nondecompression limit for a single dive to 90 feet (30 minutes). But you plan to spend 10 more actual minutes down there—remember to start timing as soon as you leave the surface. Thus, your total new dive will last an equivalent of 48 minutes at 90 feet.

To find your decompression stops and times, you must consult a separate chart designed specifically for decompression diving. Table 3, the modified U.S.

Navy Standard Air Decompression table, will cover your new dive. Find 90 feet in the depth column and, after adding 10 minutes to 38 minutes (RNT), choose 50 minutes as your bottom time. Result: you must decompress at 10 feet for 18 minutes before surfacing.

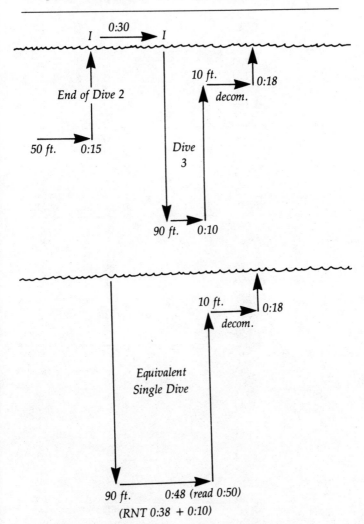

8.4. Example 4: *Summary of decompression dive scenario.*

Table 3: Modified U.S. Navy Standard Air Decompression

Depth (feet)	Bottom Time (mins.)	Decompression Stops (mins.) 20 ft.	10 ft.	Repetitive Group
40	200		0	N
	210		2	N
	230		7	N
50	100		0	L
	110		3	L
	120		5	M
	140		10	M
	160		21	N
60	60		0	J
	70		2	K
	80		7	L
	100		14	M
	120		26	N
	140		39	O
70	50		0	J
	60		8	K
	70		14	L
	80		18	M
	90		23	N
	100		33	N
	110	2	41	O
	120	4	47	O
	130	6	52	O
80	40		0	I
	50		10	K
	60		17	L
	70		23	M
	80	2	31	N
	90	7	39	N
	100	11	46	O
	110	13	53	O
90	30		0	H
	40		7	J
	50		18	L
	60		25	M
	70	7	30	N
	80	13	40	N
	90	18	48	O

Table 3: (continued)

Depth (feet)	Bottom Time (mins.)	Decompression Stops (mins.) 20 ft.	10 ft.	Repetitive Group
100	25		0	H
	30		3	I
	40		15	K
	50	2	24	L
	60	9	28	N
	70	17	39	O
110	20		0	G
	25		3	H
	30		7	J
	40	2	21	L
	50	8	26	M
	60	18	36	N
120	15		0	F
	20		2	H
	25		6	I
	30		14	J
	40	5	25	L
	50	15	31	N
130	10		0	E
	15		1	F
	20		4	H
	25		10	J
	30	3	18	M
	40	10	25	N
140	10		0	E
	15		2	G
	20		6	I
	25	2	14	J
	30	5	21	K
150	5		0	C
	10		1	E
	15		3	G
	20	2	7	H
	25	4	17	K
	30	8	24	L

(continued)

Table 3: (continued)

Depth (feet)	Bottom Time (mins.)	Decompression Stops (mins.)		Repetitive Group
		20 ft.	10 ft.	
	5		0	D
	10		1	F
160	15	1	4	H
	20	3	11	J
	25	7	20	K
	5		0	D
170	10		2	F
	15	2	5	H
	20	4	15	J
	5		0	D
180	10		3	F
	15	3	6	I
	5		0	D
190	10	1	3	G
	15	4	7	I

The Decompression Meter

A device known as a decompression meter first began to catch the attention of sport divers in the early 1970s. The decompression meter is a gauge with short straps and a buckle, worn on the wrist. The gauge indicates depth in intervals of 10 feet from the surface to 50 feet down. These are depths of decompression stops for a diver who has absorbed an appropriate amount of nitrogen. During a nondecompression dive, the indicator needle of the gauge will not move beyond the zone marked "Surface," and the diver can proceed directly to the surface at the end of the dive.

The decompression meter has been praised by some and damned by others. Those dissatisfied with the "decom" meter probably expected too much from it, and, indeed, it is misnamed. In most cases, the device should be used only to monitor nondecompression dives; the aim should be to keep the indicator out of the decompression range, or the red area of the dial. The decom meter works by simulating the uptake of nitrogen by certain tissues of the body, and because the meter performs an integrating function, responding to small changes in depth, it is useful in sport diving where depth may be shifting continuously, for instance, as a diver explores a rugged bottom.

The manufacturer recommends that the meter be used only for single dives not exceeding 130 feet. A decom meter should not be used for repetitive diving, because the meter is designed to mimic the nitrogen dynamics of the so-called "fast" tissues in the human body. Fast tissues (for example, blood and muscle), which are low in fat, gain and lose nitrogen quickly at a rate matched by the decom meter. But error creeps into the meter readings after surfacing, when "slow" tissues in the body (for example, brain tissue and liver) may actually gain nitrogen from the fast tissues. The meter, however, would have you believe that all the nitrogen leaving the fast tissues is eliminated from the body. Thus, a decom meter will not give you an accurate estimate of residual nitrogen for your whole body, and relying on a decom reading is not a safe way to start a second dive. To sum up, while it is generally agreed that the meter is okay for a single, nondecompression dive, it should be used with the diving tables for either repetitive or decompression diving.

Flying after Diving and Diving at Elevation

Cabin pressure in most high-flying, modern aircraft is maintained at about 0.75 atmosphere, equivalent to an elevation of 8,000 feet. According to the *NOAA Diving Manual*, anyone who embarks on a flight soon after scuba diving can develop the bends, since some of the body's tissues will still contain excess nitrogen. Of course, the risk is greatest for an individual who has absorbed nitrogen right up to the nondecompression limit, or who has made a decompression dive. To be safe at a pressure corresponding to an elevation of 8,000 feet, you must wait at sea level long enough to bring your residual nitrogen down to the level of a D diver in Table 2. Note that driving over mountains of any significant elevation poses exactly the same sort of problem for a person who has just been scuba diving.

Anyone who dives in a mountain lake should be aware that the diving tables used at sea level do not apply at elevation, where the air pressure is less. Significant differences in a diver's response to lowered pressure theoretically exist with an elevation gain of 1,000 feet above sea level. To put it more simply, using sea-level diving tables at elevation to plan decompression dives or dives that barely fall within the nondecompression limits will almost certainly cause the bends in some divers. Extremely careful calculations must be made, using the true atmospheric pressure at the site, to customize the diving tables. Another problem is that depth gauges calibrated to read zero at sea level do not show the true depth in a mountain lake. Accurate depth readings must be obtained by using a measured, weighted diveline. Decompression diving at elevation is so problematical that we emphatically advise you to avoid it. For any diving at elevation, seek local knowledge at a professional dive shop and avoid even approaching the nondecompression limits.

Emergency Ascents from Deep Water

Below 50 feet, divers begin to enter true inner space, a zone where they may not be capable of reaching safety by their own efforts in case of a problem with their life-support system. It is worth repeating here, with respect to deep-water emergencies, that speculation in this area outweighs reality in the proportion of whale to minnow. Fortunately, true emergencies under water are rare. Moreover, in tracing causes of major underwater accidents, experts from the University of Rhode Island and NAUI have found that equipment failure is vanishingly rare. Human error and lack of training, as well as unfitness in extreme diving environments (the roughest seas, deepest caves, and the like) account for nearly all serious diving mishaps.

Still, as we noted in our discussion of shallower dives, failure of the air-supply equipment is not entirely outside the realm of the possible. Therefore, we end this chapter with a look at the options open to a diver in trouble at depth.

Below the range of ready emergency access to the surface, mere faith in the buddy system—which has universally degenerated in practice to keeping your diving partner in sight—is no guarantee of salvation. Good buddies not only believe in, but practice their creed religiously. In fact, it may be that, with respect to the exploration of the awesome, silent regions below 50 feet, the term *buddy system*, with its casual overtones, ought to be replaced by a term with a weightier ring—for example, *deep-diving team*, or *deep team* for short. This term begins to emphasize the absolute mutual reliance of deep-diving partners upon one another.

As noted earlier in this chapter, we feel that every pair or team of divers should pause before descending below 50 feet to make a brief check of all systems, especially the octopus rigs. If octopus rigs are not carried, the pause becomes even more important. Then, it should entail a short relaxed round of *buddy breathing*. With this little ritual practiced at the start of every dive, emergency procedure will be fresh in each diver's mind and mutual trust assured. Divers who do not carry octopus equipment but who become panicky at the thought of sharing their second stage, or divers who are unable to coordinate the maneuver, should not descend below 50 feet (or their own controlled ascent limit, or that of their partner—whichever is less).

Divers practicing the deep partnership system should remain very close together. Earlier we suggested that members of a diving party remain within touching distance of one another. This might translate into an outer limit of 10 feet, even where an octopus rig is available. There is always the chance that just as you experience a problem, your partner may be facing and swimming *away* from you. Without an octopus, closeness is absolutely mandatory, for you will not be able to scoop your partner's second stage into your mouth immediately; you will have to explain yourself, using the classic hand signal across your throat (symbolizing lack of air). It may take your partner a few seconds to get over his or her shocked surprise before responding to your predicament.

Needless to say, armchair fantasies of cool, calm, and heroic behavior in an underwater emergency are seldom realistic, and you will need all the time you can save by being close to your fellow diver. Truly deep dives that invade the zone of nitrogen narcosis (usually below 120 feet) demand the most exacting cooperation imaginable between partners. Again, reaction time in an emergency can be slowed at this depth, depending on an individual's susceptibility to nitrogen's physiological effects. And, of course, both the diver in need of aid and the assisting diver are affected, doubly prolonging the time before a proper coordinated response to the problem begins.

Whole-Body Coordination

Making a controlled emergency ascent from deep water with your diving partner is not merely a matter of sharing a tank of air, whether via an octopus unit or the far more difficult practice of sharing a single second stage. Using an octopus rig seems like simplicity itself: you merely pick up the dangling extra second-stage unit, put it in your mouth, and blow the water out of it. Or, if you have no air left to exhale, purge the water, as described earlier, by placing your tongue into the mouthpiece and then pressing the purge button centered at the front of the unit. It's not quite that simple, for in using the octopus you necessarily find yourself extremely close to your partner, preferably face to face, and your individual freedom of movement becomes curtailed. Fortunately, the direction you want to take is almost always straight up, and this movement can be accomplished without swimming by using buoyancy control. Nearly always, the partner wearing the octopus rig initially controls the rate of upward movement—no more than 60 feet per minute to guard against embolism—with his or

8.5. *Buddy pair making a controlled emergency ascent while sharing a single second stage.*

her BC alone. The recipient of the air is likely to be the more flustered partner in the emergency and should ride passively, at least at first. Remember that the air originally contained in *both* partners' BCs will expand during the ascent, so if the passive partner is unable to cooperate, the controlling partner should expect to dump approximately twice the volume of air as on a normal solo ascent. Partners making an emergency ascent normally grip each other's shoulder with one hand to maintain bodily contact.

As the team approaches the surface, both BCs usually have to be manipulated. Here the coordination of the upward movement can become a major challenge. It demands that the divers remain in bodily contact, controlling their buoyancy and holding the rate of their ascent to within the limits of safety. The buoyancy of both divers should be matched as closely as possible so that neither partner tends to drag the other up too quickly, or worse, breaks away and loses control.

Sharing a single second stage on an ascent from *very* deep water is fraught with such difficulty that we feel the octopus rig is essential equipment on a deep dive. We predict that the octopus regulator will become standard in the amateur scuba industry and will probably soon be required for deep diving from charter boats.

For divers who are properly prepared and who have the necessary equipment, training, and frame of mind, deep diving can be an almost mystical experience—a voyage of human consciousness into a region where preceding generations have never penetrated. The feeling of slow, langourous flight through an immensity of space has never before been realized outside of dreams. Visitors to the deep add a dimension to their lives that is shared with few others— mountaineers, hang gliders, and astronauts, perhaps. Deep divers return to the surface with a sense of having satisfied the nearly universal urge of the human species to explore its uttermost surroundings.

Part Two

Encounters with the Underwater World

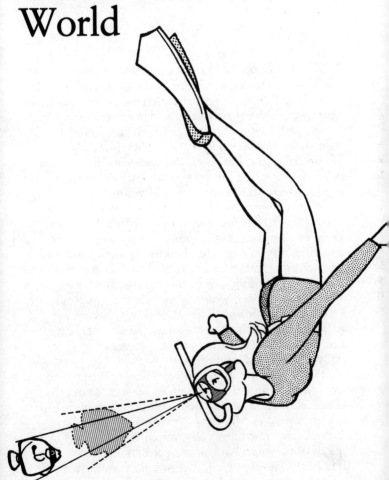

Chapter 9

Cold Kingdom

WHEN BLEAK NOVEMBER CLOSES in across the sea coasts and lake shores of the northern United States and Canada, many divers reluctantly stow their gear bags, move their wetsuits to the rear of the closet, and dream of balmy aquamarine seas and palm-lined beaches. For those souls who really love life under water, however, the cold-season blues can be transformed by the unique adventures and expeditions possible in the winter world below.

Winter divers are often highly rewarded for their efforts and sometimes come away with an exquisite high. Diving sites that are merely tolerable or even poor in summer—due to plankton blooms, turbidity from river runoff, crowds on the beach and in the water—go through a refreshing seasonal change. Visibility in winter generally increases dramatically. Fish and other forms of life slow down, becoming easier to approach. A pair or a group of divers often find themselves to be the only explorers of an essentially unbounded wilderness.

We should mention that cold-water diving is not everywhere limited to the winter season. At depths below about 30 feet, the ocean off northern New England, Canada's Maritime Provinces, and Alaska, as well as large northern lakes, remains truly frigid for much of the year. And since "cold" is a relative term, it is next to impossible to define cold water diving by a specific temperature range. A confirmed deep-tropics dweller who rarely feels the ocean cooler than a silky 80°F winces at the idea of cold water diving off central California, where the water temperature reaches perhaps 50°F in the winter. Quite different sentiments about California coastal diving are expressed by Minnesotans who routinely dive beneath the ice into 32°F water.

Equipment: Gearing Up for the Cold

For a fraction of the cost of a week's Caribbean diving vacation, you can equip yourself to dive in Arctic waters or the local equivalent at any time of year. The key item of equipment is, of course, the suit: one needs either a high-quality, custom-fitted farmer-

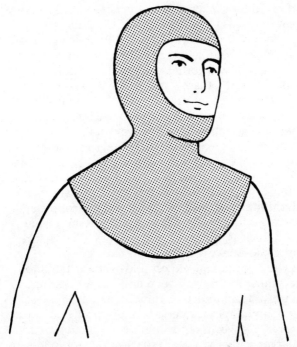

9.1. *A cold-water hood extends down over shoulders, upper chest, and upper back.*

john-style wetsuit of two-sided nylon at least a quarter inch thick (the less expensive option), or, for maximum comfort, a unisuit (see Chapter 3).

With a custom wetsuit, some divers remain comfortable in relatively shallow water (less than 25 ft.) at, say, 40°F (about 4°C) for up to one hour. Remember that the wetsuit will compress, reducing its capacity for insulation, so the deeper one goes, the colder he will get. The wetsuit must include a cold-water hood whose widely flaring flange is smoothed over the shoulders and tucked under the farmer-john suspender straps.

In braving cold water with a wetsuit, remember to tuck booties inside pant legs, thus preventing a forcible exchange of water in the boots when you are swimming forward. For the same reason, wear your gloves outside sleeves. One important option for very frigid conditions is to wear an oversized extra hood of regular (summer) length on top of the cold-water hood. For good reason, the human body is extremely conservative about keeping the head warm and will allow chill to invade other parts of the anatomy before turning down the thermostat on the nice 98.6°F supply of blood being pumped in the direction of the brain. Thus, as in any other outdoor winter sport, proper insulation for the head prevents excessive heat loss and helps to keep the whole body warmer.

Another winter option often used by professional divers is the full face mask, which keeps the face dry and conserves body heat significantly. Air enters the mask through a special coupling to the second stage. However, if flooded, full face masks are somewhat difficult to clear; therefore, only divers with special training should wear them.

If you become hooked on cold-water exploration, we recommend that you get a unisuit. A diver wearing a unisuit can remain comfortable in the coldest water at any depth for periods of up to several hours. However, it's worth repeating the suggestion, made in Chapter 3, that you learn to use a unisuit in less than Arctic conditions and that you in no case use the suit as a BC. Properly inflated, the unisuit contains a thin film of air, just enough to separate the rubber and the underwear. Excessive inflation not only brings a risk of blowup, but also tends to discomfort the diver when air forces the collar seal up around the throat, resulting in a constricting, choking effect.

Cold-Water Hazards

Hypothermia and Other Problems

The special enemy of cold water divers is *hypothermia*, a deep, sustained chilling of the body resulting in a lowering of the internal core, or trunk temperature. Even relatively warm water, with temperatures in the 60° to 70°F range, can bring on hypothermia if exposure is sufficiently long. Becoming chilled in the water should not be taken lightly, nor can it be controlled by will power. Severe cases lead to incapacitation and unconsciousness, and may even be fatal. Because cold water steals body heat so much more quickly than air at the same temperature, hypothermia rapidly becomes critical for a diver. As the condition worsens, symptoms include intense shivering and muscle tensing or cramping, poor coordination, slowed movement and dulled mental functioning, and widespread numbness. A hypothermia victim usually cannot rewarm himself, even if well insulated. Hot drinks, or hot enemas in cases of unconsciousness, are preferred treatments.

The danger level in hypothermia begins with strong shivering. As a rule of thumb, when your arms and legs begin to really feel cold it is time to head back for the boat or beach. But above all do not delay if you notice yourself shivering. Hypothermia inevitably involves the brain and spinal cord and has a progressive dulling effect on thinking and physical reflexes. It brings a real risk of drowning due to enfeeblement, poor coordination, or poor judgment.

If you find yourself becoming seriously chilled, swimming faster to warm up is a bad remedy. A body in exertion will lose heat at a faster rate than one that remains still. And the old-time practice of urinating in the wetsuit as an aid to warming up deserves no more than the snickers that this suggestion usually elicits in a beginners' dive class. Relief accrues to the bladder only. The warming sensation on the skin is momentary and valueless for maintaining body temperature. In fact, urinating may even hasten hypothermia by suddenly removing a concentration of heat from the central region of the body. And if you have a nicely fitting suit with minimal exchange, urination can cause a form of diaper rash. This condition varies in severity with the sensitivity of the skin. Habitual suit wetters come to be known by the peculiar odor of urea combining with nylon and neoprene. We have started to run across reports of damage to nylon linings in wetsuits, ostensibly from exposure to urea or uric acid. Happily, we have never heard of anyone urinating in a unisuit; since there are no leaks to the outside, a leak on the inside would be retained by the suit.

A warming technique used by many winter divers, both before and after a dive, is the pouring of warm water into the suit. A wetsuit's greatest insulating power is experienced not in the water, but in the air, where it retains heat with great efficiency. To take advantage of your suit's insulating function on winter trips, carry a large thermos that was filled with boiling water at home. At the dive site, mix the hot water in a bucket with ambient water to attain a tolerable temperature and pour the mixture into your wetsuit at the neck. If performed just before your entry, this technique will provide some warmth as well as a psychological boost; you will partially stem, or perhaps temper, the icy flow around your wetsuited body for the first couple of minutes into the dive. Some hardy souls claim that they are able to eke out a bit more bottom time after using the "thermos-bottle fix."

Some of the most experienced cold-water divers we have met are marine biologists from the University of New Hampshire. A handful of faculty members and graduate students carry on year-round ecological studies in depths of approximately 60 feet at Isles of Shoals, 12 miles off the Maine-New Hampshire border. In summer, this cluster of small islands in the Gulf of Maine is delightful to visit. Cornell University has established a seasonal laboratory on one of the islands and offers summer courses in marine science and natural history. The diving in summer is usually fine, and the submarine cliffs, caves, and rocky ledges harbor interesting fauna such as basket starfish, wolf eels, goosefish, and, of course, the delectable New England lobster. The water is usually fairly clear—visibility is 30 feet or more—but chilly. It is definitely custom-wetsuit country below the thermocline.

In winter, however, the picture is greatly changed. The islands are bleak and windswept, fringed by shore ice. On the deck of an exposed boat, the chill factor ranges far below zero. Hardy are the divers who step off the stern platform of the University's small research vessel and descend through the merciless, frigid sea water. The water here is fully representative of the undersea environment that stretches in this season all the way to the Arctic.

A number of the New Hampshire diver-scientists still wear custom-made wetsuits of three-eighths-inch neoprene. Yet even this extreme thickness—which makes wearers begin to resemble stiff, blubber-bearing marine mammals—is not proof against the cold at 60 feet. Most of the heavy-wetsuit wearers surrender to the cold after 20 to 30 minutes.

Typical cold-induced problems at Isles of Shoals include a loss of will power and acceptance of one's own poor job performance. For example, one scientist we met was occupied with recording numerical data on small tags attached to free-roving snails. He reported that toward the end of each dive he would write down partially obscured numbers from a first impression without checking closely for accuracy—a procedure he never would have tolerated under normal conditions. Another common problem is confusion regarding compass direction and familiar landmarks and, in related manifestations, the distortion of mental maps of familiar areas of bottom and the loss of memory concerning direction of travel ("Did I go north first, or west?"). Physical symptoms take the form of a progressive numbing of the muscles in the jaw and lips as cold water seeps past the mouthpiece into the mouth. Also, severe headaches form in the forehead just above the mask where the skin is exposed to the icy water, and tooth and gum pain is experienced, especially if the diver has cavities, loose fillings, or other dental problems.

The New Hampshire wetsuit divers swear by the hot-water treatment prior to the plunge. They recommend filling the entire suit up to the neck with water as hot as you can stand. These divers are among those who report that, if performed just before entry, the technique allows for several extra minutes of bottom time.

Cold-Water Diving in Summer

Although winter diving is our primary theme in this chapter, some of the discussion applies to summer conditions in certain areas mentioned earlier, including much of the West Coast, New England, and Maritime Canada, and any northern lakes deep enough to maintain a thermocline. The risk of hypothermia in such waters is just as serious in July as in January. Surprising to the uninitiated, summer diving in cold water is sometimes more uncomfortable and stressful to the body than the average winter plunge. After lugging and arranging heavy gear and struggling to don a cold-water suit on a blazing hot day, many an eager aquanaut has been overcome by heat exhaustion. This problem seems to be especially common in beach diving, where, as we saw in Part I, the level of exertion is far greater than for boat diving and where often there is no shade. Those who succumb are generally fully suited and waiting for buddies to arrive or finish putting on gear.

The remedy in such a situation is to avoid a long wait in the sun; get dressed at the same rate as your slowest partner. If you feel hot, take a swim before you start putting on your heavy gear. Wetting your head by pouring a bucketful of water on it or by splashing is almost as good as soaking your whole body. If you are fully dressed and cannot avoid overheating, peel back the hood from your forehead and slosh some water back into your hair and keep your face wet. Or, if you are going into fairly calm water and familiar environs, you can enter and snorkel near shore while waiting for your buddy. Simple pleasures are often the most clearly memorable. Everyone we know who has had the experience of suiting up on a really hot day can describe perfectly the initial bliss of cold water surrounding and starting to trickle into a wetsuit.

Beneath the Ice

The ultimate thrill in amateur cold-water diving is a descent under the ice in a large northern lake. One such lake is New Hampshire's Lake Winnepasaukee. Regional dive clubs and scuba-instructor organizations use this lake at least several weekends every winter for training and pleasure diving. In winter the topside weather controls the diving here, with preferred diving days featuring sparkling sunshine and little wind. The wind and its chill factor, of course, are only of concern for people above the surface of the ice.

For under-ice diving, we strongly recommend a unisuit. The water temperature just below the surface is the coldest possible in fresh water, 0° C, or 32° F (slightly lower in the sea, due to the "antifreeze" property of dissolved salt). Perhaps surprisingly, in a descent to 30 or 40 feet you will feel the water warming perceptibly. The coldest temperature lies just under the surface of the ice. This subsurface layer is a reverse thermocline, and is characteristic of bodies of fresh water. Through most of its seasonal temperature cycle, water increases in density as it cools and vice versa, but once cooled below 40° F (4° C), water density begins to decrease through the freezing point. Thus, the coldest liquid water and ice float on the slightly warmer and denser layers below. Even an excellent quarter-inch-thick wetsuit usually will not protect a diver under the ice for more than a few minutes. The time limit depends on the individual's particular physiology, but it should be remembered that after the dive any wet, chilled body will take some time to warm up. Drysuited, due to the suit's power of insulation, one becomes practically independent of the climate above and below.

Before you descend into the cold kingdom, be sure your equipment has been cleaned and calibrated recently. For years, diving literature has touted the old-style double-hose regulator as superior to the single-hose variety for under-ice diving. While it is true that the potential to freeze up is slightly smaller in the double-hose regulator, it makes little sense to buy and maintain this outdated item merely for ice diving. In fact, there are several good reasons for *not* buying a two-hose model: two-hose regulators in good condition are not readily available; parts are often unobtainable; the two-hose design will not accommodate a submersible pressure gauge; and even the best of the line is inferior in overall performance to a good single-hose model.

Proper dive planning alone can eliminate the problem of regulator freezing. The first precaution is to use a tank that has been filled recently. Occasionally, old summer air in a tank has a very high humidity and tends to form ice crystals in cold weather. The second precaution is, at the dive site, to keep your regulator dry until you are in the water and remember not to surface until you are ready to come out.

Many of the newer single-hose regulators can now be fitted with a special antifreezing device. It must be installed in your regulator by a professional scuba craftsman, or you can order a new regulator with the device incorporated. Note that this is expeditionary level equipment and therefore expensive. Also, maintenance work must be done on the antifreeze unit every six months, which may make it more of a hassle than most amateur divers wish to put up with.

The careful preparation of the dive site at a frozen lake involves an efficient division of labor among several tasks: the removal of snow, cutting of access holes, and setting up of a warming facility. Snow removal is necessary first, of course, before the hole cutters can go to work. Once the site for the holes is cleared, however, snow is best shoveled in paths radiating from the holes. Various patterns can be improvised, but they should all include arrows pointing back toward the holes. Such cleared patterns on snow-covered ice are highly visible from beneath, as we shall soon describe in some less dry anecdotes.

Cutting an access hole is simple, though not quite as simple as it sounds. Those who have never been intimately involved with the ice covering a northern lake may be imagining breezily sawing through a 2- or 3-inch layer. In reality, a New Hampshire or Wisconsin lake in midwinter can be solidly covered by ice 2 or 3 feet thick.

The hole cutting entails first drilling a small hole with an ice auger. This keyhole to the world below is then enlarged by a few minutes of abrasion with a chain saw. Finally, a large muscle-powered, broad-toothed ice saw is brought into play, and everyone, taking turns, gets the benefit of some fine predive warmup exercise.

The hole should be roughly 6 feet across, and the recommended shape is triangular, since the sharp Vs formed by the angles permit easy exits. The loose block of ice is submerged. Several helping hands or feet (well insulated) are useful here to guide the big block carefully under the ice where it is to be left at the edge of the hole for later replacement. The point is to make sure that the ice block is stable and won't slide back to close the hole like a bank vault door when divers are below. If more than one hole has been cut, topside snow pathways should connect them, and as an added precaution, lines strung between them by the first and most experienced divers. The lines should be securely attached topside to stakes or spikes driven into the ice. It is also standard procedure to have an experienced safety diver ready to go at each surface hole. Another reasonable rule is that only a single pair of divers be below at any given hole and that they be given a predetermined time limit which is monitored by the safety diver.

For everyone topside, and especially for emerging

divers, a warm-up shack, a van, or a tent, plus warm-ing equipment and hot beverages and soup are as es-sential as they are enjoyable. An under-ice trip is re-ally an expedition, and skimping on support facilities risks frostbite, hypothermia, pneumonia, or worse. A few other words to the wise: an under-ice diving ex-pedition is not the occasion to try for personal depth records. It's prudent to remain within 30 or 40 feet of the surface. Avoid diving in the spring during the period of ice breakup and melting. Entry points can become clogged or jammed by drifting floes or mas-sive shifts caused by winds or currents. Be wary of diving in open water near solid ice cover. A wrong turn under such ice could lead you away from access to the surface, and continued disorientation here would be fatal.

It should be clear by now that in this book we are unavoidably dealing with ice diving in lakes only. Barring a very sudden return of the glacial era, access to permanent or stable sea ice is usually beyond the reach of the amateur diver. This is probably fortu-nate, because conditions of ice movement, breakup, under-ice currents, and so on are far more severe in the ocean, and even optimal marine conditions can be hazardous.

The world beneath ice is at its best in large north-ern lakes where the water is often very clear—150-foot visibility is not uncommon there—and where big-game fishes such as pike and lake trout are found. The fish tend to be very sluggish, similar in behavior to many of the species encountered in night dives (see Chapter 14). At times you can swim up slowly and pet them.

Chance discoveries of fish and the novelty of en-countering warmer water at depth may occupy a few minutes of a dive, but the winter world, though crys-tal clear, can seem sterile and uninspiring to an otherwise experienced diver. The question arises, Is this all there is? Happily, the answer is no, but to dis-cover the rest it is necessary to orient yourself to a very strange mode of diving.

Imagine it is your turn. You and your partner are ready to go, standing at the edge of the large triangular hole in the ice. You wave to friends and a couple of incredulous ice fishermen, glance down at the still, dark water and a few clots of floating slush, and step off.

You are below in a dim, green world—the absolute visual antithesis of the brilliant, glaring winter day above the ice. Your unisuit is functioning perfectly. You imagine that your lips are already turning blue, but everything else is warm as toast. Then you look up. The ceiling is glowing with what look like enormous fluorescent lights extending into the distance. Viewed from a few yards down, the access hole is a mirrorlike gem, a brilliant triangular cell of light from which all the fluorescent trails radiate like sunrays. The scene surpasses achievements of cinematic wizardry in such films as *Star Wars* and *2001*. Wherever the deep snow was shoveled off the ice, light from the other world above comes through with stunning effect. Elsewhere under the ice there is only a diffuse grayness, nearly dark by comparison with the glowing pathways on the ceiling.

Under the ice, you can experience other-worldly sensations and alien perceptions more readily than in any other diving situation. If you approach the underside of the ice and increase your buoyancy, you will find yourself pressing gently but firmly against the smooth, almost glassy surface. Try floating up against the ice so that you are lying flat with your stomach against the surface. Simple. Buoyancy keeps you there nicely, and after a few seconds your perceptions have already changed. Slowly you shift to your hands and knees and deliberately remove your fins. The ice, having become your floor, extends flat and smooth into the distance. Hesitantly you get to your feet and stand, perhaps blinking a few times as you adjust to the fading residual sense of upendedness, particularly if you glimpse your partner still in the normal diving orientation. But you are feeling almost natural by now. It seems advisable to move cautiously on the slick surface. You shuffle slowly out onto one of the huge fluorescent pathways and follow it, the light winking from thousands of crystal facets in the ice and shining up from your feet.

At the same time, floods of bubbles keep falling in rhythmic cascades *down* your body to gather in silent splashes around your feet. You can get down on your knees and play with the iridescent globules, reminiscent of giant blobs of mercury. Holding your fins as scoops, you can push together a huge mass of bubbles as more keep falling through your arms and adding to the pile; then you shove them across the glassy surface and they tumble and roll like pools of quicksilver.

You and your partner can have a hilarious, clumsy soccer game, kicking and herding a mass of gleaming bubbles back and forth on one of the bright raceways. If you have traveled any distance down one of the radiating paths, the way you came will be strewn here and there with pools and clusters of bubbles like outlandish silver mushrooms.

Sooner or later in your wanderings, you will approach the entrance hole. Take a closer look at the bubble pools and you will see them slowly creep toward the hole because of the reduced pressure there. Eventually, they are pulled over the edge and disappear. You can bend down and collect another big pile of bubbles from the surrounding area, and guide them toward the edge of the hole, which will probably seem about 2 feet deep. A large pool of air makes a beautiful show as it cascades over the edge like a perfectly smooth and silent waterfall and vanishes through an evanescent opening in the blue mirror.

On a sunny day, the hole is filled with bright cobalt blue. As you stand at the edge looking out, the large triangular opening seems to be nearly filled with sparkling water. Like Alice, you find a scene that is partly familiar, partly psychedelic. The blue in the hole is very unlike the color of any water you have ever seen. It glows with light, and the ripples and ruffles caused by an unfelt wind are marked by shifting streaks of silver. There is something strange about the shapes of the ripples too. The small troughs and ridges seem inverted in texture; troughs look steeper and deeper than they should be while ridges are rolling and more rounded.

By this time, people from the other world on the other side of the hole may have become curious about all the activity. You begin to see diffuse, ripply images of red-faced beings weaving about near the edge and puffing great clouds of steam. Some of them may bend down to stare at you closely, their distorted faces looking up from all around the blue hole. Communication with the other dimension may take you by surprise as a gloved hand reaches up by your feet. Perhaps you are handed a note on waterproof paper or a token offering such as an apple. Don't worry if you drop the apple. It will float nicely on the blue surface, and you can easily pick it up again unless someone plucks it down from the other side.

The ultimate excursion into fantasy comes when you are ready to exit. Again, you are standing at the edge of the triangular blue and silver mirror. The prescribed technique for ending the dive is to jump into the hole. Without fanfare or countdown you step off the edge. There is a long moment of slow motion as you follow your bubbles into the blue hole. Your feet break the surface first. Then comes a sensation of entering another dimension. Because of greater buoyancy in your upper body, you revolve suddenly and forcibly at the boundary between air and water. There is total disorientation for a few seconds—a chaos of disconnected perceptions and a lack of spatial awareness—until finally you discover you are floating head-up and feet-down in the world of red-faced beings. In your last look below, the underwater scene appears dim and barren of interest.

One dive per day under the ice is enough for most people. However, if you can't resist another trip into the submerged winter wonderland, it is usually necessary to start with a fresh, dry regulator, not to mention a well-warmed body.

The final mandatory activity of the diving day is to slide the big triangular block of ice out from its resting place at the edge of the opening and back into place. Usually the last divers below push it out at the edge, just far enough so that ice picks can be used from above to pull it into place. Normally, the cake will freeze in solidly within a day, but it's a good idea to put up ropes and warning flags to alert unwary snowmobilers, iceboaters, one-horse-sleigh drivers, and the like.

Winter diving days are short, and so you have plenty of time to retire to your favorite warming spot for some *après*-dive refreshments, conversation, and perhaps a planning session for the next excursion into the strange inverted world below the ice.

Chapter 10

The Amber Jungle

WITH ITS TEEMING and immensely diverse forms of life, the marine environment has frequently been compared to a jungle. Nowhere is this comparison more apt than in the cool-temperate coastal waters along the western edge of North America, where giant algae (mainly several species of kelp) form unique forests in the sea. These environs are eminently accessible and include some of the most popular diving sites in the United States. For the knowledgeable enthusiast, kelp diving is safe and highly rewarding. Here are found some of the most mysterious and beautifully alien seascapes on the water planet. Thanks to the lush growth of kelp, marine life of enormous variety abounds. Many of the fish and shellfish are esteemed as seafood.

So our advice to sun-crazed tropic dwellers, Easterners, and lake-locked divers in the interior is to head out West to places like Catalina Island, Half Moon Bay, and Pacific Grove in California, and to points northwest reaching clear to the Aleutian Islands. Here the big amber jungle, the "dark continent" of underwater exploration, stretching in a coastal band for thousands of miles, awaits you as a new challenge and a delight.

Kelp is classified as a brown alga (plural, algae). Like other algal species, some of the peculiarities of its anatomy and life cycle are not typically plantlike. Beginning at the bottom, the kelp is anchored by a tangled, spreading array of ropy-looking strands. The whole thing closely resembles a root system snaking over and around and under rocks, giving the plant a firm grip on the bottom. But this is its only function, and the structure is called a holdfast, not a true root, which carries out a nutrient-gathering function as well as an anchoring one. Kelp, of course, absorbs fertilizing elements directly from the surrounding sea water.

What appear as stems rising through the water are termed stipes by marine botanists. Stipes have no physically supportive function. Instead, thousands of small gas-filled floats, or pneumatophores, keep the huge plants upright in the water. Finally, the long leaflike organs that sprout at intervals from the stipes and that are most lushly represented in the canopy of the plant, spreading across the surface, are simpler in structure than true leaves of land plants, and are termed blades. An inclusive term, shared by palm trees, is frond; it refers to an entire length of stipe with its attached blades.

The organic productivity of kelp is immense. Recent measurements have revealed that more than 13 pounds of organic matter were generated yearly in each square meter of the canopy layer of a giant kelp bed in Monterey Bay. It is not surprising that kelp forms the base of one of the richest ecosystems in the sea. The kelp forest is not only rich in numbers of plants and animals, but also in numbers of kinds of organisms. This species richness nearly rivals that of some coral-reef environments, where the occurrence of myriads of life forms is legendary.

Those who are not acquainted with the kelp environment should first be aware that kelp diving anywhere is cold-water diving. These largest of marine plants flourish only far to the north and south of the equator. California kelp forests have their counterparts along the coast of Chile in South America. Off the eastern United States, kelp may be found from New Jersey northward, but it only grows luxuriantly in very cold waters beginning north of Cape Cod. Thus, anywhere a diver encounters kelp, even in the summer, he or she will be grateful for superior insulation (we recommend at least a custom-fitted wetsuit for treks into the sea forests in most areas).

Entering the Kelp Forest

If your dive is being staged from shore, look for an entry point that is relatively free of boulders and nearshore seaweed cover. Before the dive, find a high vantage point on shore, if one is available, and look for a break in the band of kelp offshore; such a break often reveals a sand channel leading out from the beach. Here you can approach the edge of the kelp in open water of a comfortable depth, say 15 or 20 feet. Try to avoid entries through weed-choked shallows filled with hidden rocks. Such an entry is especially disconcerting to new divers, and if any significant surge is present, it can lead to multiple abrasions and contusions, bruised and battered bodies and gear, or worse.

A boat-based dive in kelp is delightful, and, from the standpoint of the diving itself, is basically the same as any boat-based dive. The major precaution relates to the parking of your boat in the vicinity of the unique environment you are privileged to explore. Always anchor your boat outside the area of kelp. This rule has nothing to do with the boat becoming stuck; rather, it is aimed at protecting the kelp forest itself. Most determined boaters would have little trouble pulling an anchor free of the kelp, but the damage to the deceptively robust-looking plants can be all out of proportion to a single incident of entanglement. To live, kelp must remain free and upright in the water, although a considerable intermeshing of the leafy fronds occurs at the surface. Plants that are detached from the bottom, however, are doomed. They drift through the kelp bed, entangling others and pulling them loose in turn. Surge and storm waves accelerate the damage, and a chain reaction may result that decimates a portion of the kelp forest. Diving biologists have reported finding as many as eighteen giant kelp plants dead and dying in a huge, ragged, tangled ball.

Although it may be possible to anchor the boat off the seaward edge of the kelp, the depth of water here (often 80 or 90 feet) and exposure to swell and chop sometimes make an anchorage difficult or impossible. It's better to look for a shoreward opening into the kelp and anchor in as shallow a depth as possible in a channel or cove. You can then begin your dive along the lateral edge of a forest grove, as suggested for the shore-based excursion. If the scope of the anchor line allows the boat to drift into the kelp canopy beside the channel, this is usually all right. Disruption of the kelp is primarily a function of the anchor's placement. The boat itself will glide easily out of the canopy.

Inside the Kelp Forest

Regions where kelp flourishes are not known for exceptional water clarity. Kelp plants are usually biological indicators of fairly fertile ocean water. The same fertilizing elements that promote lush growth in kelp also stimulate planktonic algae. Sometimes the plankton undergo population explosions called blooms. Needless to say, kelp divers never encounter the "gin-clear" conditions of the tropics, where a lack of open-water fertility often results in an extremely small plankton population.

Generally in kelp forest areas, the best visibility can be expected in late summer or fall, when the fertility of the water has been partially exhausted for the year. The poorest visibility, due to plankton-caused turbidity, is usually experienced in the spring. Winter explorers in the kelp often find very clear water unless there has been a recent storm causing local rivers to discharge mud into the sea or causing waves to stir up the bottom sediment. Also, kelp environments around offshore islands lacking rivers, canals, or other major drainage outlets often feature better visibility under water than those along mainland shores.

Even if the water is very clear, however, the country beneath a dense canopy of kelp will be dimly lit at high noon. Detecting and identifying some of the marine life in the forest may be difficult, given the available light. Shallow caves, deep cracks in the rocky bottom, and spaces beneath ledges, where the biggest lobsters, octopus, and abalone may be hidden, are nearly in total darkness. Many kelp divers, therefore, carry an underwater light and use it intermittently as needed.

Despite a light and reasonable visibility, it is very easy to lose track of one's buddy in the depths of the marine jungle. Therefore, it's a good idea to work out a plan in case of separation. Typically, in open water, the disappearance of a buddy should prompt all the divers in a party to surface and rendezvous. Surfacing in dense kelp may not be the best alternative, especially for fairly new divers, who may be prone to "weed claustrophobia." Consider that while divers may be out of each other's sight, they may still be in close proximity. Before surfacing, then, one of the divers (or one member of a team) should try searching for the missing person. That person, presumably aware that he or she is lost to the others, should stay in one place, preferably signaling by tapping a knife or stone against the tank. Although underwater sound signals do not give a good directional cue, they can serve to initiate the search process. After a while, if the search is unsuccessful, a pause or change in the signaling frequency, agreed upon before the dive, can be used to say, "Enough of this; let's surface." Needless to say, all signaling codes as well as active or passive roles in a search in case of separation should be decided upon before the dive.

One potential problem, often of great concern to first-time divers in the kelp environment, is the possibility of becoming hopelessly entangled in strands of the huge seaweed. In most cases, this is a nonproblem. Except under the most unusual circumstances, kelp of any given species is readily breakable or else growing sparsely, so that a diver of minimal strength and finesse can easily avoid an extended entanglement. Some differences in tensile strength do exist among kelp species, however. Divers should be aware that the predominant New England laminarian kelp (straplike, with an inch-thick tubular stipe) may, under unusual circumstances, be able to hold up one's progress in the water. The thick, short laminarian stems do not break nearly as readily as those of the giant *Macrocystis* in California. One of us had a brief unsettling experience of being trapped by shrub-sized kelp near the end of a dive in Massachusetts Bay. In this case, the plants were projecting outward thickly from the top of a small cliff, and the diver, ascending very close to the wall, came up under the vegetation without realizing it. There were a few anxious moments of reaching back to untangle kelp fronds from the tank valve and first-stage assembly.

Eliminating from your person as many projections and protuberances as possible is the key to smooth, unhindered kelp diving. You will never be as sleek as a seal, but keeping your knife on the inside of your calf and keeping dangling gauges, collecting bag, and the like tethered with some sort of Velcro closure or elastic loop will go far to promote uninterrupted swimming in the kelp.

In discussing entry, we stressed that a kelp dive should begin in open water. Usually you will return the same way at the end of the dive. A few words are in order here regarding currents and surge, which are nearly always muted within a stand of kelp. It is possible for a strong current or large swells to occur outside kelp while little water movement is noticed by divers within. Thus, if you began a dive at slack tide, you might emerge from the calm depths of the forest into unexpectedly swift or turbulent water, especially where tidal channels or shallow submarine canyons lie along the outer edge of the kelp. In such a case, stay in the kelp while working your way back to shore or your boat. Reaching shore is always possible. If a boat operator is aboard, surface and signal to be picked up.

Occasionally, we are asked about night diving under kelp. We answer that only advanced divers should consider exploring the kelp forest after dark. Divers should gain experience in night diving in open water before entering kelp. And, as with any form of night diving, it's best to choose a site familiar from daytime dives and to dive first with an experienced night stalker. Chapter 14 covers night diving in more detail.

The deep seaward edge of a kelp forest is an exhilarating place, the border of a Tolkienesque realm where a diver can soar slowly beside an immense leafy-stemmed jungle and perhaps meet some of the peerless denizens of the sea. Marine mammals, in particular seals and sea lions and, increasingly in California, sea otters are most reliably encountered in and around the kelp habitat. If we were to select the most adventurous overall diving environment, it would probably be the kelp forest. The mystery, enchantment, and exhilaration are as fine here as anywhere, and the spectacular close encounters with large marine creatures can include a glimpse of a California gray whale, an orca, or, far less likely, a great white shark.

A Personal Account

The first West Coast kelp dive for one of us was in December 1977, in a beautiful marine preserve established by the state of California near the south end of Monterey Bay. The scene from shore before the dive was striking. Just offshore from a small rocky peninsula, a marine wildlife tableau spread itself across tangled seaweeds and massive rock forms of the intertidal zone. Between two and three hundred birds were concentrated into perhaps a 200-yard band along the coast. Most were gulls of at least two species; many cormorants were also present. Fifteen to twenty large pelicans stood out sharply from the crowd. Large solitary grebes patrolled in patches of open water, and a single loon repeatedly dove and reappeared in a zone farther offshore.

The mammals were represented by twenty or so harbor seals sprawled on nearshore rocks or drifting, heads up, in the water. Beyond the rocky area in the unbroken kelp canopy appeared about a dozen sea otters. Once, the panoply of living abundance and diversity was punctuated in silent, exclamatory fashion by a large gray whale, which spouted, then showed its flukes as it sounded about 300 yards offshore. My dive partner, Tuck, was a research biologist from the University of California at Santa Cruz. We lugged our gear down to a small sandy beach from which an open-water passage extended seaward between two large patches of kelp.

We waded slowly into 50° F (10° C) water. I donned my fins and clenched my teeth as the icy fluid seeped slowly into my rented wetsuit. The day was cloudy bright, with virtually no wind, and the water near the shore was almost glassy smooth. Diving conditions were nearly ideal. Tuck had mentioned that this area often experienced strong winds. We began to snorkel out and found the water to be quite clear; approximately 25- to 30-foot visibility was immediately apparent, excellent for an area where visibility sometimes closes down to less than 5 feet.

Almost immediately we were greeted by seals. Three of them approached closely to look us over. They almost seemed eager to join us—though very different behavior is exhibited by their cousins (of the same species, *Phoca vitulina*) in Maine and New Hampshire, where, according to local scuttlebutt, they are frequently shot at by fishermen.

Under water, the seals were transformed from the familiar floppy shapes they assume on land. Here in their element they were lithe, dappled swimmers, moving with languid grace, looping under us and gliding in for a closer look, sometimes halting no more than 5 feet away and hovering, staring wide-eyed with apparent curiosity. If we turned toward them or reached out an arm, they executed a neat flip, turned, and swooped away effortlessly. They moved so well that I wondered how they could fall prey to great white sharks, which often look obese in photographs. Perhaps the obesity is only an indication of a large and recent meal. And if lean great whites are underrepresented in photographs, it might only mean that photographers are less successful in bringing back their portraits. In these waters, such thoughts were more disquieting than usual. Earlier Tuck had told me that a wildlife biologist friend of his had recently found a small but unmistakable tooth of a great white embedded in a sea otter carcass near the north end of the bay.

On either side of the sand channel as we swam out, we could see kelp plants rising from the bottom 15 or 20 feet below. These plants are *Macrocystis pyrifera*, one of the world's largest kelp species, capable of growing to more than 100 feet in length. *Macrocystis* is also one of the fastest-growing plants known. Elongation rates of 6 inches per day are common. One measurement of sustained growth over 120 days revealed an addition of 82 feet to the height of one of these plants.

At the edge of a large stand of kelp bordering the open channel, we purged our BCs and descended slowly through clear water to the bottom. Surprisingly, the view below the surface as we looked into the silent amber forest did not appear choked or impenetrable at all. Rather, the scene was open, inviting, and the swim into the forest easy and unhindered. My diving partner, however, had told me that kelp in this area had been thinned greatly by a storm about two months before. Mainly, however, the effect was to thin the canopy and allow greater light penetration below.

The spacing of the plants ranged from about a foot apart to a couple of yards. The bottom was a wilderness of large and small boulders with interspersed sand patches, sudden ledges and drop-offs, and sunken, room-sized pits. Everywhere the kelp plants rose vertically and motionless in the calm water. Each plant consisted of many slim parallel stipes with occasional leafy blades projecting outward; most of the stipes began to sprout from a main axis a few inches to a few feet above the holdfast. However, individual stipes rose so closely together in each plant that from a short distance away they appeared to form a single thick trunk, several inches in diameter. The eye was deceived, and the scene indeed seemed that of a dim, hazy forest of strange, leafy-trunked trees.

The great variety of animal life in the kelp revealed itself as we glided through the yellowed glades. Close up, we found that the plants were crawling with snails. At least six species were readily observable on the fronds. According to studies by diving biologists at nearby Hopkins Marine Station of Stanford University, the snails, like small birds in a tall tropical forest, occupy preferred zones on the plants from the sea floor to the canopy.

Much of the bottom in the kelp grove was the stronghold of the starfish. Some were large and strikingly patterned and colored, showing many shades of yellow, red, and other decorative hues. Most common, and in places virtually covering the bottom like exotic floor tiles, were 3- to 4-inch batstars. Viewed closely, they resembled in size and bulk some sort of fancy, five-tined potholders in a wide choice of colors from yellow-brown through orange and red, to purple. Often, the background color was broken by blue and tan blotches.

Fishes seemed as varied as the snails and starfish, but nowhere near as colorful as the latter. On the average, they seemed as numerous as the bottom fishes of a coral reef tract in Hawaii or the Caribbean, but again not as colorful. In the beam of my underwater light, we spotted a cabezon, its gray-brown, 2-foot sculpin form lurking in a vertical crack between two boulders. Several large basslike fishes let us approach very closely, an indication that the spearfishing ban had been enforced in this area for a long time. Small lizardfishes, up to about 8 inches long, were everywhere on the bottom. These fishes have slender, cylindrically tapering bodies on which the head seems slightly overlarge. They blended well with the texture and color of coarse sand. In most of the area we traveled through there seemed to be at least two lizardfishes per square yard, and we were not necessarily seeing all of them. Several times, when we stopped momentarily, we were approached by wrasses of a moderately large species, up to about a foot long. These fishes are immediately recognizable by their unusual swimming behavior, extensive sculling with the pectoral fins while the rest of the body is held nearly rigid. They seem to dart and swoop over stones and around kelp plants like nervous birds. Some of the smaller wrasses are also well-known as cleaner fishes because they make a living by picking parasites from the bodies of larger fishes, even entering mouths and gill chambers to perform their service and obtain a meal. Cleaner wrasses are more common in coral reef environments (see Chapter 11).

Several of the common animals here were giants of their kind. Throughout the dive, we came upon huge sea anemones (*Tealia*) sprouting above the rocks. Some of the anemones, with brown or gray columns and white tentacles, were as big around as dinner plates. Another, less common colorful red anemone was about the size of a coffee mug. In the kelp forest, molluscs were represented by several outsized and outlandish forms. During the dive, we discovered a primitive-looking *Cryptochiton* as large as a man's shoe (about a size 10). The creature appeared black under natural conditions at 30 feet, but in our artificial lights its color was revealed to be dull red. Chitons are well known for their segmental shells of overlapping plates. A gentle, sluggish grazer, the animal often superficially resembles a miniature, flattened armadillo with its head and tail tucked under the shell. This giant chiton, however, covered its shell completely with a tough, leathery sheath. The giant keyhole limpet (*Megathura*) and giant sea hare (*Aplysia californica*) extended the roster of large molluscan oddities that we encountered in the kelp off Monterey.

Surely the most famous mollusc here and on most of the West Coast is the abalone. I wondered whether we would see any, given the presence of sea otters in the area and their reputation for devouring the delectable "abs." As expected, there were none of the characteristic flattened, domelike shells in sight on the open faces of the rocks. But as we got into increasingly rugged terrain, with jumbles of boulders and deep vertical cracks in massive rock ledges, the abs suddenly appeared. They were way down inside the cracks, farther than I could reach without dislocating my shoulder. (I imagined sea otters backed into the crevices, groping for them in vain with their hind feet). Some of the shells appeared to be at least 10 inches in diameter. Inch-long black or dark red tentacles projected out past the edge of each slightly raised shell in an encircling fringe. These were the red abalone (*Haliotis rufescens*), and they were anything but scarce if one looked in the right places. Thus, the fisherman's complaint that sea otters wipe out the abalone is not strictly true. They have just made them less accessible.

The other famous (or infamous) creature that rates highly on the sea otters' menu is the sea urchin. Two species can usually be found in the kelp here, but when sea otters are present the urchins are very scarce indeed. They too find safe haven only deep in cracks and crevices.

Urchins have the reputation of destroying kelp, and when very large numbers of these animated pincushions accumulate, the loss of kelp can be enormous. Most sea urchins begin to feed on the holdfast. When its anchorage is cut away, the kelp plant will slowly die as it drifts through the forest entangling and killing other plants. Recent scientific studies from California, Alaska, and Nova Scotia indicate that large numbers of sea urchins may keep coastal areas barren of kelp indefinitely by grazing down young plants as fast as they sprout.

Sea otters, which were hunted nearly to extinction on the California coast by the late nineteenth century, have slowly made a comeback. Estimates of the California population of sea otters, ranging between Morro Bay and Santa Cruz, now fall between 1000 and 2000 animals. No other natural sea otter populations remain on the rest of the entire West Coast north to Prince William Sound, Alaska. Recently, however, experimental introductions of sea otters have been attempted in Oregon, Washington, and British Columbian coastal waters.

Sea otters returned to the southern end of Monterey Bay in the early 1960s. By 1969, the population had increased to about fifty animals per square mile. The increase is believed to be responsible for an approximately 30 percent decline in the abundance of abalone and a far larger reduction in local sea urchin populations.

Marine biologists now view the otters as the major "keystone" species of the North Pacific kelp regions. The otter's multifarious diet—fish, octopus, crabs, snails, clams, sea urchins, and so on, helps to keep the numbers of many prey animals in check, thereby assuring that kelp eaters do not overbalance their food supply. With the arrival of sea otters in a new area, kelp forests, which are being severely overgrazed by urchins and snails, begin to expand. Diving biologists at the University of California at Santa Cruz suggest that central California kelp forests, which had been degraded for over a century, are being returned with the reestablishment of sea otters, to the lush condition of ecological balance that existed in the early nineteenth century.

These relationships among species help to explain the unusual abundance of abalone off California in the first half of the twentieth century. Lack of consumption by sea otters led to the ab population explosion. But human greed and poor fishery management, not the return of the sea otters, are primarily responsible for the decimation of abalone along much of the coast. The decline of the big shellfish was apparent in the 1950s, well before the rapid phase of sea otter recovery and expansion. And, as any southern California diver will admit, abs are scarcer than sunken treasure and nearly as valuable, even where nary a sea otter has been seen in living memory.

The otters we had seen in the kelp canopy as we looked out from shore before the dive had given me hope that we would spot one under water, but it didn't happen. Tuck told me that otters are infinitely more shy than seals, and that he had yet to see one on the bottom in the kelp. My goal for a truly complete kelp dive remains—to observe one of these elusive and intriguing marine mammals wild and free in the amber jungle.

Chapter 11

The World of Living Rock

GROWING SLOWLY UPWARD and outward from coastal waters is a strange landscape built by corals and small brittle plants called coralline algae. This ecosystem is found around the globe in shallow tropical and subtropical seas. The reef environment is an ancient one. Enormous fossil reef deposits, very similar in structure as well as types of corals and other organisms, have been discovered in many parts of the earth, even in present-day cold regions such as Greenland, an indication that balmy tropical waves once washed these icy shores. Presently, coral reefs are limited to zones where water temperatures remain above about 65°F (21°C) in winter. Occasional short episodes of cooler temperature are tolerable, but reef development in general is bounded north and south of the equator by latitudes not far outside the Tropics of Cancer and Capricorn.

The coral reef has been called an oasis in the sea. Typically, where reefs are found, the surrounding sea is desertlike in that dissolved nitrate, phosphate, and other fertilizing chemicals are less abundant than nearly anywhere else in the world ocean. It follows that in such waters there is little growth of plankton, and to the diver this means that underwater visibility is usually excellent.

In part, the coral reef oasis functions due to a unique living partnership between the coral animal and single-celled plants. Numerous species of stony corals incorporate tiny cells of algae called *zooxanthellae* within their polyps. The polyps form an interconnecting network over the surface of the coral's limestone skeleton. The algal cells and the coral animal work together in a symbiosis, each supplying what the other can use. The algae use carbon dioxide, nitrogen, phosphorus, and other wastes of the coral to manufacture simple sugars and proteins. Some of these in turn are absorbed by the coral, whose growth rate is thus greatly increased. Only the uppermost surface of a reef mass is alive. Beneath the living coral branches, pinnacles, and domes, a kind of gritty humus—sand and shards of former organized skeletons—accumulates and is slowly, naturally cemented into rock.

The term *coral* is used imprecisely by nearly everyone, including many biologists, to refer to a variety of animals and even plants. Precise application of the term requires modifiers; it is perhaps most often applied to the reef-building species that produce rigid, massive colonies and grow rapidly in symbiosis with algae to provide a foundation for the reef. Other stony corals lack the symbiotic algal cells and contribute relatively little to the structure and mass of the reef. Some of these small, slow-growing species even occur in cold northern waters. Other forms, the so-called soft corals, grow into treelike, whiplike, or fan-shaped colonies, or networks of thousands of tiny cup-shaped, tentacle-bearing polyps. Many of the soft corals are brilliantly colored, with yellows, reds, and purples often dominating. Soft corals still contain crystals of calcium carbonate, the stuff of limestone, but it is much less dense than in the stony corals; soft corals are usually flexible enough to sway gracefully in a slight current.

On some reefs, the living rock is not coral at all but rather stony sponges, called *sclerosponges*, a distinctive type of reef-forming organism that was only discovered, or recognized, in the late 1960s. Other sponges are more true to their image. Remaining soft and flexible, they do not contribute to the skeletal structure of the reef, but may be large and showy features of the landscape. Finally, to round out the tropical reef-builders, the coralline algae, plants that secrete hard limestone crusts or else grow in small "heads" resembling stony corals, may actually be the dominant contributors to the reef substance in some areas. Coralline algae grow fastest in the brilliantly illuminated buttress zone—the outer reef crest—and here their mass usually greatly exceeds that of coral.

In a sense, the reef-building corals and algae concentrate basic nutrients from vast surrounding areas of ocean. The abundant life of the reef oasis locks up nutrients that trickle in with the currents from the fluid desert, and the nutrients are then recycled extremely efficiently. Once trapped in the life of the reef, the vital substances make the rounds endlessly through algae, coral, invertebrates, fish, even man (when he formerly operated within the natural economy of the system), and only a very small proportion is again lost to the waves and winds.

However, all who love the cool, dappled underwater vistas of exceptional clarity and seascapes of the most intricate beauty should be aware that the reefs and adjoining shore areas are now being irreversibly cropped and stripped. Fish and shellfish are being exported for sale, as are land-based crops whose nutrients formerly remained in reef-island systems. On many tropical islands, the native plants are cleared away to provide acreage for non-native crops for export, such as peppers, cotton, and macadamia nuts. For a time a cash-crop economy promotes population growth far beyond what the island could support in its natural state. The ensuing economic boom spells doom for the natural ecosystem, as pollution in the form of concentrated sewage, oil, and chemicals spreads out from the shore across the reeflands. Excess chemical fertilizers wash off the land to choke the organically nurtured bays and lagoons. Organic wastes—the naturally composted remains of vegetation, the bodies of fish and shellfish—from the harvest of the sea and land are not returned to the system. The vital substances that sustain the reef and that normally recycle so completely are being lost wholesale, and reef environments that were once in ecological balance are slowly losing ground. The next generation of coral and algae will not be as lush. The next crop of fish will not be as large.

On other islands, sections of reef are dynamited and dredged to create boat basins and sterile artificial beaches, while shore vegetation is bulldozed away to be replaced by hotels and parking lots. Even the laudable economic gains that have been made by native island peoples can have direct negative effects on the ecological balance. Formerly, Micronesian turtle hunters were prevented from sailing to uninhabited outlying islands during the dead-calm doldrum season, when green sea turtles came ashore on those islands to nest in great numbers. However, now that powerful outboard motors are available throughout Micronesia, the nesting islands are quickly reached in windless weather, and the turtles are severely endangered despite new conservation laws.

We became angry as we began to outline this chapter. According to the latest scientific reports from around the world—the Caribbean, Red Sea, Micronesia, Australia—at the present rate of damage, the reefs of the world will virtually be decimated in thirty years. So we are including this capsule description of ecological crisis on the reefs and are revealing our emotional involvement in the hope that this will pique the conscience of readers the next time they slip into their favorite part of the coral kingdom. By joining together with such organizations as The Oceanic Society, the Audubon Society, and the Sierra Club, which lobby internationally for the protection of reefs, divers can have a powerful voice. If the effort is not great enough, we may be the last generation to know the reefs in all their glory.

But for now, let's assume that it's a fine day. The tropical cumulus is a fancy scrollwork on the horizon; the sun is reflecting blindingly from the white sand of the beach and subtly in blue-green tints just off the shore. What could be more inviting than to step into the silky-warm water, adjust your gear, and push off over the magical wilderness of the reef?

Diving Environments on the Reef

The Reef Flat

Much of the reef-flat environment—the shallow zone nearshore—is ideal country for even the novice snorkeler. The depth here usually averages only a few feet, though occasionally you will come to deeper channels that may require scuba for ease of exploration. However, at certain times and places, shallow reef-flat exploration can be limited by wave action and surge, typically where a site is exposed to strong wind. Not only can you be swept about uncontrollably by the waves in such areas, but visibility can be reduced practically to nil by stirring of the bottom sediment.

In most shallow reeflands, currents are seldom a problem for the diver. An exception occurs where strong winds blowing toward shore move masses of water over the reef into a longshore channel or shallow flat behind the reef crest. Such a combination of factors can cause a strong current to run parallel to shore. Deceptively, there may be little wave action in the channel or on the reef flat, most of the turbulence having dissipated on the outer edge of the reef, or buttress. Where the longshore channel intersects a pass, or an outflow channel through the outer reef, a strong seaward current may develop, and here weak swimmers will find themselves in trouble.

Tidal currents—reversing about every six hours—are generally not of great concern to divers in most reef environments, in particular those that surround oceanic islands where the range of the tide is often smaller than 2 feet. Exceptions to this statement occur where narrow passages or channels receive the tidal flow from a broad expanse of water. For example, an almost imperceptible flow of water across a wide flat or lagoon (a deeper, enclosed body of water inshore of the reef edge) will reach several knots in a narrow channel piercing an atoll, or ring of coral islands. Another area where the tide can be important to divers is in a waterway between islands, or between an island and a mainland shore. For example, in the Florida Keys, the deep channels between the islands are increasingly popular dive spots, especially for foraging for lobsters and spearfishing. However, during the highest tides, which are roughly 2.5 feet in the Keys, currents up to 4 knots (about 5 mph) have been observed in some of the interisland channels. Therefore, in the Keys, unless you are prepared for drift diving, it's a good idea to limit channel excursions to periods close to the slack tides.

The life forms on a shallow reef flat may vary greatly in abundance and diversity, even within a short distance. The areas of abundant life are usually found around small, isolated areas of reef called *patch reefs*, or at the edges of channels. Extensive beds of seaweeds, or sea "grasses," may conceal a variety of fishes and invertebrates. Even a barren-looking bottom, however, may yield some surprises. Turn over a rock and numerous bizarre representatives of the animal kingdom will usually begin trying to burrow, crawl, or swim to safety. Rare and beautiful shells can be found in this way, as can the odd, the weird, and the ugly—things to fascinate anyone interested in marine biology. You may well come across clusters of eggs, left glued to the underside of a rock by some unknown denizen of the reef. But if you become hooked on rock turning, the most important thing to remember is to turn it back again the way you found it. This practice will help conserve the eggs and the many life forms you find, all of which mesh intricately with the living structure of the reef.

Most of the life you encounter on the reef flat will be wholly benign, but there are a few exceptions. If you are pushing aside seaweeds and turtle grass with your hands, and especially if you are turning over rocks, you would be wise to wear gloves. Cheap cotton gardening gloves give sufficient protection from the stings and spines of most of the militant creatures, but these gloves will usually begin to wear through from contact with the rocks themselves after a few dives. Neoprene wetsuit gloves can be uncomfortably hot in tropical waters; many divers prefer gloves of lightweight leather.

Sometimes the greatest pains come from the most peaceful-looking sources. The aggressively spiny, scuttling brittle stars that swarm out from under a turned rock are harmless, while some of the exotic, day-glo-colored patches of sponge that adhere passively to the rock release thousands of microscopic glasslike needles into human skin at the merest brushing contact. Sometimes these penetrate even the relatively thick skin of the fingertips, and they can burn and itch maddeningly for a week. Gloves offer complete protection against such irritating experiences. However, you still have to watch out for the spines of some of the sea urchins, and much more rarely for those of the small, venomous scorpionfish, which can pierce a cotton glove. Simply learning to recognize the venomous cone shells will prevent any trouble from them. We would like to emphasize that none of the creatures mentioned above is actively antagonistic toward divers, and any "attack" is entirely the fault of the victim.

Most kinds of animals that you see on the reef flat are hardy enough to live in home saltwater aquaria. If you are stocking an aquarium, first find out if collecting live marine organisms is legal in your area. Check with authorities, variously listed in different states under Departments of Natural Resources, Fish and Game, Conservation, and the like. You may need a permit. In planning to set up an aquarium, start with very few animals. Crowding can be deadly. If you have to transport marine life any distance, use generous-sized covered buckets but put only a small amount of sea water in the bottom of each. Surprisingly, the partially filled bucket will maintain a much higher concentration of oxygen over an hour or two than will a full one. Better yet, use a battery-powered aerator sold at any pet shop or fishing-supply store. One fairly subtle pointer to those starting out with an aquarium: if you choose animals found during the day beneath a rock, they will stay beneath a rock in your aquarium. Or, if you don't provide a rock for them, they will cower in the corner or burrow in the sand. In nature, these are night-active animals and they are very light-shy. It's better to look instead for the relatively few, easy-to-catch creatures that are out and around in broad daylight.

Inshore Bays and Lagoons

The main feature distinguishing bay and lagoon environments from a reef flat is depth. True lagoons, which are enclosed by atolls, can be as deep as 300

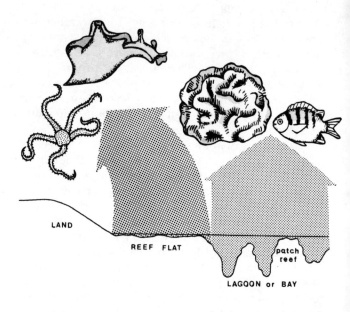

11.1. *Cross section of a coral reef, indicating relative depths of water (shaded areas) and organisms representative of four zones.* **Reef flat:** *brittle star* (Ophiuroid) *and sea hare* (Aplysia). **Lagoon:** *typically rounded, massive coral heads, and damsel fish*

feet. Inshore bays, as in Bermuda and Hawaii, may reach depths of 50 to 60 feet. Tropical bay and lagoon diving can be excellent—one of the best features is the almost perpetually calm water—but at certain times and places it can be unrewarding. Fortunately, the quality of the underwater exploration in bays and lagoons is often predictable.

The best approach in an area that is new to you is to look for patch reefs. These may appear dark in relatively shallow water (20 feet or less) over light sand bottom; in deeper water, they often appear to be light colored, especially if there are areas of dead coral and

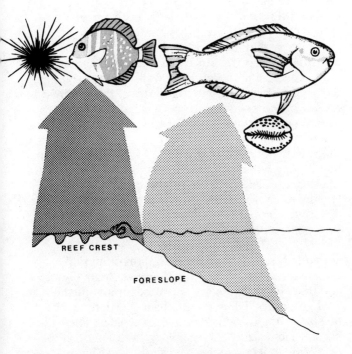

REEF CREST

FORESLOPE

such as the sergeant-major (Abudefduf). **Reef crest:** long-spined urchin (Diadema), and small surgeonfish, or tang (Acanthurus). **Foreslope:** large parrotfish (Scarus), and large cowrie shell (Cypraea).

sand on the shallow portions. Typically, patch reefs rise to within a few feet of the surface. Where they border deep channels, the edges may be vertical, even overhanging, due to the tendency of corals and algae to grow upward and outward faster near the surface. Most of the colorful and active life in the bay will be concentrated around the patch reefs. By contrast, the deeper lagoon or bay bottom will almost invariably be muddy and barren-looking

Underwater visibility in bays and lagoons ranges from excellent during dry seasons and at certain times of day, to poor after heavy rains, particularly in bays receiving runoff from streams. Divers who spend some time in the tropics become aware that the calm waters of a bay or lagoon show a nearly constant daily cycle of turbidity. The water early in the morning is crystal clear, but this changes gradually during the day, and by midafternoon visibility can be reduced by half due to the appearance of a uniform cloud of white specks and flecks in the water. This puzzling but predictable change in the clarity of the water is caused by very slight shifts between daytime and nighttime levels of dissolved carbon dioxide in the water. The tiny particles that appear in the water are a precipitate of calcium carbonate, which builds up during the day when plankton use carbon dioxide during photosynthesis. The more carbon dioxide in the water, the more acidic the water is (like a carbonated soft drink); the less carbon dioxide, the less acidic. The precipitate actually dissolves in slightly acidic sea water; thus, during the night, when carbon dioxide is added to the water by the respiration of myriads of marine creatures, virtually all the precipitate dissolves and disappears. It begins to reappear only during daylight hours, when plant cells begin to photosynthesize, using carbon dioxide in the water. The water becomes less acidic and unable to hold the calcium carbonate in its dissolved invisible state. The precipitate begins to build up during the day until the light starts to diminish in the afternoon. Night divers in the lagoon several hours after sundown again find very clear water.

Common marine animals at a depth of about 35 feet on rocky terrain off New England. Small bloodstars (Henricia) crawl among plumose anemones (Metridium) about 8 inches high. Gray-white sea pork (Amaroecium), a colonial tunicate, covers the rock. Photo by Edward S. Crockett.

An underwater photographer at about 30 feet amid Southern California giant kelp (Macrocystis pyrifera). Photographed at Flower Gardens Reef off the west end of San Clemente Island, California by Emerson Mulford.

A clownfish (Amphiprion) hovers over the dark gray tentacles of its symbiotic host, a large sea anemone (Ftoichactis). Colorful sponges, soft corals, and tunicates complete this scene in Truk Lagoon. Photo by Edward S. Crockett.

Divers explore the famous wall in Bloody Bay, Little Cayman Island, about 180 feet down. Photo by Edward S. Crockett.

The wreck of the **Balboa**, a large interisland freighter sunk in a hurricane, lies in about 30 feet of water only one-quarter mile out-side Georgetown, the capital of Grand Cayman Island. Its accessibility makes it one of the best-known wrecks in the Caribbean. Photo by Emerson Mulford.

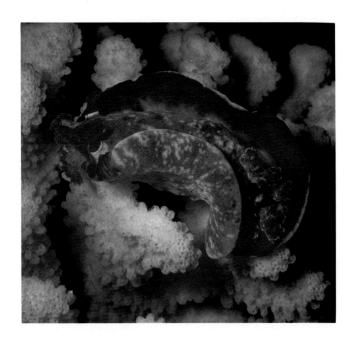

The Spanish dancer (Hexabranchus) is a large nudibranch that ranges widely in the tropical Pacific and Indian oceans (see Chapter 14). Here it crosses a coral head (Pocillopora) about 15 feet deep in Hawaiian waters. Photo by Dale Sarver.

An underwater photographer off Bonaire Island, in the Dutch Antilles. He is using a Nikon F in an Ikelite housing, an Oceanic 2001 strobe with a sea light on the top for focusing, and a Seconic marine light meter. Photo by S. Tecci.

The large moray eel, Gymnothorax undulatus, *inhabits reefs and rocks at shallow depths throughout the tropical Pacific and Indian oceans. Photo by Dale Sarver.*

Occasionally, large, spectacular marine animals are seen in a lagoon or bay. We have found sea turtles resting at the bases of patch reefs in Kaneohe Bay, Hawaii. Several species of sharks enter protected inshore waters to breed, although sharks are much more likely to be seen on the open-ocean side of the reef. Mantas, the huge, harmless "bats" of the sea, occasionally swim through channels in the reef; whole flocks of them have been seen in inshore bays and lagoons. The most spectacular inshore denizen we have heard of is the 50-foot whale shark that lived for more than a year in the lagoon at Canton Island, an atoll in the South Pacific. A number of diving scientists from the University of Hawaii, as well as the military people stationed at the U.S. missile tracking station on Canton, had the once-in-a-lifetime experience of swimming with this near-mythical creature free in the marine wilderness.

Across the Top: The Reef Crest

Many fringing reefs—reefs built outward like shelves from a sloping island edge—are narrow enough to allow a swimmer from shore to cross the reef flat easily and approach the reef crest from the inside. Under certain conditions, it may be possible to cross the crest and continue the dive on the outside, or ocean side, of the reef. The reef crest itself ranges from a few inches high and sometimes dry, to a few feet submerged. Most reefs have crest sections extending both above and below the surface. The depth of submerged portions varies with the tide and changes rapidly and continuously with the wash and suction of waves, and the terrain is always rugged.

The crest is a fascinating area of wave-eroded limestone pinnacles and small channels, often teeming with fishes that somehow live happily here amid the often extreme turbulence. Attempt to swim here only if you are very agile in the water, and then only if the sea is very calm. In some areas exposed to nearly constant trade winds, only a few days in the year are calm enough to allow a good swimmer to cross the crest safely. No one should ever try to swim over the top of the reef with a scuba tank on his or her back. Here we are talking about free and unencumbered exploration only.

On some reefs, you may be able to walk across a very shallow or dry section with or without a tank and, under very calm conditions, continue the dive on the outside. The Smithsonian Institution's marine laboratory at Galeta, on the Caribbean side of Panama, is located on a shallow reef flat. Here diving marine biologists can pick up their gear at the door of the lab and walk about 75 yards through shallow water to a mostly dry reef crest. On the outside, they simply step off into 20 feet of water. At Galeta, however, the prevailing calm conditions are set up by a second reef several hundred yards further offshore. This outside reef breaks the backs of any large ocean swells before they reach the inner reef.

If you do find yourself in the shallows of the reef crest zone, it's best not to linger. Be alert for occasional large swells or surges. If you see one coming, position yourself in a channel or open area away from shallow rock masses or coral heads. Aim your body head-first into the oncoming swell and just try to hold your position in the open area until the wave has passed. The effect of any wave, of course, is to pull you toward it at first, and then, more powerfully, to push you back as it reaches you. Your goal should be to minimize the distance across which you are pulled and pushed. Often, larger-than-average swells come in sets of five or six in succession, so you should be prepared to go through this little maneuver several times before placid conditions return. Even though being caught on the reef in surge can be scary, this technique of free-swimming works quite well if you have a little open-water "breathing room" around you. However, on most reefs, most of the time, and for most divers, we do not recommend swimming in the crest zone. Look for a nice, deep, safe channel through the reef (and be sure you won't have to return against a current). Better yet, plan to make your dive outside the reef from a boat.

On the Outside

Normally, diving on the ocean side of a reef, whether free diving or scuba, is done from a boat. To marine biologists and geologists, the seaward edge of the reef is known as the *foreslope*. Here, the terrain ranges from gentle to steep and rugged, but inevitably, the bottom drops away toward the open sea. Nearly always, the foreslope exhibits the greatest diversity and abundance of corals and other "reefy" invertebrate life and of fishes. This is the zone most often depicted in spectacular underwater photos of the coral kingdom.

Besides the photogenic qualities of the foreslope, the best spearfishing and foraging opportunities are usually found here. Fishes tend to congregate near several types of irregular features found along the outer reef: large depressions, ledges, minicanyons, and coral ridges or pinnacles. Lobsters and octopus inhabit holes and small caves in the sloping floor of the reef or along the edges of the minicanyons. The small canyons may be mere rills or sand channels. Nearly always, they are aligned in roughly parallel tracks, sometimes only a few yards apart, sloping down the face of the reef toward the deep sea.

Outside the reef's crest lies the open-ocean environment. Except near major channels through the reef, the influences of land—muddy runoff, local pollution, and so on—are usually nil. Typically, the water is very clear. Bottom features 70 or 80 feet or more down may be visible to a diver at the surface. Surge is never a problem at such depths, but closer to the reef crest, in 20 feet or less, snorkelers in particular should be cautious around holes or caves in the bottom. It is possible to become temporarily pinned in such holes by the powerful forces generated by large ocean swells. Ascending scuba divers, too, should be mindful of large swells overhead and the potential for embolism represented by sudden changes in depth of several feet.

Sounds and Sights of the Reef

The sights of the reef vary in fine detail depending on where you go in the oceanic tropics, but many of the same kinds of terrain and wildlife will be found by reef divers the world over. One of the most interesting characteristics of a reef, especially at relatively shallow depth, is the almost constant low background noise that fills the water. Not really a silent world at all, the reef is alive with sound-producing creatures, the most numerous of which are small (1 to 2 inches long), shrimplike crustaceans. Each square yard of reef bottom usually harbors dozens of these animals. They live in holes and crevices and are almost never seen unless a diver breaks open a lump of dead coral. The little creatures possess a knucklelike joint in one claw that is noticeably larger than the other of the pair. When flexed, the knuckle pops audibly—hence, the common names snapping shrimp or pistol shrimp, describing the conspicuous behavior of these animals in defending their burrows against intruders. The sound is believed to constitute a warning signal, but it may also have some significance in mating behavior. Often a diver is within hearing range of tens of thousands of snapping shrimps, which together produce a continuous crackling in the water.

Louder, more occasional crunching and scraping sounds are audible in nearly every tropical reef environment. These are made by large fishes (chiefly parrotfishes and puffers) with beaks formed of fused bony plates that enable them to feed on hard coral. The sounds tend to be produced individually against the undertone of the blended crackling of the snapping shrimps, but in the midst of a large parrotfish population, bony fish beaks against limestone, the skeletal stuff of the reef, can produce a surprising din. Coral-eating fishes, of course, are after the thin layer of living tissue at the very surface of the coral head or branch, so they must scrape large areas of coral to obtain a meal. When you are diving, look for the white oval scars left on the surfaces of coral branches by the fish bites, which have scraped away the usually brown or yellowish living tissue. Left alone, the coral tissue will grow back over the scar, but in a few areas, large parrotfish populations actually stunt coral growth and can virtually prune away certain preferred species of coral.

Also, follow a parrotfish or puffer for a while and you will see it defecate a white cloudy mass that slowly diffuses in the water and settles down toward the bottom. This waste is pure coral sand and silt, cleanly divested of the fraction of organic material formerly contained in the fish's stony fodder.

Other occasional natural sounds in the sea include squeaks, grunts, and thumps produced by various fishes and crustaceans. Tropical lobsters are famous for squeaking, or stridulating, when captured. The most impressive sounds in the sea are those made by marine mammals, especially large whales. In the winter and spring months, off the southwest coast of Maui in Hawaii, especially at night, divers can hear (and feel) the songs of the humpback whales, which migrate to the area in large numbers. The whoops, locomotive sounds, and staccato boomings of the humpbacks—often overwhelming to humans—can be felt vibrating through the body as much as they are heard. Being surrounded by the rumbling music of the whales is a stunning experience in the ocean wilderness.

While the reef's many-hued landscape is made up largely of stationary invertebrate animals (corals, sponges, and so on) and algae, the endless spectacle of color-filled motion on the reef belongs to the fishes. Serious fishwatchers may be starting to outnumber birdwatchers. It is easy to find any number of true-life dramas, serious and comic, being played out along a short stretch of reef. A juvenile barracuda cruises with sinister nonchalance beside a terrified school of silvery small fry. A pair of angelfishes briskly evicts a lone intruder of the same species from their territory.

One of the best places to fishwatch is where you notice a brightly colored, hyperactive little cleaner wrasse, flipping around doing loops and turns in one spot, seemingly trying to attract attention to itself. This is indeed the object, or the result, of the fish's behavior. The spot it occupies on the reef is known to marine biologists as a *cleaning station*, and with its bright colors and peculiar antics, the small fish is advertising its services. Large fishes of many species are attracted to the scene, and they sometimes line up and wait as if in a barber shop while the cleaner swims all around them, picking off and consuming small parasites. Even dental services are provided; it is startling to see the little cleaner fish swim casually into the mouth of a large grouper, pick at something, and then emerge a moment later from the gill opening. Sooner or later, at a cleaner station, you will see most of the larger fish species of the reef.

The end of a reef dive comes all too soon. Many divers feel that a hundred lifetimes could be spent on the reefs, and still new sights, insights, and adventures would remain. When you finally turn your boat toward shore, and later, as you rinse your gear, daydream in front of your aquarium, or look over your newest underwater photos, chances are you will already be planning your next drop into the exotic tropics of the sea.

Chapter 12

The Wall

IN A FEW REGIONS of the world ocean, island chains were born, evolved from volcanic to coralline stature, and then were drastically altered by movements of the earth's huge crustal plates. This pattern occurred in the Caribbean Sea, where a number of islands and shallow platforms bearing groups of islands have become truncated by massive faulting—a pulling apart and slipping downward of the earth's crust.

Extending approximately due east-west across the central Caribbean Sea is the boundary between the North American and Caribbean crustal plates. The back and forth shifting of these plates' stony edges, which extend several miles beneath the sea floor, has created perhaps the most spectacular diving environments in the world, characterized by enormous scarps, or cliffs, 2000 to 6000 feet high.

The cliffs, usually referred to by divers as *walls*, are highest where islands were split asunder by the earth-moving forces at the plate boundaries. The island remnants now lie atop ridgelines with sheer sided walls that rise from the deep to very shallow water startlingly close to shore. Along the great walls, more than in any other underwater landscape, a diver comes face to face with the awesome scale and overwhelming dynamic forces that shaped the ocean. Nowhere else does the mystery and loneliness of the deep outer sea press so heavily against one's back.

Yet nowhere else can a diver achieve such a powerful sensation of free motion, of flying, of unencumbered mastery over boundless space. These are feelings shared only with hang gliders.

The only special requirements for divers planning to explore the wall environment are deep diving experience and a thorough familiarity with the techniques and precautions it entails. Walls frequented by divers are found in the Bahamas, near the island of Eleuthera, and in the South Pacific, near Palau. But perhaps the best place in the world to take the ultimate plunge over the edge of inner space is in the Cayman Islands, about one airline hour south of Miami.

The Vertical Wilderness

Our adventure begins at Bloody Bay, off Little Cayman Island. The name of the bay never fails to intrigue visitors, and speculation is rampant on board our party's Zodiac (a popular motorized rubber craft) as we head through the shallows toward our dive site. Possibly the christening traces to an early British arrival (irate gentleman or drunken seadog are equally likely) venting his ire of the moment on the bay. Perhaps the name refers to an old pirate battle, once, it is said, a common enough event in these islands. The least popular suggestion has to do with sharks, and this ends the speculation as we head out slowly over the reef flat.

The shallows possess absolute clarity, an excellent omen for the coming dive. Viewed from the boat, the water inside the reef, 8 to 10 feet deep, has a background color of cool, light turquoise, reflected from the white sand bottom. Some dark, almost black-looking patch reefs, with pinnacles reaching nearly to the surface, stand out sharply, and we steer among them as we aim for the channel through the breakers ahead.

Our anchorage is in approximately 25 to 30 feet of water outside the reef's very shallow crest zone, with its line of constant surf. The ocean is benign today under a zephyr of trade wind; the Zodiac shrugs and weaves gently against the anchor in light chop covering an easy swell. Nobody has the slightest difficulty on entry.

Thirty feet below the Zodiac, we rendezvous on a nearly flat shelf; turquoise water appears all around. Colorful little reef fishes are abundant over coral heads. A large grouper or two appear in the middle distance. But these typical reef scenes hardly seem of passing interest to the group in view of what's in store. Someone seems to know the way, and the rest of us follow slowly, skimming a few feet above the bottom.

Quite suddenly the view ahead changes. We are about 30 feet from where the bottom appears to end. One's line of sight is attracted over the obvious break in the terrain ahead. Downward, turquoise gives way to a deep and darkening blue. As if in a dream, we glide out over the lip of the ocean, on the verge of a geologic yawn 6000 feet deep.

The visibility is well over 200 feet downward and the scene is awesome. The emotions it engenders, especially in a first encounter, are difficult to describe—mind-blowing, unreal, incredible—most people are at a loss for meaningful words. Here is the ultimate underwater wilderness. The stupendous fluted cliff dominates everything; all one's past diving memories are lost, swallowed up by the panorama below. The wall extends impossibly far down until lost in the remotest blue. Horizontally, along the edge of the shelf where we hover, the wall disappears into a lighter blue haze in either direction.

Suspended above the abyss, one becomes suddenly, powerfully aware of the profundity of depth in the sea. Gravity seems to be a drawing force from the abyss. One can almost feel it in the legs, tugging insistently downward. Two by two, we vent our BCs and start to drop slowly into the blue vastness. The feeling is very dreamlike. Imagine stepping off the edge of the Grand Canyon, enveloped in a thin blue fog and drifting down beside cliffs, and you may begin to approach the effect of a wall dive. The water flowing gently past the body feels so pleasant, a diver might wish to continue down forever.

This is a world of utter contrast. On one side is deep inner space, extending empty to the antipodes, as far as one can tell. On the other is the wall, festooned with life, a silent, hanging jungle, a sudden vertical oasis in the marine desert. Most of the weird "trees," "shrubs," and "mushroom" forms are really animals: corals and sponges in huge variety. Around them and through them the fishes, shrimps, molluscs, and others soar and jump, walk and glide.

The wall is a unique jungle; tilted upward 90 degrees, its ridges and valleys run vertically, forming a regular pleated or folded relief. As far as we can see along its face, the wall resembles the partly expanded surface of some colossal weathered accordion, frozen silent in stone.

Descending very slowly past the canopy of upended forest, we view one of the richest concentrations of marine life on earth, representing the entire animal kingdom. Sponges, corals, fanworms, molluscs, crustaceans, echinoderms, fishes are all featured here, interweaving their growth forms and movements in an endless kaleidoscope of shifting pattern and color. Only a few of the creatures here are capable of extensive movement, and many are fixed permanently to the rock. But it doesn't matter; in its unfathomable variety the scene is anything but static.

A short way down the wall, we pass below an overhanging brow of stone; beneath it is a shallow cave, which prompts us to pause briefly in our descent to explore with the aid of diving lights. Artificially illuminated, the colors here at about 50 feet down are breathtaking—yellows, reds, oranges, blues, turquoises, purples in every shade imaginable. In the shallow cave, the colors seem more vivid than outside on the open wall—probably the effect of the diver's light being more penetrating and the eye more receptive to color in semidarkness.

We emerge from the dazzling color show in one of the recesses of the wall and again face the deep blue and the immensity of the sheer, scalloped mountain extending into ultimate dark and silence below. As we roll over for a view of the receding surface, we can make out a tiny boatshape and doll-like human forms silhouetted against a remote, pale, and expanded orb of sunshine. Long wispy columns of bubbles seem to rise endlessly from them toward the light. No other diving environment places a diver in such true perspective with the sea.

Between about 80 and 100 feet is a zone of more extensive caves and true tunnels. The tunnels were probably formed long ago when sea level was much lower and rain water seeped and ran for millenia through cracks and fissures in the reef, dissolving away the limestone. Many of the tunnels are nearly straight and slant upward at a steep angle. At least some of them open far above on the shallow reef flat close to shore. Divers have descended through a few of the wider passages and have emerged raving about the fantastic interior decorations—overlapping frescoes and splashes of encrusting marine life in indescribable colors. Some of the tunnel walls are covered solidly with sponges that grow in a circular, spreading manner, rather than into an upright structure, and resemble a display of lurid pizza pies. Pausing inside, near the middle of one of the shorter tunnels, a diver feels suspended between two worlds. Above, the view telescopes to a small, far-away opening of bright aquamarine. Downward, the opening appears as an unutterably remote circlet of deepest blue. Surrounded by living walls resembling an alien art, one feels like a futuristic traveler caught between dimensions of normal existence, exploring a blue hole in inner space.

Descending again with 100 feet of water overhead, it seems we have barely left the shallows. One-twenty, 130 slides past easily, almost too easily, and the nitrogen fuzziness behind the eyes begins to be ever so slightly noticeable. As usual at such depths, the intervals between the hiss of inhalation and the burbling of exhalation are filled with the immutable silence of the deep. If people are prepared for deep diving, this is one of the finest places in the world for it. Not only are the weather and underwater conditions usually fine, but the learning opportunities are superb; the wall is a living instructional display, an immense blackboard of information on the natural history of marine life.

Beginning about 100 feet down, several kinds of hard coral appear to be taking on a horizontally spreading and flattening form of growth. These so-called table corals are actually of the same species that form massive or ball-like heads, usually with short branches, in shallow water. On a ledge near 150 feet, we find a very large and thin table coral, about 6 feet long by 3 feet wide, supported by a short irregular pedestal and extending from a narrow ledge out over the abyss. This peculiar flattening of coral growth in the depths is thought by marine biologists to be a reaction to diminishing light intensity, analogous to the way many trees produce extra-large leaves deep within and beneath the forest canopy. Only species of coral whose growth depends on a symbiosis with tiny single-celled zooxanthellae show the flattening and spreading with depth. This growth response results in maximum light exposure for the algal cells, which carry on photosynthesis as they lie embedded in the soft tissue, mainly concentrated in tiny pits, on the coral's upper surface.

Below about 150 feet, the wall seems predominantly decorated with sponges. We are leaving the largest of them behind, however. Now their collective effect is of a giant's patchwork quilt or an immense display of overlapping, multicolored cushions. Some of the sponge forms are actually hard and brittle, the sclerosponges that form the primary framework of deep zones of the reef environment. Among the thickly bedded sponges on the wall sprout long sea whips studded with tiny stinging polyps. These are a type of soft coral, and they project several feet out from the wall like huge, coarse hairs. Nestled in clusters here and there, a surprise at such depths and conspicuous for its color, is the bright green alga *Halimeda*, consisting of small sprigs of interconnected flattened platelets.

At 175 feet, a grove of rare black coral extends along a ledge. Also a soft coral, these animals resemble nothing so closely as miniature oak trees in winter. Leafless, bonsailike, they form extensive forests in some places along the wall. For a time, divers in the Caymans routinely carried handsaws down to the black-coral zone and ruthlessly stripped certain areas. Fortunately, a conservation ethic has replaced the frontier spirit that originally prevailed on the deep walls. In most areas, even spearfishing is now suppressed, and nearly everyone agrees that killing the fishes and plundering the scenery in such a showcase wilderness is criminal behavior. Punctuating the starkness alongside the thicket of black coral appears a slow, sinuous parade of silvery fishes, weaving its way past the shadowless pattern of branches, a moment of living Oriental art, simplicity of form in black and white.

The buzzing sensations behind the eyes and the cottony-headed feeling from the nitrogen take hold more strongly as we approach 200 feet. Lips are tingling, fingers feel numb, air tastes strangely sweet, and bubbles sound like bells as they fly upward past the ears. Looking up, we can see friends in the distance soaring like birds through diffused sunshine that gleams dully like cracked pewter and seems impossibly far away. There is a thermocline here; a cooling sensation on the skin can be felt at first, but then it seems to disappear. This is probably another effect of the bottled-up nitrogen, which conveys a false impression of warmth.

At 200 feet, disturbing sensations of nitrogen begin to take over. The air has begun to taste somewhat bitter. A slight apprehensive feeling takes shape as a very large barracuda appears from the back of one of the massive infoldings in the wall. The fish approaches slowly, deliberately posturing in a peculiar way, presenting himself in side view at intervals. Close up, he is a very impressive 6-footer, with very prominent and wickedly sharp-looking teeth; his jaws work slowly with his breathing. But most impressive is an incredible display along his flanks. Silvery patterns of splotches, streaks, and bars oscillate rapidly along his skin as he hovers a few feet away. The patterns resemble a neon sign gone wild, flashing meaningless bits of a message continuously at random. We are partly disadvantaged by nitrogen, but we can interpret the fish's message. It almost has to be a territorial warning signal. The huge neon barracuda is not afraid of us and is definitely telling us to leave the area—or else, what? We decide not to speculate.

We were intending to leave anyway and return to the upper, more hospitable layers of the sea, but just for a moment we move horizontally away from the fish and take a last look downward into the abyss, where we cannot go. The deepest impression is one of the remotest reaches of the water planet. Here, at 200 feet, the exuberantly colored life forms clinging to the wall have thinned out and are much smaller than those above. Areas of apparently bare stone can be glimpsed a short distance below us. In the distance, a silent fall of white sand pours down out of a recessed hanging canyon and diffuses like a small cloud of dimly seen snow, falling into the depths. Far down the cliff, perhaps between 400 and 500 feet, is a large irregular shelf which has caught drifts of the sand like a mountain ledge catching snow.

The deep conveys an ultimate loneliness. In the perpetual oceanic dusk below, the utter implacability of physical forces and alien biology can be sensed. There is something there, as in the highest mountains, the farthest deserts, the barren surface of Mars, that is as yet beyond the reach of human emotion. In such places we sense no hostility or cruelty, only an elemental indifference. Once, however, this indifference was reflected everywhere, a constant quality of the universe. That has changed; the indifference has retreated in a few small areas, but it still hovers near at 200 feet along the Cayman wall. We turn our faces upward and begin the long, slow climb back to the light.

Chapter 13

The Lure of the Inaccessible: Shipwrecks and Caves

D IVERS, LIKE ODYSSEUS, may be tempted during their sea travels to explore certain exotic locales where extra preparation and precautions are needed against foreseeable dangers. Descending on a large wreck or probing a drowned cave, especially in deep water, poses unique problems and challenges far beyond those encountered in normal open-water diving. Divers new to caves and wrecks are advised never to approach these environments without at least one experienced and locally knowledgeable person along as a dive-team member.

Of course, on any dive where the difficulty is greater than usual, prior planning assumes a correspondingly greater importance. Every detail of the dive plan must be clear to every diver and to people remaining on the surface in supporting roles.

Aficionados claim that wreck and cave diving can differ greatly from each other, and this is certainly true in terms of their overall settings and in some of the details that go into planning. But when one is actually on site and exploring, avoiding physical encumbrance and encountering overhangs at close quarters with other divers in silty surroundings, the two diving environments have much in common. We have decided to treat wrecks and caves in the same chapter because of the similarities of the practical problems they present, and, more importantly, the high degree of underwater competence and judgment they demand.

Exploring a Shipwreck

To illustrate the major points and problems of a wreck dive, we will describe a visit to the well-preserved remains of U-853. Sunk by American destroyers at the end of World War II, this German submarine lies on a sandy bottom, 130 feet deep, on the New England continental shelf, about 7 miles southeast of Block Island.

Finding the U-boat is our first problem of the day. Reaching the approximate location requires an experienced skipper using Loran navigation. Once there, a good depth recorder guides the approach and sooner or later pinpoints the sub itself as a large, smudgy bump showing against the smooth bottom.

With the dive boat positioned as directly above the wreck as possible, a light marker buoy is dropped. The buoy is simply a brightly colored plastic lobster fisherman's buoy tied to a half-inch nylon line half again as long as the depth of water here. Anchoring the marker is a cluster of diving-belt weights totaling about 25 pounds. The essence of the operation is that once the boat is in position, the anchor must go down fast, so that a current will not displace it more than a few yards from the target.

With the marker in place, the skipper idles his engine and drifts as divers line the rail and watch the buoy for signs of a surface current. Currents are nearly always observed here on the open continental shelf. Because we are in fairly deep water, a complex system of currents, involving subsurface or bottom flows moving in different directions from those at the surface, can occur. But offshore on a gentle day such as this one—midsummer to early fall is the best season for diving in these waters—currents rarely present difficulties for competent divers who are prepared for them. The offshore currents rarely show the extreme fluctuations found closer to the coast in areas where the tides become compressed in narrow bays and channels.

A fairly standard procedure for descending to U-853 has evolved over the years and is followed by most dive clubs and charters visiting the sub. A diver guide or a buddy pair with prior on-site experience makes the first descent along the marker line. These divers carry a second half-inch line, which they tie directly to the sub's conning tower at 90 feet, the shallowest portion of the wreck. The lead team then returns without delay to the surface, noting briefly conditions of currents and visibility below.

All conditions are within acceptable limits for our dive. The original marker float and anchoring weights are hauled back on board to avoid confusing and possibly entangling the divers. Everyone makes final their preparations and partnerships, and, as the skipper maneuvers close to the marker and idles his engine once more, we step off into the cold, blue-green depths to begin the dive.

The marker line is white for maximum visibility. From the surface, as we look down, it trails off at an angle into nothingness. Instead of being taut, it forms a leisurely downward bow, casually tethering the unknown. Seen from a distance, the nearly identical, wetsuited figures, descending slowly along the thin curving line, would appear to be some ritual procession from another world.

The divers drift down close to the line. Visibility seems good but is hard to gauge, unless one remembers to look up at the surface. Someone below hauls on the line, hand under hand. Reassuringly, the line tightens. Thermocline hits at just under 30 feet. Dimly perceived, the cold envelops us all and begins to probe thin seams of warmth. We are in the nether layer now, somewhere between sand and sky. The water is a graying world; the loss of color here seems to occur much more rapidly than in the aquamarine tropics. Water clarity, however, is exceptional, as is the silence between trains of exhaled bubbles. A brief pause at 50 feet for tightening weight belts and check-ing the octopus unit is standard.

As on any deep dive, the silence is impressive—it is not merely an absence of sound, but a positive force, an assertive quietness unmatched in any other wilderness setting, including the deepest canyon and farthest desert.

Suddenly from ahead and below, the visual uni-formity of water is broken by a hulking pattern be-ginning to form out of featureless space. One's ten-dency is to disbelieve and blink hard to clear the visual field. But the image is solid and will not dissi-pate; the mind immediately switches tactics and has-tens to resolve the mystery and identify the looming mass.

At first glance, from many positions close to its roughly 230-foot-long hull, U-853 looks as if it might suddenly start up its engines and move off into the gray-green haze. The sub appears to be merely parked on the bottom. With good visibility, perhaps 65 feet in these waters, descending divers in the right place can see at a glance the conning tower, the forward-deck machine gun, and a number of hatches; viewed from the conning tower, the bow finally ta-pers off into dim obscurity.

The dive plan is to remain in buddy pairs and make an optional abbreviated circumnavigation of the wreck. Since this is a nondecompression dive, there is barely enough time to swim entirely around the sub, that is if one wants to pause to look at anything. One pair in the group is aiming to do some photography. Bottom time is limited to ten minutes.

Before the dive, everyone was cautioned to beware of fishing lines caught on and tangled around the sub. Entanglement is one of the most serious hazards in wreck diving. Because they attract fishes, submerged wrecks also attract fishermen and become crudely fes-tooned with monofilament rigging—sometimes miles of it—an invisible trap for unwary scuba divers. Much of the line is of high-breaking strength, 40-pound test or more, giving neither fish nor diver a sporting chance. A knife is therefore essential for a wreck diver—again, worn strapped to the inside of the calf to prevent the protruding knife handle itself from catching on tangled lines.

Another admonition, less important for safety but significant for the quality of the dive, is to avoid stirring up silt, which tends to settle in sheltered areas of the wreck and beneath it. Silt, of course, is an anathema to photographers, and the clumsy or careless souls who fail to trim their buoyancy and wallow on the bottom risk being roundly cursed after the dive. As a rule of thumb, according to one veteran of U-853 and other northeast shipwrecks, a good wreck diver "ought to be able to thread a porthole touching only his fingertips."

Of course, U-853 has no portholes, and we have not planned for entry. To do so safely on a wreck of this sort would demand expeditionary logistics and skills comparable to those needed for a minor Himalayan climb. Despite this, U-853 has been entered by a few hot-dog divers whose crude operations even included, on at least one occasion, violating the dead German crew. (A skull and portions of a uniform were removed and later displayed as souvenirs in Rhode Island.)

The American destroyer that sank U-853 did so with finesse. The hull of the German craft was not noticeably marred by the attack, but apparently some vital internal system was irreparably damaged and the sub was left to drown quietly on the bottom. It might be noted in passing that simple submarine-escape technology developed by Captain Cousteau and the French Navy just after World War II could easily have saved the U-boat's crew from a depth of 90 feet. But in 1945, 90 feet might as well have been 900.

Years later, diving vandals attached dynamite to the hull of U-853 and blew an irregular hole, roughly 3 feet in diameter, in the upper deck of the stern section. Prior to this, divers were able to enter U-853 through a hatch on the foredeck, but entry necessitated removing one's tank and lowering it through the hatch separately, or else relying on an extra-long regulator hose to supply air from a tank left with a buddy outside. Entry at the dynamited section is hazardous due to torn and twisted metal around the opening and large accumulations of silt inside. Local diving instructors regard entering U-853 at the stern hole—"a scaled-up version of someone having punched a hole in an oil drum with a pickaxe"—to be as difficult as a cave dive, but with added risk from the jagged metal and possible structural weakness inside from the blast. So far, however, the sunken submarine has claimed no victims beyond the original combatants.

Entering a submerged, nearly intact wreck is in the realm of professional diving—for rescue or salvage purposes, insurance investigation, movie making, and so on. Making such an entry is highly technical, precise, exhausting, and dangerous work beyond the scope of this book. Also, we feel that a wreck in which people have died should be treated by divers with sensitivity in a manner reserved for a gravesite. However, anyone still harboring a fatal fascination for the thought of penetrating shipwrecks in the deep should obtain the highest-quality professional training in the specialty. Captain Jacques Cousteau's vivid account of exploring wrecks in *The Silent World* should be required reading for anyone contemplating entry. Although the technology of diving has changed greatly since those early days, the pitfalls and problems encountered by the first divers to reach the deep wrecks are the same today.

The prospective explorer of wrecks might also be enthralled or sobered by accounts of expeditions to the *Andrea Doria*, perhaps to wreck-minded divers the Mount Everest of sunken ships. The *Doria* too lies on the New England shelf in 160 to 230 feet of water. In 1972, divers with a professional salvage team gained entry to the ship, but found the interior badly deteriorated—"a death trap," in the words of one of them. To date, no attempt to recover a significant portion of the valuable ship's stores has been successful.

Conveniently, our unhurried outside tour of U-853 takes ten minutes, precisely our allowable bottom time. In addition to the dynamited hole in the sub, the highlights include the periscope, part of which has been sawed off by souvenir hunters. The remaining basal portion still looks smooth and untarnished in the beam of a dive light—a tribute to the quality of German stainless steel forged nearly forty years ago. It is surprising to find the metal so little touched by the sea; neither corrosion nor obvious encrusting life is visible. The explanation may be that the wreck is swept clean nearly continuously by the currents, or perhaps it still retains some superior chemical anti-fouling coat. On the bow, the large numerical insignia of the sub is also clean and clearly visible in the gloom.

Of wildlife, we encounter relatively little. A small cod moves along the side of the sub just above the bottom. A flounder or two lie scattered on the sand; the pattern of their skin matches the background and the fish remain inconspicuous even to a trained eye. A small "stand" of white hake, propped on their long stiltlike pectoral fins, completes the fish roster, except for one spectacular encounter near the stern. There an enormous goosefish lurks in a depression that curves under the side of the ship near the propeller shaft. Ugly as sin and demonically repulsive, this one looks as if it could indeed swallow a goose. Fully half of its 3-foot length appears to be head. Its eyes gleam evilly green, reflecting the beams of several lights. A thin fleshy fringe just below the wide half circle of its mouth palpitates ever so slightly, perhaps in response to a gentle current or the breathing rhythm of the fish itself. The inevitable silt accompanying the stirrings of several divers begins to drift through the scene, and the monster assumes a theatrical air; it resembles a smirking goblin seeming to fade and reappear amid Hadean vapors.

At 130 feet, one's objectivity is partly preempted by the onset of rapture of the deep, but even at shallow depths where the soft nitrogenous fuzz is not an influence, a goosefish is just as sinister looking. By comparison, a shark of this size would be admired by most divers. In form, the fearsome goosefish closely resembles its relatives, the much smaller scorpionfishes, many of which are venomous. Scorpionfishes are most common in shallow tropical waters, where careless barefoot waders are "stung" when they step on the fish's venom-injecting spines. Even tiny scorpionfishes are usually deemed ugly, repellant, and vaguely dangerous-looking by fishermen or divers seeing them for the first time.

The goosefish is the largest of the anglerfishes, famous for a slim, flexible "fishing rod" and attached wispy "lure" that grows from the top of the head and that can be extended forward over the mouth from its normal folded position. The goosefish, with its bodily design selected and maintained by nature, is superbly adapted for a mostly sedentary life, ambushing fishes, shrimps, and perhaps squids that come within gulping range. Despite its name, even the largest goosefish would probably choke on a goose. Besides, an encounter between the two is unlikely. Goosefish, however, might confront and attempt to swallow an occasional diving duck.

The silt, which first became noticeable by the goosefish's lair, seems to have spread, probably from several points of interest. By the conclusion of our tour, the scene back at the conning tower appears somewhat more hazy than on arrival. Visibility here is probably down to 25 feet. The beams of diving lights at a distance of more than a few feet appear dim and yellow, as if seen in fog. Cold may be weakening the lights' batteries as well. The cold is also steadily slipping through our pressure-thinned wetsuits, becoming a powerful presence. It's time to go up. The bulk and outline of the submarine is lost to view almost immediately as we form the same ghostly procession as on our descent a few minutes past and climb out of the dark and cold toward light and warmth.

Cave Diving

Cave diving is similar to wreck diving in that attention is primarily focused on a single unique aspect of the environment. Were it not for this uniqueness, few divers if any would visit the site. Freshwater caves are frequently nearly devoid of visible life—they are far more barren than even freshwater wrecks. Except in rare instances, when a cave has very recently filled with water, a diver will never see the fantastic arrays of stalactites and stalagmites and exposures of crystals and unusual minerals known to conventional spelunkers. These attractive features have either dissolved or been concealed by sediment in most underwater caves. Submerged caverns, especially the freshwater variety, are often dark and claustrophobic with muddy walls and floors.

What motivates people to swim into cold, muddy passages? Occasionally, scientific research will bring some intrepid souls into this improbable realm. Most underwater cavers, however, simply have the explorer's urge—crying, "Because it is there," and wondering, "How far does it go?" and "What's on the other side?" The appeal of this most womblike of diving environments is strong: hundreds of divers now enter caves yearly.

Except for simple quarry or chimney diving (straight vertical configurations), a cave dive usually involves a loss of *overhead* (unobstructed vertical access to the surface). Where this is the case, the dive should be treated as a deep-water expedition, no matter what the actual depth to be reached. Necessary equipment is the same as that for deep diving, including octopus regulators, calibrated depth gauges, lights (one member of each buddy-pair should carry an extra light), BCs with autoinflators, plus a lifeline to the surface.

Necessary prerequisites begin with a professional attitude and a special preparedness for cave diving, along with the highest degree of underwater competence. Anyone attempting an excursion involving loss of overhead should be an expert diver, preferably with some open-water nighttime experience and a few deep descents under his or her belt. A cave diver's positive state of mind and physical abilities must mesh well. If you can remain extremely cool in dark, silty conditions and swim with finesse amid obstructions, ropes, and close encounters with your partners, you pass the first test. The next step is to seek local knowledge if you are new to a cave site. The best way to obtain information is to visit the nearest professional dive shop.

Before entering any cave, check carefully for currents. Caves connected to the sea nearly always have currents; normally, they follow the local tidal cycle and are roughly predictable. However, cave tides may precede or lag behind those in nearby open water, so get local information and then make your own predive observations at the site. Freshwater caves may have unpredictable currents or no detectable currents at all. Currents in a freshwater cave that forms part of an underground river or system of springs will usually be strongest in spring or early summer. Watch for outflow or suction at the cave entrance. Some divers use a line tied to a water-filled, neutrally buoyant plastic bottle to test for suction. *Never* go into a cave where suction is present. A very slight current in a wide passage can quickly become irresistibly powerful as the cave narrows. In a sea cave, plan the dive for slack low tide or during the outflow phase of the tidal cycle. The suction in a sea cave will eventually reverse, but each phase typically lasts six hours.

A person tending the lifeline at the surface is absolutely necessary. This person should pay out line as the divers progress, keeping the line free of coils and preventing slack from accumulating in the water. Use light climbing rope, preferably white for high visibility. Light snap links or carabiniers on short lengths of rope are recommended for attaching divers to the lifeline whenever they are without overhead. Never tie yourself to the line, since it could become stuck in a crevice or looped around a rock, leaving you struggling to untie a knot in the dark with water-softened fingers. The alternative to a carabinier-type of attachment is merely to use the lifeline as a guide, holding it by hand and not letting go. In a muddy passage with 1-foot visibility, we emphasize: *don't let go!*

Stationing a reserve or safety diver at the surface with the dive plan firmly in mind and a watch synchronized with yours is highly recommended for all but the simplest cave dives. Even a minor accident or slight diving problem, such as difficulty in clearing the ears, can be serious in a cave and require you to call for outside assistance. Of course, the line tender should not double as safety diver.

Before the dive, one member of the team is designated lead diver, responsible for advancing the lifeline, which is tied to a light anchor, usually a 5-pound belt weight. The other diver or divers all monitor time and depth.

In the cave, your mobility will be enhanced by an inflator-equipped BC. You will need to make very cautious, deliberate movements if you encounter overhangs and major obstructions, and attention to buoyancy will tend to minimize the amount of silt you stir into suspension. To get maximum mileage from your cave excursion, you may choose to wear double tanks, though these will restrict your access to tight passages.

In some caves divers encounter air pockets and sometimes larger air-filled natural vaults. It is a popular fantasy that a diver may surface to breathe virgin air happily and indefinitely in such places. This is rarely true. Much of the air may not be virgin, particularly in caves frequented by divers. The air in such places has probably already passed through others' lungs. Small pockets will soon go stale, and breathers in them will experience a rapid onset of carbon dioxide poisoning. Large air-filled rooms in drowned caves have been found, but they are very rare and usually remain the closely guarded secrets of a few local divers.

Not surprisingly, air-reserve logistics for cave diving, recommended by NAUI, are highly conservative. Calculate a safe air allotment by first subtracting the standard reserve of 500 psi plus a 100 psi emergency reserve from your starting pressure. Then halve the remaining pressure to find the pressure drop that limits your excursion into the cave. This means that if you start the dive with 2500 psi, you should turn around after your gauge shows a drop of 900 psi—that is, when you have 1600 psi left. Note that this calculation is a little conservative, which is always a wise approach to cave diving. Not surprisingly, running out of air before clearing a cave is nearly always fatal. Buddy breathing with an octopus rig is very difficult to coordinate during a horizontal swim and can be impossible in narrow passages. On exiting a cave, the same diver usually handles the safety line with its 5-pound weight, and the line tender at the surface hauls in the slack. Signals to the surface, for example to announce that the divers are returning, usually consist of a coded series of tugs on the line. It's always a good idea for the first divers out of the cave entrance and into the zone of free overhead to wait for the last person. When everyone is in the open, all ascend together.

Diving into a Chimney Cave

Only one of us has had any experience in cave diving, and that has been fairly well limited to sinkhole or chimney-type sea caves in the Bahamas. One of the more memorable of these was unique for its seclusion in the interior of a mangrove forest on a small outer island. The way to the dive site was a pleasurable excursion in a Boston Whaler through winding, woodsy channels. Birds called from the trees and an occasional bonefish or snook cut the water as it veered away from the oncoming boat. Suddenly, in a widening part of the channel, the very light aquamarine color of the water was interrupted by a deep blue and jagged-edged circle roughly 30 feet in diameter. We experienced what was almost a sensation of falling as the boat drifted over the hole. Ripply limestone walls dropped straight down to vague shapes and shadows far below. The water was crystal clear.

Anchoring the boat was no problem here. If it drifted it would go gently aground within a few yards in nearly any direction. The descent began along great, ragged, eroded ledges of limestone that once formed part of the coral reef that became an island. About 40 feet down a stone archway crossed the chimney, leaving irregular twin passages about 4 to 6 feet wide on either side. The chimney narrowed at this depth, but further descent revealed a widening trend, and on the bottom, at 80 feet, the whole structure could be visualized as resembling a rough-hewn hourglass, perhaps with a very slight curve.

During the descent, life was evident in the form of a few watchful moray eels backed into holes in the walls. A few lobsters carried on their surveillance in a less self-confident manner. Also backed into holes, the big crustaceans twitched their antennae for odors and vibrations that might signal the intentions of the human invaders. Spider crabs scuttled slowly at the rear of a shallow recess here and there down the walls. Near bottom were growths of sponges and what were probably nettlelike hydroids. Something left a mild stinging sensation after my arm brushed the surface of the stone.

With the stirring of some silt at the bottom, visibility was reduced from more than 80 feet to perhaps 30 feet. Light could still be seen above, though the bottom was dim. Through the silt, we could see that three tunnels opened laterally from the base of the chimney. Two of these tunnels opened near each other on one side. The other was nearly directly opposite. The mouths of these tunnels averaged about 6 feet high by 9 or 10 feet wide. The openings were again irregular in shape. Local lore had it that alternate sucking and outflow currents reached half a knot in the nearer parts of the tunnels, and that the currents alternated on a six-hour tidal cycle. The origin of the chimney and the tunnels is believed the work of groundwater during the glacial epoch of eighteen thousand years ago, when sea level was lower by about 350 feet. An underground stream may have dissolved the limestone and flowed through these tunnels to the sea. Local theorists believe that the tunnels now open two miles distant in deep water on the edge of the reef that surrounds the island.

A school of gray angelfishes paced nervously just inside one of the tunnels. Entering the tunnels is not recommended. It would be safe only with precise knowledge of the tidal cycle here, and proceeding against the current. A friend had recalled seeing a 7-foot nurse shark here, apparently sleeping in one of the openings. In general, however, fishes were not common at the bottom of the chimney. Their number and diversity increased noticeably very near the surface, with colorful little tropicals and occasional gamefishes, even including, at times, a small tarpon or two.

The most rewarding part of the dive came on ascent. Shutting off our lights at the bottom and looking up toward the surface lent the chimney an air of alien architecture or perhaps of an archaeological ruin. We could have easily imagined ourselves to be in a mystical setting as we rose past walls of a watery city toward a curving bridge across the weakly scintillating sunshine.

Chapter 14

Undersea by Night

OUR VOTE FOR THE MOST ADVENTUROUS kind of diving excursion goes not for the brief, carefully monitored plunge to 200 feet, or for the tedious roped-in probe of a silt-laden cave. Rather, we favor the usually uncomplicated descent to familiar bottom that has become wholly mysterious after dark.

If you can recall your childhood fears of the dark or habit of looking under your bed before you went to sleep, you may have to fight down a few qualms about dropping into black inner space for the fun of it. But inevitably you will experience a terrific mounting thrill in approaching some dark overhanging ledge, playing your light down over its face, and then peering beneath to suddenly discover a large prowling octopus or a fantastic school of motionless silvery fish.

For all its strangeness and sense of adventure, night diving, for properly trained people (we recommend a course in this specialty with a professional instructor), is much safer than deep descents and exploring inside caves and wrecks. Preparations and planning for a night dive are only a little more complicated than those for a daytime plunge. The first considerations involve the diving site and water conditions.

Planning a Night Dive

A familiar site is best, especially if you are making a shore dive. Even if you have been under water in a particular place dozens of times in daylight, don't worry about being bored on your first few night dives; nearly everything you encounter will be or seem different—a world transformed and enchanted in the watery night.

For enjoyable and safe diving after dark, the sea surface should be relatively calm. It's a good idea, where possible, to arrive at the site before dark, since it's difficult to make accurate judgments of the level of chop and surf. Turbulence barely within the acceptable range for a given diver in the daytime should rule out a night dive. While an individual may find open-water turbulence tolerable, problems of surf entry and exit loom to unexpected heights in the dark. Excessive bottom surge is also harder to cope with at night. Bumps, bruises, scratches, scrapes, punctures, and equipment loss may follow, so to ensure that diving remains fun and to maintain your unblemished skin, choose a calm night.

Night diving from a boat eliminates some of the difficulties associated with turbulence, but if you have a problem with surface choppiness in daytime, be especially wary of it at night. When you are immersed with a literal sea-level view, it is next to impossible to judge the speed and distance of oncoming waves; thus, they break over you suddenly without warning. Before entering the water, nocturnal boat divers should be extremely well aware of any currents and potential changes in current strength or direction associated with the tidal cycle.

Night-diving equipment, beyond that needed for basic daylight diving, is not elaborate. Each diver should possess his or her own light having fresh batteries, or, if rechargeable, a fully charged power source. Underwater lights are available in several brands, shapes, and sizes. The rechargeable varieties are preferable if you are really hooked on diving after dark or on daytime deep diving, cave exploration, and the like. For the occasional night swimmer, a battery-powered light will do. The battery, typically the 6-volt, block-shaped type, should be stored in a sealed container in a refrigerator to prolong life. But be sure to let it warm up completely before use. A cold battery will provide far less power and will discharge more rapidly than one that has been allowed to warm fully.

Some underwater lights are slightly buoyant. This quality is a safeguard against loss if you fumble at the surface, but frequently a source of annoyance to a diver on the bottom. Some prefer to counterweight a buoyant light with strips of leadfoil or a couple of large fishing sinkers. Lights that are neutrally buoyant or heavier than water are also available. A weighted light can be placed on the sand in front of you, freeing both hands for a task of the moment: taking a picture, stuffing a big lobster into your sack, or cinching up your weight belt.

Many divers secure the light to a wrist with a thong or cord. Be aware that this convenient, innocent-seeming little habit is potentially dangerous. A cord attached to the wrist or any other part of the body should always be thin enough to allow you to break it with conscious effort. Better yet, use a strip of flexible rubber tubing for a wrist thong so you can slip your hand out with a hard, quick pull. The danger is that in rocky, bouldery terrain, while a diver is intent on close exploration with both hands, perhaps after seafood or shells, the dangling light will slip into a crevice or crack and stick or wedge itself tightly. This insidious little problem is especially critical for nocturnal snorkelers.

In most situations, night divers are well advised to enter the water fully clothed. In warm water, long pants and a sweatshirt may substitute for a wetsuit. The object is literally to save one's skin. At night, a diver seems prone to many more brushes and bumps against rocks and coral. And in the nighttime sea, the spines of sea urchins and the stinging tentacles of other creatures are much more apt to appear in the diver's path than during the day. These animals switch into their active mode at night, emerging from rocky crevices, burrows, and other hiding places, including their own protective skeletons, after dark. It seems ironic that these creatures cower by day and go about armed at night, but it is comforting to know that they are never aggressive. An active sea urchin travels at perhaps 2 feet per hour; thus, in a collision the diver is always at fault.

One other noteworthy piece of personal equipment that has been picked up by many night divers is a small, sealed, pressureproof strobe flasher. Putting out a very powerful flash at short precise intervals, the strobe is a terrific attention getter underwater— say, if diving companions begin to separate too widely. On the surface, the strobe serves as an emergency signal to guide rescuers in case a diver is unable to return to the shore or boat. We recommend that all night divers off open coasts carry such flashers.

If you contemplate diving at night from a boat, the most critical item to bring along is an extra person who will sit and wait for you to come up. The sitter in the boat should keep an extra underwater light or a strobe flasher in the water aimed downward toward the divers. The importance of leaving someone in the boat with a light cannot be overstressed. Of course, the person should be able to operate the boat if, for some reason, the divers need to be picked up at a distance. But note: the presence of a boat sitter does not relieve the divers of the responsibility to secure the anchor at the time they first reach bottom. We know of cases in which a boat has drifted from an anchorage and the person sitting topside did not even know he was moving. We also know of a case in which several experienced divers descended from an untended boat at night and returned to the nastiest of surprises: the boat had drifted out of sight. Because an offshore current had come up, the divers also drifted, BCs inflated and arms linked, through an entire night and part of the next day until they were picked up several miles offshore by the Coast Guard. For added safety in case of the slightest current, a long lifeline ending with a large white or luminous float should be deployed from the boat.

An assessment of the environmental considerations on a night dive should take into account the depth and clarity of the water. It is foolish to go deeper than about 50 feet at night, and wise to require that the bottom be visible in the beam of your light before you leave the surface. In other words, safe night diving does not include deep diving of any sort as defined in this book. A descent through the nether layer at night is not recommended for amateur divers. Of course, it's impossible for you to become totally disoriented, as suggested by the vicarious Hollywood school of diving. You can always tell up and down, even if your light is off, by the movement of your bubbles. Nevertheless, judging the speed of descent in turbid water is hard without visual cues, and encountering rough bottom quite suddenly at night is to be avoided.

On a shore-based dive, the trick is to find your way back at the end. In many cases, an underwater compass is the ideal tool for the job. With it you can return close to the beach before surfacing. After surfacing, first-time night divers are usually powerfully surprised at how hard it is to see details on the shore and sometimes the shore itself from, say, 50 yards out. Usually a sandy beach will be visible in starlight as a faint trace. It becomes a bright band under the moon, but a low coast of dark rocks or one with extensive seaweed or other vegetative cover is virtually invisible. From your sea-level vantage point, you may only be able to make out the white breakers in the shallows. The blackness beyond can be an unknown obstacle course.

A preselected shore location that provides an easy exit is a must when the water is fairly rough and the coast fairly rugged. Before the dive, pick out landmarks—trees, rock formations, houses, or other structures behind the shore—and note their locations relative to the exit point. In the water before descent, again check your landmarks against the sky and commit the pattern to memory. Even a starry sky will reveal these silhouettes. An even better idea is to take along a shore sitter with a flashlight or fire-making skills.

The easiest night diving possible is from a large boat with an underwater lighting system. We have savored this luxurious night life in the sea and found it to be interesting but not as adventurous as exploring with just your own narrow beam showing the way, perhaps under a refracted moon. In clear water, powerful lights easily revealed the coral landscape 50 feet below and extending around the boat for 30 yards. From below, the surface appeared to be ablaze with light, and the water all the way to the bottom had a greenish tint. This craft, as is true of most big boats, was also noisy, and the sound of generators was another alien intrusion in the dim, tranquil night world of the sea.

Surprisingly, most of the common nocturnal creatures did not seem to react to the unusual craft with its raw technological power hovering overhead. We found typically night-active fishes, lobsters, octopuses, and so on going about their business as if nothing unusual were happening. It may be, however, that in particular sites used as overnight anchorages by charter diving boats marine life adapts to the bright lights and other disturbances in the night. Some of the local denizens of popular diving areas, as Jacques Cousteau has pointed out, quickly become tame and expect food scraps to be available at certain times of day and night.

In the following section, we illustrate the alternative type of night-diving experience, that which is less controlled and hence a little more difficult, but which is also more readily available to those who wish to encounter the sea by night. The dive described here was made in Hawaiian waters, but the kinds of experiences and impressions related are open to divers after dark almost anywhere.

A Nocturnal Excursion

Huge rock forms loom over us as we lug our gear down a steep, gullied path from the "scenic overlook" where we parked the car. The path ends about 100 feet below the parking area on a tiny beach at the head of a narrow cove—little more than a deep cleft in the stony bluffs that make up this portion of the coast. It is a clear night. The moon, almost full and nearly overhead, reflects dully in the wet sand, and the lightly ruffled water nearby sprays a thousand shards of light every second across the cove.

Laden, we trudge out along the rough edge of the cove to the mouth and stand on a rocky shelf 5 feet above the ocean. Forty yards away, across the cove's mouth, is a small cliff about 30 feet high. The cliff is not sheer; the wall rears back from the sea and is broken by large cracks and several ledges. A climber would not find the ascent at all difficult; a scuba diver would. Both sides of the cove would make severely strenuous and potentially dangerous exit points. The only reasonable exit is on the beach at the head of the cove. Both my partner Frank and I have come diving here in the daytime several times. The site is often rough, sometimes too rough to be safe, but the surf and surge seem gentle now. Incoming swells rise only halfway up to the shelf where we stand; wave height seems between 2 and 3 feet as we don our gear in the moonlight.

As soon as we jump off we can see bottom. The water is very clear and about 10 feet deep directly below the ledge. Frank and I drift with the ebb and flow in the channel just inside the cove's mouth as we check our lights by flicking them on and off several times. We both notice that with lights off, the bottom is visible in the moonlight. The rough, rocky terrain below is vague with shadows and soft highlights reflecting the moon.

We snorkel out a little past the mouth of the cove. A few small fishes caught momentarily in our light beams perform evasive maneuvers amid a labyrinth of boulders. The fishes seem sluggish and somewhat poorly coordinated, not their daytime selves, as they seek to hide from our probing underwater search-lights. Just before descent we reconnoiter the shoreline, which rises steeply, black against the sky. We have to come back this way; no safe and sane exit exists anywhere else on the sheer rock formations for at least a quarter mile in either direction. Holding my light high overhead and shining it into the cove, I can just make out the reflection from the tiny beach. Aligned with the cove and beach and looming against the sky behind them is a triangular-shaped hill. We choose this as our last-chance directional aid. Then, after checking and setting the sighting aid on my compass, we submerge.

Fifteen feet down is a gently sloping bench of rock. Smooth and apparently often wave-swept, it sprouts only a closely cropped turf of algae. The slope of the bench is toward the open sea, and we follow the contour outward and down. Frank finds a car-nivorous cone shell—he's doing research at the uni-versity on these predatory snails—and a few other snails, consumers of algae. All are extended from their shells, crawling actively, seeking food or feed-ing. Shortly, we see a noticeably brighter reflection of our lights ahead of us. Abruptly the sloping rock sur-face ends on a level bottom of white sand that extends in a pattern of undulating wavelets. We are 25 feet down.

The sand wavelets, about 6 inches high and 4 feet apart, are parallel to shore and indicate that large waves "feel" bottom here frequently. I turn my light toward the surface and look up. A startlingly bright, wide, waxen yellow glow comes back at me as if from a fractured mirror. My dive light's beam is dull white by comparison. The overhead illumination, broken into countless glints and facets by the surface chop, is moonlight transformed by the simple process of penetrating the sea. The scintillating glow is spread into a circular pool at least 20 feet across. How com-pletely changed is an underwater perception of the familiar moon. Astronomy developed by an intelligence restricted to the sea would be very different from that which has been pieced together from our vantage point above sea level.

Inspired at very nearly the same moment, Frank and I both shut off our lights. The effect is that of late twilight. We can see each other clearly but as silhouettes, no more. Details are absorbed by the watery night. The sand is dull white, like snow seen at night except for the telltale wave patterns, which are too regular for snow. Streams of bubbles rise with an unusual appearance, like dimly seen smoke. Toward the surface, however, the view is very different, with no familiar referents. Distance is hard to judge. The dazzling dancing spears and pennants of moonlight form endlessly shifting patterns within the bright circle. It is powerfully hypnotic. One imagines being drawn closer and closer to the pattern of light within an enormous, monospectral toy kaleidoscope.

Frank is about 5 feet away from me and I notice that he is moving a hand rapidly back and forth. Suddenly in the agitated water bright sparks and tiny curving comets appear—luminescent plankton. I create some miniature cold pyrotechnics of my own just in front of my mask. This is biological light, virtually identical in manufacture to that of fireflies or glowworms. In the sea, certain single-celled algae are the most common light producers. Often, animal plankton and bottom creatures, which are not themselves light producing, consume the luminescent plant cells in such quantities that they begin to shine in the nocturnal sea. At certain times of year and in some parts of the world, environmental conditions foster massive concentrations of the minute, glowing cells. A swimmer in Puerto Rico's Phosphorescent Bay can be literally bathed in eerie underwater light. Unfortunately for the diver, such areas are rare and becoming rarer. Phosphorescent Bay is becoming grossly polluted and its original brilliance is fading fast.

With our own lights back on, we can see massive rocks in the outer range of the beams' power, about 40 feet away. We approach across the sterile-seeming sand, and the scene becomes dominated by great irregular blocks of volcanic tuff. Some of them are larger than railroad freight cars and are lying in jumbled array as if dropped from high above the sea. Actually, they were probably carried down in landslides from the steep hills when the shoreline stood approximately in this place a few tens of thousands of years ago. A closer look reveals that the igneous rock here, an accretion of material originally ejected in colossal fire fountains of the past, is now studded with accretions raised by slower metabolic fires—those within the coral colonies and other organisms that cling or crawl across the rough surface.

We begin to encounter some of the exotic nighttime inhabitants of this place. Nearby, the edge of an enormous slab forms a cliff about 10 feet high, and crawling, or rather flowing, over the stone and coral surface is a spectacular nudibranch. *Hexabranchus*, or Spanish dancer, is bright red-orange with delicate cream-colored markings. A giant among nudibranchia, this species reaches 9 inches long—the one in front of us measures about 6 inches long. It ripples effortlessly over the uneven surface, its cluster of lacy gills visible near the rear of the animal.

Frank lifts the nudibranch gently off the rock and frees it in open water. We shine twin spotlights on the creature in hopes of seeing the performance evoking its namesake, a flamenco dancer in red petticoats. *Hexabranchus* immediately obliges, twirling and gyrating and flapping its gorgeously hued mantle with seemingly aimless abandon. However, this behavior is believed to have a serious purpose—to advertise and establish the nudibranch's identity with a potential predator. If successful, the creature will probably be spared. Most nudibranchia are poisonous or extremely distasteful to fish, crabs, and other predators. *Hexabranchus* is considered relatively scarce in these waters, yet we are to see three on this single dive. Statistically, these creatures are likely to be more active and exposed at night than in daytime. We also discover an egg case, or egg mass, deposited by this species. Neither of these terms captures the delicacy of the soft, loose coil of thin tissue, pink in color and arranged on the rock like a fancy chiffon dessert. Embedded in the tissuelike material forming the 4-inch-diameter coil are thousands of tiny eggs and developing embryos waiting to hatch into the flowing sea and make their way among the plankton. Eventually, a few of them, the survivors, will settle back in some rocky or reefy place to grow into the beautiful red adult form.

Just beyond and below the territory of the Spanish dancer, I find a small recess that extends along the wall and deepens and widens beneath the rock. Movement in the shadows toward the back of the recess attracts my eye, and in the beam of light a school of large blue surgeonfish, or tangs, swims slowly back and forth above the white sand floor. The fish act nervous, but dopey, perhaps sleepy. The light reveals in them a sort of wide-eyed torpor. Of course, most species of fish sleep with their eyes open, but these fish do not have the precise and wary movements they exhibit during the day.

The rock face suddenly turns a nearly right-angled corner, and I find myself in an alley between two of the megaliths. Frank is slightly ahead of me, searching for live cones. Across the alley, another shadowy wall begins. I probe its nearer features with my light level and swinging slowly—to reveal suddenly an enormous, motionless fish resting in a narrow horizontal crack. Splashes of blue and green, brilliant as fluorescent paint in the beam of light, give the creature the air of a gaudy clown. It is a sleeping parrotfish, a real grandaddy, close to 3 feet long. I know it is not a grandmother by the color—females of this species are reddish brown—but the strange thing about the parrotfish and some of its relatives is that, for example, this magnificent male was probably once a grandmother, and before that a mother, and perhaps a father as well. The species goes through phases of natural sex change and may revert from female to male more than once. The largest blue-green fish, however, are thought to be terminal males, patriarchs of the reef. They can live 20 years.

The fish I am watching is not yet asleep. Movement of the eye facing me reveals wakefulness and suggests apprehension. The eye twitches and rolls slightly. Whenever I move a little it seems to follow me; then it rotates forward suddenly, apparently focusing on Frank's form as he drifts in beside me. Later, after the dive, we both agree we could detect no sign of the mucous cocoon these fishes often secrete around themselves at night. Neither were cocoons visible around several other parrotfishes we found that night. Possibly it was too early (about three hours after sundown), or perhaps we were visiting a group of insomniac parrotfishes. Scientific speculation has it that the purpose of the cocoon is to protect the sleeping fish from detection by nocturnal predators such as morays and sharks. The mucus may conceal the odor of the parrotfish even when a large hungry prowler is in contact with the cocoon. At any rate, the predator seems to remain unaware of a potential meal within the flimsy shelter of the cocoon. The situation seems a little reminiscent of a grizzly bear and a sleeping backpacker separated by merely the thin nylon wall of a tent.

I make my first mistake of the night when I gingerly reach a hand in to touch the fish. I have visions of lifting it out carefully and then holding the huge exotic animal in one hand, a scene I saw in a photograph somewhere—a diver posing with a supposedly live parrotfish in his hand. With no more warning than a few nervous twitches of his large eye, the fish bolts out of the crack to our right and is gone. A cloud of silt is left in his place and we definitely feel the wake of his departure. I am lucky he wasn't inclined to bite. The force of the bite of this coral eater, directed by powerful muscles in the large head, has been estimated to exceed 400 pounds per square inch. One or more of my gloved fingers would have been gone or pulped in a twinkling.

Frank has found several cones. He displays them as we shine our lights through the mesh of his collecting bag. Two of them are the large fish-eating species *Conus striatus*, about 4 inches long. These cones harpoon their prey with a hollow dart, fired by a hydraulic mechanism. The dart is actually a specialized tooth derived from the lowlier snails' basic feeding tool, the radula. A typical radula is a ribbon of hard mineral material bearing numerous scraping teeth along its length. Most snails feed by running the radula out of the mouth, scraping up bits of algae and other organic matter, and then returning the food to the mouth all in a continuous motion. Some cone shells, however, have coupled the extreme hypodermiclike modification of radular teeth with the development of a powerful venom for paralyzing active prey. Generally, the large fish-eating cones are the ones posing the greatest potential threat to humans.

Frank has several other species of cones in his bag, and he hopes they will lay eggs in his experimental aquaria. Having searched the base areas of the terrain, where sand laps up against rock, he wants to cover some of the plateau country, and we rise slowly up one of the rock faces.

The uplands here consist of broad rocky surfaces atop the huge blocks, and the terrain is covered with coral growth. This is not a true reef, merely a rugose cap of coral over volcanic rock. The surge is more noticeable now, unbroken between us and the surface. Small, sleepy-acting fishes cower in nooks and crannies formed by the profusion of coral heads. Several times I shine my light upward through the clear water and catch reflections from numerous, fairly large, silvery fish, well over a foot long. They are not grouped in a tight school, but are well dispersed, twisting and turning as they apparently pursue prey in midwater. When they pass through the shattered moonglow, they turn dark as shadows and we never come close enough to see what kind they are.

One of the revelations to me is that the warm colors—reds and yellows—of fishes, corals, sponges, and other organisms stand out in the beam of my light more brightly than they ever do in daytime. This, of course, is due to the close direct illumination. Even at shallow depths in daylight, the spectrum is narrowed and faded by the absorption of light in the overlying water.

For a while during the dive Frank and I both hear unusual sounds in the water. None of them are loud and they are probably coming from a long distance away. Afterward, discussing this, I recall that what I heard sounded like muffled grunts and human voices in garbled tones. Frank recalls thinking he heard a dog barking. We believe that the sounds could have been coming from distant whales, since this dive was made in winter, the season when the migratory humpbacks frequent the Hawaiian Island area. The typical crackling background sounds produced by snapping shrimps in reefs or on the rocky bottom and heard nearly everywhere in the shallow tropics and subtropics are not as intense at night as during the day.

Up to this point in the dive, we have seen no lobsters, perhaps because of other distractions, but now we pick up their distinctive eyeshine at the openings of holes and small caves. A mirrorlike layer in a lobster's eye reflects light powerfully, throwing back a concentrated glow resembling a miniature electric arc. I manage to lay hands on a monster over 2 feet long and wrestle him back down to the sandy bottom, but my bag is too small to hold him. After what must resemble a drunken tussle—with my light dangling and swinging wildly from its rubber wrist thong and the lobster protesting bodily and vocally, his loud squeaks resembling the sound of a thumbnail on a blackboard—I lose the struggle. The lobster twists free and careens off into the night with frantic flaps of his big tail. Somehow, possibly due to all the commotion and the threatening vibrations of the battle, all the other lobsters in the area seem to have become extremely wary, and I am unsuccessful in even getting a hand on any more that night.

We find that our air supply is finally dwindling and turn shoreward. In an alleyway Frank finds his way blocked, or so he wisely decides, by a large moray eel, fully out in the open. The creature remains perfectly still in our lights, head raised about a foot off the bottom. Overall, it is about 5 feet long, thicker than a husky man's arm. Its motionless body ripples with potential energy, and the deceptively small head is hesitantly poised but performing the jaw-clenching, toothily aggressive breathing motions of all its kind. Morays generally stay in holes in the rocks or reefs during the day but have the reputation of prowling actively at night. We are thankful not to have seen any other big ones and detour quietly back the way we came.

Approaching shore now, we feel occasionally strong surge. Time to go up for a position check. Almost. First I find a huge pock-marked slab being combed over by numerous sea urchins. I am quite shallow, perhaps only 10 feet down, and, conscious of the swells above, try to breathe accordingly shallowly. In my beam of light is a large cowrie, its soft, frilly black mantle fully surrounding the shell. I reach out and touch it, and the mantle parts at the center line retract quickly down and underneath to reveal a beautiful polished pattern of brown and beige and yellow on a shell the size of a goose egg.

I am still studying the cowrie, about to pluck it from the rock, when I make the second mistake of the evening. Surge is building behind me. I feel it coming and brace myself. It builds powerfully, sweeping past the nearly vertical rock face. My handhold is secure enough but my mask is not. I am facing in the wrong direction. The massive rush of water pulls the mask partly away from my face; the mask instantly floods. If my head had been tilted forward the mask could have been torn away completely, hardly a way to end a night dive with finesse and safety. I should have turned when I felt the surge coming. Facing directly into moving water is the best way to ensure that your mask will stay in place. The other way is to remain free in the water, drifting with the motion, but this practice holds some risk at night, particularly if one is near the shore and around rocks.

I regain control, clear my mask, and rise toward Frank's light at the surface. We inflate BCs and bob in the tossing chop and backwash from the nearby cliffs. The unusual pyramid-shaped hill is directly in front of us, in line with the mouth of the cove. What is sobering is that from our vantage point, floating low in this rough water (which seems rougher than when we entered), we cannot immediately tell we are at the cove's mouth without the skyline cue. Only sporadically, when a swell raises me a couple of feet can I catch a glimpse of the little white beach far inside the cove. With success assured, we submerge again to escape the surface turbulence and follow the small channel leading into the cove and to the beach.

Chapter 15

Diving with a Camera

QUITE POSSIBLY THE LARGEST SOURCE of frustration for a diver lies in trying to describe underwater adventures to friends and acquaintances. While some nondivers, listening to one's tales of the deep, may seem rapt, even incredulous at times, there is a feeling that they aren't really getting it. Skepticism is much harder to take and impossible to counter unless you can dredge up an appropriate episode from *The Cousteau Odyssey* (assuming that at least some of your listeners have seen it too and can back you up). Alas, frustration can be almost as severe in communicating with diving colleagues—in describing a new site or trying to remember the pattern of a recently observed rare fish, a coral, or the lay of a newly explored wreck. Thus, nearly every diver has an understandable longing to photograph the strange and stunning sights of the underwater realm and bring back a lasting, visible record from his or her expeditions to the frontier.

Equipment

Cameras

Outfitting yourself for underwater photography is fairly expensive. At the outset, ignore any foolish suggestion or temptation to take a camera under water sealed in a clear plastic bag. Believe it or not, this idea has been proposed with apparent seriousness in at least one popular diving manual. Instead, explore the two safe and sane options: either use a simple, self-contained submersible camera, for example, Nikon's *Nikonos III* or earlier models, or use a conventional camera in a rigid, watertight housing.

The self-contained underwater camera has a lot to recommend it. It is lightweight and easy to handle on the way to the dive site. It is ruggedly built, and available lenses will produce good photographic images in both air and water. Thus, it serves well as a field camera anywhere. Drop an underwater camera in the mud of a swamp and just rinse it clean in a stream or under the tap when you get home. The simple sealing mechanisms use rubber O rings, and the lens and other camera parts are actually squeezed more snugly together under pressure, thereby forming a progressively tighter seal with depth. Perhaps its chief advantage is that the self-contained camera is very compact, which makes it extremely easy to swim with and manipulate under water.

Conventional cameras protected by a housing offer a greater range of adjustability and choice of special lenses, from very wide angle to telemacro. Photographers who have a superstitious or occasionally well-reasoned devotion to a particular make of camera will probably prefer a housing to fit the instrument of their choice. Assuming you already have a camera you like, a good housing will cost you somewhat less than an underwater camera. The best, off-the-shelf housings will cost you up to twice as much as the self-contained camera.

If your camera is of an uncommon species, it may be worthwhile to explore the option of having a custom housing built for you by a reputable firm or a local entrepreneur. Be especially careful about the latter. Check out his references, in particular the prevailing opinions about his work, at nearby professional dive shops. Remember, even the slightest leak at depth may prove fatal to your camera.

The disadvantages of a housing are its weight in air and its bulk and fluid drag under water. Expect to swear at your housing fairly frequently. Another occasion for blue language arises when you have to change film. The typical housing requires five times the usual sweat and film-changing time—for drying and opening the housing, detaching the camera from housing controls, changing film, reattaching the camera to the housing, and resealing the housing.

Housings should be tested for leaks before every dive. When you are using one for the first time, test it empty. On a boat dive, it's a simple matter to tie the empty, sealed housing to a line and, before the dive, lower it overboard to the approximate diving depth, then haul it in and check it. Even after you have grown to trust your housing, however, don't forget to look through the lens port a couple of times as you descend, just in case.

A tiny, even unnoticed, bit of water in a housing is immensely aggravating, for it tends to vaporize in the warm interior of the housing just before the dive, condensing on the inside of the lens port as it cools during the first part of the dive. The only way to prevent condensation is to ensure that no moisture at all is in the housing before the dive. If you think a drop or two of water got inside, or if noticeable condensation appeared inside after you opened a very cold housing in warm air, leave the housing open and empty in the hot sun for several minutes, and then bring it into the shade and let it cool to the surrounding air temperature before loading. When you first open the housing after a dive, beware of drops of water falling off your body, especially your hair. Wear a watch cap or towel around your head to prevent dripping into the open housing as you extract the camera.

According to some experts, there is hope of saving a drowned camera. If the mishap happened in the ocean (the worst-case situation), you are advised to flush the opened camera immediately with warm fresh water. Total immersion in a sink or very clean bucket is best. Then, as soon as possible, place the camera in a bath of isopropyl (rubbing) alcohol, again in a bucket or a sturdy, leakproof plastic bag. (Use double bags to be sure.) If alcohol is not immediately available, packing the camera in ice after the fresh water treatment will help to retard corrosion, but not for long. Then take your pickled camera to a professional camera store or dive shop for further advice on where, how, or whether it can be restored to life. Inundation by clean fresh water is only a little less serious. Again you should quickly place the camera in alcohol, then seek to have it professionally dried and lubricated.

The Light Source

Above or below the surface, light is the photographer's medium. Available-light photography can be satisfying in the shallows, and a submersible light meter is invaluable here. If a fish you are following won't stay still and let you get close enough for a reading, pick a nearby stationary object of the same approximate shade, and then pursue your subject ready to shoot. Remember, though, that water scatters light immensely (air does not), so the same subject and background over a light sand bottom in shallow water will not be much more brightly illuminated than over a dark bottom.

With depth, however, the brightest daylight quickly becomes subdued and narrowed in spectrum. Well within the depth range of a scuba diver, available light becomes essentially monochromatic and too dim for good photography, except perhaps for recording silhouettes in very clear water.

Sooner or later, most serious underwater photographers acquire a submersible strobe or other flash unit. A good strobe costs as much or more than a good camera, so shop carefully. Extremely high power is seldom necessary for good close-up underwater photography. On the other hand, even the most powerful strobe is useless at a distance of more than about 15 feet, so panoramic scenes are nearly always disappointing on film. Warm colors revealed by artificial lighting are lost beyond the radius of the flash, which dies out quickly due to the scattering and absorption of light by water and drifting particles, including plankton and silt.

Should you run into money and really become dedicated to documenting the underwater world, *slave synchronization* (where the flash of one strobe triggers a second unit) may be a very useful feature. With two strobes flanking a subject, you can simulate studio lighting. Some of the best portraits of sea dwellers are made with this technique.

An alternative to strobe lighting is the old-fashioned flashbulb. Standard flashbulbs can be carried to depths of 100 feet or more without being crushed. Underwater flashbulb attachments are available at generally lower prices than good underwater strobes. The disadvantages of the flashbulb option are that the bulbs themselves are expensive and that significant time and air are lost in bulb changing. Flashbulbs are inordinately clever at escaping benumbed fingers and vanishing irretrievably upward with your bubbles. Runaway bulbs even represent a litter problem along shores near popular dive spots. If you do use bulbs, plan to use the more powerful ones such as the "M-3." Some types simply do not provide enough light in water—even for close-up photography—and therefore you will have to open the lens and sacrifice some depth of field.

A final option for the undersea photographer is underwater floodlights. However, due to their high cost and their need for considerable power, floodlights hardly represent a reasonable choice for the amateur diver.

To use a flash under water, be sure to hold the unit or units at an angle, to the side of or well above the subject. If the light source is aimed straight ahead at the subject, either just above or below the camera, the scene in the picture will resemble a snowstorm. Why? Because the light will reflect straight back into the lens from the numerous tiny particles, even microscopic ones, that are always suspended in the water. There is no such thing as perfectly clear water. To be sure the flash unit, set off at an angle, is pointing precisely at the scene, you might want to strap a small spotlight to the top of the strobe. Then, when you're setting up a shot, you can switch on the small under-water light and adjust the strobe until the spot is within the frame.

Calling each shot accurately with respect to f-stop and distance from light source to camera takes a lot of experience. These two variables, together with the ASA rating of the film, are the major considerations in most underwater photography. Theoretically, it's possible to calculate exposure settings in perfectly clear water, but this is seldom practical, because of the light-scattering particles that are always present. Therefore, even good photographers bracket their ex-

15.1. *Underwater photographer demonstrating use of a framer.*

posures (taking several shots of the same scene at different f-stops, or light intensities), often extensively. However, it's still a good idea to carry a small slate and record the set-up and exposure data for the most memorable shots.

Have you ever noticed how a large majority of beautiful underwater photographs are still lifes, dynamically no more difficult to photograph than a vase of cut flowers placed under water? Many kinds of marine life, starfish, nudibranchia, corals, anemones, sponges, plumed worms, and the like, because they remain essentially still, can be photographed in a very routine fashion. A device called a framer, usually a squared, U-shaped wire that projects ahead of the lens is mounted on the camera. The framer encompasses an area just barely greater than the scene to be recorded on the film frame. The distance from framer to lens can be adjusted to correspond roughly to the minimal focal distance of the lens, but the trick is to stop down the lens to its narrowest aperture. Now, with the maximum depth of field available, the scene enclosed by the framer will be automatically sharp and clear. The framing technique leaves only one variable to bother with, the strobe distance, and, to ensure adequate lighting, you can change this factor methodically as you click off several shots of the same scene. Later, you can select the best exposure, and if you kept notes of strobe distances, narrow down the bracketing range for next time.

Special Techniques

A good underwater photographer learns to move with the finesse of a ballet dancer. Movement must be slow and deliberate. The necessity for fingertip control applies not only to equipment handling, but also to maneuvering on the bottom. Nothing photographs well through a silt storm caused by sudden kicks or twists of the body. Where possible, in searching for shots, move into a slight current. Thus, as you discover scenes and subjects you want to shoot, the sediment you have stirred up will be carried away to your rear and your pictures will remain clear.

The other reason for keeping your movement slow and easy is to avoid frightening sensitive wildlife, which range from the beautiful plumed, or "feather duster," worms to fishes and marine mammals. The small bottom creatures, such as the worms, sense pressure waves ahead of a human swimmer and quickly snap back into their burrows or tubes at a too-sudden approach. People who thrash their way over the reefs often complain that an area looks barren, while a quieter swimmer, who makes numerous pauses, finds that the opposite is true.

Among fishes and porpoises, divers using slow, gentle swimming movements can approach very closely. One of us recently enjoyed several minutes among a large group of spinner porpoises in a secluded Hawaiian cove. The water was about 40 feet deep and very clear. A pod of about twenty-five or so of the sleek marine mammals, including some very young ones, milled around slowly between the surface and about 20 feet down, and tolerated the human presence until two other snorkelers leaped off a nearby boat and churned their way, full speed ahead, into the tranquil scene. The porpoises turned toward the open sea and vanished like shadows within 30 seconds.

In a likely place—beside a large coral head, an obvious burrow, a hole in the reef, or stand of kelp—the practice of sitting or lying on the bottom for several minutes often pays off with something interesting to photograph. Terrestrial naturalists often report that when they do this in the woods, inevitably small animals emerge from their hiding places, go about their business, and can be observed and, with care, photographed. A wrasse's cleaning station for larger fishes, described in Chapter 11, is an excellent place to lie in wait for photographs, for you are likely to encounter a variety of local fish species arriving here. In choosing a place for yourself, you can sometimes even select the best backdrop in front of which your subjects will "sit" for their portraits.

Have you ever wondered how professional travel-ad pictures are made in which a pretty model swims surrounded by clouds of attentive fish? Simple, the model carries some bait down, and crumbles and disperses some of it in the surrounding water. Bread works well; chopped squid or fish flakes are even better. To lure some photogenic creatures to your underwater studio, carry some bait in a small plastic bag in your pocket. Instant schools of fish will be at your service, but don't spread the bait around too liberally or it will show up in the picture.

Capturing fish and other creatures in nets and cage traps and then releasing them in a photogenic setting with camera ready is another technique used by professionals. Some exceedingly rare species, such as the chambered nautilus, a swimming, shelled relative of the octopus, have been captured on film in this way. More often than not, the photographer never acknowledges that dramatic or wholly unusual shots were staged. To enhance his reputation, a photographer may even indulge in some misleading fantasy: "Suddenly it appeared, swimming in the beam of my diving light; with time for only one shot, I whirled, focused, framed, and scored with this flawless photograph of rare and endangered species X . . . ." It is more likely in such a situation that he took over a hundred shots over several days using several dozen animals retrieved from a net.

Underwater photography at night often produces better results than in the daytime. Most marine animals do not react to divers visually at night. There are no shadows, and only your diving light is visible, which often has a hypnotic effect on fishes and octopuses. Lobsters and other crustaceans seem oblivious to artificial light at night, though they still react to pressure waves. At night, too, many lesser creatures are up and about, whereas during the day they may never be seen. For the most part, you can get much closer to wary animals at night and take more time to set up your photographs.

Baiting at night is strictly for the adventurous. You may get some fabulous photos, but depending on the bait, you may also attract large eels or sharks. Some photographers leave an open can of bait on the bottom, and then revisit it at intervals. Approach carefully at night. The same applies to a gill net or cage trap where agitated, trapped fishes may attract something larger.

Performed with the proper frame of mind and finesse, underwater photography can be very rewarding and immeasurably exotic. However, this pursuit is a specialized art that demands hard work and the development of new skills, and there is no guarantee that a good photographer above the surface will make the grade down below.

Safety Principles

A good underwater photographer is first a good diver. If you are a learning or newly certified diver, it's wise not to invest in an expensive housing and strobe until you have become very much at home under water and until using scuba and the routine activities of diving become nearly automatic. Only then will you be able to focus your concentration safely and effectively on photography. In other words, an underwater photographer should be experienced enough to allow photography to occupy 80 or 90 percent of his or her consciousness, with the remainder taken up with the routine mechanics and necessities of diving.

We are wary, however, of promoting any underwater activity that takes a diver's mind off his or her surroundings and the sometimes subtle margins of health and survival inherent there. Photography is just such an activity, and we want to offer two general caveats. The first concerns photography in very deep water; the second involves the opposite end of the depth range.

Any photography involving intense, prolonged concentration in deep water is problematical. Don't attempt anything but a few snapshots on a bounce dive. If you plan to do some serious, complicated picture-taking at depths over 100 feet, you should have your partner watch the time, depth, and air supply for you. Also, you should have made arrangements for decompression, even if a mere bounce dive was the plan. Nitrogen narcosis may play havoc with your concentration and subjective judgment. Therefore, you should be prepared for the possibility that scenes that wowed you at the time will be less than prize-winning compositions. Rumor has it (beginning with Jacques Cousteau's speculations in *The Silent World*) that the more artistic a person's temperament, the greater the distortion of reality that comes with breathing nitrogen under pressure.

The second dangerous situation to avoid is a lapse into total preoccupation with photography in open water near the surface. The danger here may even be more subtle than at great depth. Example: you are framing a school of fish in midwater at 20 feet. The school is a fantastic silvery kaleidoscope of patterns, shifting moment by moment as it rises slowly at an angle, and you swim alongside trying to keep pace. You have the photographer's urge to hold your breath as you squeeze off shot after shot. This scenario, readily recognizable by any experienced underwater photographer, holds the potential for embolism. The general rule of scuba diving—"Do not hold your breath"—should apply especially to photographers whose concentration is necessarily focused primarily on their art.

Breath holding is a temptation to underwater photographers largely because of the noticeable changes in buoyancy during the breathing cycle. A diver who is in perfect trim at a given depth will rise slowly on inhalation and sink on exhalation. This motion is most aggravating to photographers attempting to hover motionless in midwater or along a wall. If holding your breath is absolutely necessary for a photograph, be sure you don't do it on a full inhalation. Rather, the best place to hold is on full exhalation.

On the bottom, you should be somewhat overweighted to counteract the tendency to rise with each inhalation. When you want to ascend or move to another location, simply blow some air into your BC to trim yourself. Some photographers greatly overweight themselves to cope with surge. Of course, having to deal with this problem implies fairly shallow water and fairly rough surface conditions, so you should be an expert diver before risking your equipment and physical well-being in such a situation.

There is a lot more to be learned about underwater photography than we can cover in this short chapter. The fine details of the art, ranging from routine use and care of cameras and housings to comparing the underwater performance of various brands of film, wait to be discovered on your own. Probably the fastest and most efficient way to educate yourself in underwater photography is to take a course offered by one of the professional instructional organizations. Occasionally, a big-name underwater photographer will teach a course in some photogenic locale, typically one of the Caribbean diving resorts. Tuition for such courses, which are generally advertised in such diving magazines as *Skin Diver* or *Sport Diver*, usually borders on the exorbitant. Before you send in a deposit, it's a good idea to ask diving instructors and any experienced underwater photographers in your area if they have any firsthand acquaintance or reliable impressions of the big-name teacher. Some of these personalities, it is rumored, are neither very good nor very committed teachers. Still, no matter what path you follow in refining your picture-taking below, your camera will provide you with a satisfying record and some exquisite memories of your adventures in the deep.

Chapter 16

The Undersea Hunter

FOR MANY UNDERWATER EXPLORERS, the sight of a
school of snappers cruising slowly over the bottom, or of a behemoth flounder half hidden in sand,
brings an atavistic urge. There springs to mind the
thrill of the chase and the image of a delicious platter-
ful of very fresh filets, acquired, if not exactly free of
charge, at relatively low cost, given the proficiency of
the spearfisherman. On the next visit to the dive
shop, you wander over to the racks of spears and
spearguns and start looking seriously.

Most divers who go down to the sea with spear in
hand probably find the motives of sport and food-
getting inseparable—and this, we feel, is as it should
be. There seems to be a rapidly growing sentiment on
the part of those who enjoy natural surroundings,
whether above or below the waterline, that slaughter-
ing wild creatures just for fun is archaic and barbaric,
behavior that is now beneath the evolving civilized
standard. We applaud the obvious decline of trophy
hunting in the sea and wholeheartedly echo the spirit
of respect for all creatures large and small. The late
Dr. Ken Read of Boston University, a transplanted
Britisher, biochemist, and noted underwater film-
maker, epitomized this respect for the underwater
wilderness. In the Caribbean in the late 1960s, before

conservation was really in, Read, a diminutive man, once confronted a hulking Philistine of a frogman twice his size. The man was posing on a pier with a 700-pound jewfish, which he had speared and landed after an epic battle and which, he clearly indicated, would be discarded after the picture taking was over. Read asked the man if he knew how old that fish had been, how rarely one of that size was found, and how much energy of the coral reef had been focused and fixed in that one magnificent creature. There was no appropriate response to these probings for environmental awareness, so Read concluded for everyone in earshot, "You ought to know, that's not a fish you killed; it's a bloody monument!"

Our own philosophical feelings about spearfishing are complex. The most emphatic recommendation we wish to make is to shoot only what you will eat. This dictum assumes good local knowledge of which species are good to eat. Some types of fish in some areas taste very bad, and some are even poisonous (more on this later). Furthermore, spearfishing is incompatible with underwater photography and just plain enjoyable sightseeing. Most fishes are very quick to react to a hunter's presence, to blood in the water, and to the sinister metallic clunk of a missed shot hitting rocks. They make themselves scarce, and if you are responsible, your presence will often not be tolerated by nonhunting divers in the area.

It is also our feeling that in most spearfishing situations, the only really sporting way to go is without scuba. Good spearfishermen routinely work in depths to 30 feet without breathing gear. Very good spearfishermen reach 50 feet or more with enough time to spot, stalk, and hit their prey—all on a single breath. Generally, the best spearfishing, whether off a continental coast or along an island's fringing reef, lies in the upper 50 feet of water. Shooting fish while wearing scuba gear is disgustingly easy in many of the best diving areas. An exception is deep hunting, below 50 feet, for rare large species—groupers, solitary jacks, big snapper, and so on. For these reasons, our discussion is limited mainly to free-diving spearfishing.

Spearfishing is controlled by law in most diving areas, with limits on the species that can be taken, minimum size, and number caught per day. Be sure to familiarize yourself with local regulations (see Appendix 2 for more information).

Equipment

Underwater hunting equipment comes in three common types: the pole spear with an attached elastic power loop (commonly surgical rubber tubing); the Hawaiian sling, also elastic-powered; and the speargun and shaft, employing any one of several power sources, including elastic tubing, springs, compressed gas, and blank firearm cartridges. The business end of a spearfishing weapon comes in a wide variety of shapes. Spearpoints are available with single barbs, double barbs, and swivel fittings. For big fish, over about 10 pounds, detachable spearpoints are preferred to keep a fish from bending the shaft and levering itself free. Heads or gigs with several tines or forks are also available, mainly on pole spears.

The pole spear is effective only over a fairly short distance, usually from about 3 to 6 feet. To fire a pole spear, you hook the loop of elastic between the thumb and the rest of your hand and stretch it roughly two-thirds of the way toward the head of the shaft, gripping the shaft at this point with the same hand. Aim at the target, arm extended, and release your grip. The spear will fly where you aim, and with practice you will still have the elastic in hand when the shaft has hit its mark. One big advantage of the pole spear is the ease and speed with which you can reload and fire a second shot if you miss the first time.

The Hawaiian sling is a longer-range weapon composed of two elements: the shooter, a short, open-ended, hollow tube with attached elastic loop; and the free shaft, usually just a slender steel rod, pointed at one end, with or without a barb. To operate the sling, you insert the shaft in the shooter, engage the elastic, draw and aim as with a slingshot, and release the shaft. The chief disadvantage of the Hawaiian sling is that a lightly wounded fish may swim out of sight with your shaft. In turbid water, a missed shot can be dangerous if other divers are in the area. You may also lose your shaft if you fire it out of sight. Given such conditions, common sense would dictate shooting your quarry from above, but be mindful of the background; a hard, direct hit on rock will damage the point and, even worse, bend the shaft. With a simple sling shaft, you can salvage a mashed point by cutting a little off the end and grind-

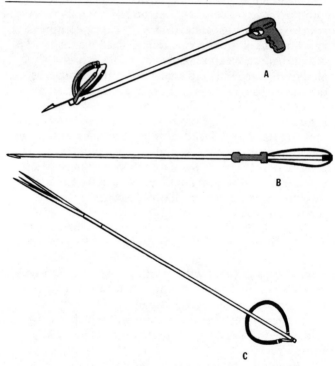

16.1. *Three types of spearfishing devices.* A, *speargun and shaft, showing two bands of elastic tubing that, when stretched and cocked, propel the shaft.* B, *Hawaiian sling with shaft inserted through shooter and abutting elastic loop (ready to draw and fire).* C, *pole spear with attached elastic loop.*

ing a new point, but a bent shaft, even though you try to straighten it, usually performs poorly in flight. It tends to curve, wobble, whip, or quiver, with resultant inaccuracy or loss of penetrating power due to drag in the water. Best get a new shaft.

The speargun is probably the weapon of choice for a majority of divers, although in some local areas there are exceptions. For example, pole spears seem to be the most popular option in Hawaii. Spearguns vary greatly in power and effective shooting distance, although no underwater hunter expects to hit much at distances greater than about 15 feet. After traveling 20 feet, shafts from even the most powerful, elastic-equipped guns slow so much that a hit on a large fish may have negligible effect. Some of the compressed-air guns propel a shaft with penetrating force for 60 or 70 feet, but we feel such James Bondian equipment is dangerous and inappropriate for spearfishing.

As the spearshaft is fired, it trails a neutrally buoyant line that pays out from a loose coil released below the gun. Free divers should carry enough line to be able to play a big fish from the surface. Some divers equip their guns with canisters for holding loosely wadded, extra line. A few spearguns even sport heavy-duty fishing reels for handling the lunkers. Just be sure the reel is made entirely of noncorrosible materials. It's best not to skimp on the test strength of your fishing line. A fish struck by a spear hasn't much chance of survival if it does escape, so it's not really sporting to go with very light fishing line that may be abraded against rock and cut through. Two- or three-hundred-pound test line will secure the largest edible species nearly anywhere; even consider splicing in a short length of stainless steel leader (with swivels) to avoid the rock- or coral-chafing problem.

While the strength of your fishing line should be on the heavy side, it is more reasonable for the power of the speargun itself to match the size of the fish you are after. It is cruel and probably wasteful to attack big species with an under-powered gun and small point that may wound the fish and allow it to escape, only to die later. On the other hand, it is ridiculous to pursue panfish with the undersea equivalent of an elephant gun. Generally, the longer the speargun (of the elastic and spring-powered variety) the greater is the penetrating power of the shaft and the farther it will travel. Like the Hawaiian sling, a powerful speargun can be dangerous in murky water. Be sure the shaft matches the gun; a long shaft that protrudes more than a few inches beyond the end of a short gun tends to vibrate or whip in flight. This motion slows the shaft down, and it may not fly straight.

In case your quarry is too large to be brought to the surface readily, it's a good idea to carry a small float that you can use to buoy your gun and the line leading down to your prize catch, which might be well wedged among rocks and tangled bottom vegetation. Some divers merely inflate their BCs to play a big one, but if a 50-pound fish is determinedly trying to pull you down as your inflated BC tugs inexorably upward, your body, in the middle, may feel the strain. Ron Merker, California spearfisherman and writer on diving subjects, reports that the crotch strap of a BC can be most uncomfortable in this situation.

If your speared fish has holed up and has successfully resisted your initial efforts at extraction, you and your partner may have to make several dives to get him out in the open. In this case, it's virtually essential to have your line to the fish originate at the surface, so you don't have to leave and relocate your gun on the bottom each time you go down.

To carry their catch, undersea hunters usually employ either a stringer, a mesh bag, or a floating basket or boxlike affair, often made by fastening a wooden or wire-mesh bottom to an old rubber inner tube. Fish stringers of various styles are available commercially, or you can make your own. The simplest type is a three-foot length of cord with a loop at one end and a short rod like a knitting needle at the other. To use, push the rod through the fish's gill cover on one side and pass it out the mouth and then through the loop. Floating baskets are convenient, but for large lively fish or lobsters you may have to rig a cover to prevent escape. A disadvantage of a large floating rig is that it will drag severely if you have to work against a wind or current.

A few words on using your equipment safely: it's good to get into the habit of keeping spears pointed down when you are swimming at the surface, and when you are returning toward the surface from a dive. Never enter the water or exit with a cocked speargun. Caution is also particularly important when you are near a boat, with other swimmers in murky water, or at night. In these cases, it's best to arm your weapon only when there is something definite to shoot at.

Hunting Techniques

To be a successful free-diving hunter, you must be in good physical shape. Only frequent swimming and breath-hold diving will maintain your body in the condition necessary to sustain one- to two-minute prowls at 30 feet or more. Unless you are in an exceptionally productive fishing area, don't expect to subsist on your catch. The balance sheet in calories of fish gained against those expended in swimming (and sometimes shivering) almost always shows a debit. This is even true of most spearfishing with scuba, as was first discovered by Jacques Cousteau during his World War II "hungry period," and related in his first book, *The Silent World*.

We feel we cannot overemphasize the value of spearfishing with a partner. This is especially critical when you are going fairly deep and where the hunting is good. An excellent habit to inculcate is for divers to go down alternately, with the person at the surface serving as the spotter. It is the spotter's job to hold the line to the stringer, catch bag, or basket (more on this later), and to watch his or her buddy, or time the dive if the spearfisher goes too deep to be seen. A spotter for a free-diving hunter should be aware of his buddy's approximate breath-holding ability, allow a margin of about 30 seconds, and, if he has not reappeared, go down to investigate.

Perhaps not surprisingly, one of the occasions for underwater blackout is success in hitting a fish near the end of one's bottom time. Example: You are down 30 feet and beginning to feel the urge to surface when you spot a nice sea bass, approach, and score a hit under the dorsal fin. But the fish, although secured to your spearhead, dives into a rocky, scrubby jungle, and the line becomes fouled. Hitting the fish has given you a surge of adrenalin; you temporarily lose the breathing urge in the flush of excitement as you work the line up through the seaweed—until you begin to see stars. . . .

Although this scenario represents an extreme case, anyone can experience this type of reaction. Even veteran spearfishermen report that they get a rush of confidence and lose the sense of breathing urgency when they hit a target. Just the expectancy of a good shot can have this effect, although the fish may be continuously moving slowly just out of range. Another insidious temptation to stay down beyond your limit strikes when you suddenly find a cave with lobsters just out of reach, but spy a big one that looks reachable with a squeeze and a stretch and a few more seconds. It is at this point that your spotter can be a lifesaver.

A few more caveats. Be careful of lines attached to your body. It's a good idea to trail your catch at the end of a light line to avoid a direct confrontation with a toothy denizen of the deep. But hold the line in your hand, or use an easy-opening snap link to fasten it to your belt, and do not dive with a line fastened to you. In other situations, be alert for places where your spearshaft line might become snagged—in rough terrain, in kelp, or around moorings for boats, lobster traps, and so on. The ultimate safeguard against entanglement is to carry a sharp knife.

Also, be wary of excessive surge, in particular where the bottom features caves, narrow alleys, and arches in rocks. There tend to be lots of fishes in such places, but they are more agile than you are and can move with ease through surge that will stop you cold. Though you might get lucky and manage to come close, firing of your weapon accurately in sudden gusts of water and tricky crosscurrents will usually prove impossible.

The ideal setting for breath-hold spearfishing is clear water where every feature of the bottom is plainly visible from the surface. Concentrations of fishes usually appear around irregularities of the bottom such as rock outcrops in sand or large holes, sand channels, and so forth on the sloping face of a reef. The general preference by fishes for a break in the terrain can be exploited by a hunter. One profitable search technique is to cruise over the bottom until some prominent irregularity is seen. Even though fishes are not visible from the surface, this doesn't mean they are not there. Make a scouting dive and inspect dense weedbeds closely, check beneath overhanging ledges, and shine a light into large holes and caves. As often as not in a productive area, you will spot worthwhile prey that was hidden from the surface. And as often as not the fish will be in virtually the same place when you come down again with your spear ready.

Another search (or stalking) technique begins at the surface when you see suitable quarry in the open, typically moving slowly away from you. Many kinds of fishes show a territorial behavior. Over open bottom, they often seem nervous, and your intrusion will start them moving toward "home base," the central, most secure part of their territory, which is usually one of the kinds of environmental irregularities we have mentioned. So don't waste your energy diving at them over open ground. Rarely will you get a shot as the fishes keep moving ahead of you, effortlessly staying out of range. Follow them at the surface until they stop. Then watch for a while before making an approach. You may have to make several "stoops" at them, like a hawk testing his prey, before one goes to ground in a hole or a crack or beneath an overhang. This kind of behavior is associated with members of the wrasse family and closely related tropical parrotfishes, many sea basses and members of the perch family, some members of the porgy family, some groupers, and some snappers—all good eating fishes.

By studying fishes' habits you may evolve your own search and stalk techniques. One scuba-equipped hunter we know catches the elusive, but curious, gray snapper in Hawaii by what must be a unique method. Spotting a school of the practically unapproachable fish, he gets their attention by going into a series of gyrations like a frenzied disco dancer, all in one spot on the bottom. After a few seconds, he lies down perfectly motionless as if dead, except that he continues to breathe normally and holds a cocked speargun firmly aimed in a fixed direction. Invariably, the school of fish drifts over to investigate after two or three minutes of watching at a distance. The fish come quite close, nearly always enabling the hunter to get one very good shot. The teaser is to wait as several relatively small fish cross your aiming window, and hope that one of the bigger ones will do the same.

Other methods may work well with species that move through their terrain on certain preferred paths. Another astute spearfisherman we know is adept at predicting the movements of parrotfish over complex reef bottom, and often manages to set up a successful ambush behind this or that coral head or ledge. Two divers can work together, one driving the quarry in a certain direction, while the other times his dive and lies in wait by a sand channel or other likely fish freeway.

Some fishes hide in caves by day and emerge at night to forage. In most tropical areas, the common daytime cave dwellers include a variety of species of the squirrelfish family. Many members of this family are reddish in color and have extra-large eyes, adapted for their nocturnal activities. All the larger squirrelfish species (reaching lengths of a little over a foot) are excellent food fishes. Lucky undersea hunters sometimes find small caves whose interiors flash red with dozens of these delectables reflecting in the beam of a diving light. During the day, the fish will not leave the cave and are easy targets for a hunter with a pole spear. A squirrelfish shoot is not exactly a sporting event for the snorkeling hunter—and is much less so for a person using scuba—but taking only what you can eat will assure the continuance of the local population.

Northern divers go after flounders of various species, whose typical habit is to lie motionless on the bottom, an easy mark for a pole spear, hand-held gig, or even a knife if it weren't for this fish's incredibly sophisticated talent for camouflaging itself. By expanding or contracting millions of special cellular capsules of pigment in the skin that yield a nearly infinite variety of possible patterns and shadings, the flounder makes its upper part come to resemble the surrounding bottom. Consistent flounder detection takes experience; many divers swim within touching distance of a resting flounder before noticing it. Many of the fish may be missed altogether. But once you have acquired a flounder sense, these fish tend to crystallize out of the background before your eyes like the Cheshire Cat.

Along the New England coast, flounders can be exceptionally abundant in shallow water (roughly 8 to 10 feet) during late spring, when they come up from deep winter refuges to breed. During a twenty-minute swim along an appropriate stretch of bottom (typically mixed sand and algae-covered rock) in Massachusetts Bay in early June, you may easily find a hundred or more large flatfish.

In the very cold waters of winter and spring, some New England divers catch flounders using no other equipment than a large catch bag. The type with a wire-framed mouth that stays wide open is best. The technique requires a very slow and easy approach by the diver, who gently brings down the open bag to the bottom right in front of the fish. At winter water temperatures between 35° and 40°F (about 2°-4°C) the "cold-blooded" flounders seldom move unless physically touched. Hence the last phase of the operation: tap the fish's tail with your free hand, and it will bolt right into the open bag. We have caught flatfish this way in Massachusetts Bay until about June, but as water temperatures begin to exceed 50°F flounders become much less tolerant of a diver's approach to arm's length. For a spearless flounder hunt, we carry two large bags: one for holding several fish, the other for use in the actual catching.

Other Kinds of Quarry

So far we have failed to touch on the nonfish quarry, a variety of delicious aquatic edibles ranging from types of animals loosely designated shellfish to seaweeds. While desirable oceanic and freshwater nonfish food species are too numerous to mention, they fall into the following major categories:

● Decapod crustaceans: chiefly lobsters, crabs, prawns, and shrimps
● Bivalve molluscs: clams, scallops, and mussels
● Gastropod molluscs: abalones, conchs, and other large snails
● Cephalopod molluscs: octopuses and squids
● Echinoderms: urchins and sea cucumbers
● Sea vegetables: numerous species of green, brown, and red algae

Not surprisingly, a whole book would be needed to describe in detail the habits and habitats, catching methods, and modes of preparation for all these kinds of underwater dwellers. Such information is already available in many scattered reference books for different ocean and freshwater areas. It's fun to browse through the foraging information for your area and to build up your own lore as you become an experienced undersea hunter. To begin, simply knowing where to look for many of these delicacies is the key to a successful hunt. With a few exceptions, these species are easily caught; some merely wait to be picked up. Once you have learned the preferred local habitat for a given seafood species, say, spiny lobster or bay scallop, you'll often find it or related species in similar locations in other regions.

Catching methods, hunting seasons, size limits, and bag limits for seafood species are often subject to intricate local legalities. The taking of lobsters (both the clawed New England variety and the very different tropical spiny lobsters and slipper lobsters) may be subject to the greatest variety and volume of regulations. Spearing lobsters is prohibited practically everywhere. Usually they may be taken by hand only, although diver-operated nets are allowed in some areas. A minimum-size law, usually specifying a carapace length—the carapace is the solid upper shell of the thorax—is in force in most lobster waters. Typically, the minimum carapace length for most lobster species is around 3 inches, but it varies, often minutely, from place to place. Some states are picky enough to specify the measurement to a sixteenth of an inch. For quick, accurate reference under water, you can carry a small measuring device—a strip of aluminum or section of plastic ruler—perhaps taped to your knife handle. Some divers simply scratch the local lobster size specs into their knife blade. Other regulations protect females in berry (carrying eggs), and some specify a closed season and prohibit night hunting, when lobsters are out of their holes and caves and catching them is easiest.

Devices to lure or pull lobsters out of their holes are allowed in some areas but banned in others. Luring devices—for example, lobster whisks or ticklers made of thin cloth or plastic strips fastened in feather-duster fashion to a short stick—are waved and brushed lightly against the antennae of a lobster backed into his hole. The animal's usual reaction is to come out at least part way to challenge this flimsy-appearing threat, allowing you to reach around and grab him from above. Lobster hooks are actually small gaffs that can be inserted into a hole beside the animal, even reaching behind him, and used to coax or pull him out. Savvy lobster hookers use the hook sparingly, merely to tickle or lightly irritate their prey into moving out of the hole. An injured specimen may wedge itself in so tightly that attempted forcible removal with a hook will only produce shreds and fragments.

Some states require a special permit or license, purchased for a fee, for divers taking lobsters, and a couple of states with a powerful commercial fisherman's lobby completely prohibit diving for lobsters. Of course, the latter is ridiculous from the standpoint of both competition and conservation. The trap fishermen waste uncountable numbers of lobsters by careless mishandling of eggers (gravid females) and shorts (smaller than legal-sized specimens). Even greater waste is incurred by the continuous loss of traps that go on catching lobsters, as inmates progressively die and serve as new bait, sometimes for years—the so-called ghost-fishing problem. The toll taken by even a large diver population, few of whom ever become expert lobster hunters, is minuscule by comparison with the commercial take. Nevertheless, until enlightened public interest can be served everywhere by rational conservation laws, it is wise to abide by the regulations. Fines for undersea poaching, use of prohibited equipment, and other transgressions are notably stiff in many coastal states. It's possible to lose the equivalent of a summer's diving budget or a week's Caribbean vacation for being caught with an illegally foraged dinner.

Poisonous-to-Eat Fare

Our short discussion of poisonous food species is largely limited to fishes, since relatively few invertebrates and, we believe, no seaweeds likely to be eaten are poisonous. The invertebrates to watch out for are bivalve molluscs—clams, mussels, and on rare occasions oysters—inhabiting coastal waters in two major areas of North America: the Pacific Northwest from San Francisco northward to the Aleutians, and the Northeast, from Cape Cod northward into maritime Canadian waters. The toxic condition rendering the bivalves unfit to eat and sometimes lethal is known as paralytic shellfish poison, or PSP, and it occurs chiefly in the summer and early autumn. PSP does not originate in the molluscs, but is produced by tiny plankton organisms called dinoflagellates. Very few species of dinoflagellates, among the many that exist, produce PSP, but at certain times and places the toxic organisms undergo population explosions, or blooms. The extreme form of a dinoflagellate bloom is called a red tide.

Bivalves are virtually unaffected by PSP and feed on the toxic plankton, filtering millions of the organisms from the water in a few hours. PSP is thus highly concentrated and, for some reason, stored in the shellfish, making them highly poisonous to eat for as long as six weeks after the bloom has disappeared. Symptoms of paralytic shellfish poisoning appear in humans between two and twelve hours after contaminated shellfish is ingested. A victim usually feels trembling and numbness in the lips and often the fingertips and toes. Paralysis begins in the limbs and, in fatal cases, reaches the chest muscles and diaphragm, causing respiratory failure. Artificial respiration—even mouth-to-mouth—will keep a badly affected person alive, but a transfer to a hospital and maintenance with a mechanical respirator should be sought as soon as possible. Recovery usually occurs, with no aftereffects, in about twenty-four hours. Contrary to certain old-fashioned culinary advice, cooking does not destroy PSP.

A different variety of dinoflagellate causes red tides along the Florida Gulf Coast and occasionally in Texas coastal waters. Massive fish kills frequently result, but human illness due to consumption of contaminated shellfish is rarely reported.

Poisonous-to-eat fishes are largely found in warm seas. Poisonous fishes should be distinguished from venomous fishes (discussed in the next chapter), in which hollow or grooved spines serve as defensive mechanisms, injecting venom directly into a careless predator or diver who handles the fish. The flesh of many venomous fishes is eaten and even savored in certain localities. On the other hand, poisonous fishes can be handled with impunity; they usually elicit no toxic skin reaction.

Scientifically, two general types of natural fish toxicity affecting human consumers internally are recognized. The first involves tetrodotoxin, a virulent poison found in puffers or balloonfishes and some of their relatives, collectively called plectognaths. Puffers, especially the large tropical species, make easy targets for a spearfisherman, but they are best left alone. In many areas, it takes an ichthyologist to tell apart the rare edible puffers from the poisonous ones. Certain Japanese seafood recipes feature puffer, but the selection of the individual fish to be cooked is reportedly made by highly experienced chefs who taste their dishes before serving them. The puffer problem is a more intricate one than the identification of wild edible mushrooms. The strength of the toxin may vary with the species, the geographical region, and even the time of year, but a pufferfish dinner is commonly fatal. Other fishes related to the puffers, including some of the triggerfishes, filefishes, and boxfishes, are also reported to be variously toxic.

The second major category of toxicity in fishes is less predictable than that associated with plectognaths. Termed *ciguatera*, the poisonous condition can be widespread in numerous tropical species that are unrelated taxonomically, but that usually inhabit coral-reef environments. Unlike tetrodotoxin, which is produced by the fish itself, *ciguatera* toxin appears to come from certain blue-green algae. The toxin is ingested by small reef fishes that browse on the algae. Immunity to the toxic effects prevails among fishes, as the toxin is passed up the food chain and concentrated ever more strongly in predators such as jacks and barracudas. A human making a meal of one of the larger species harboring *ciguatera* toxin can be fatally poisoned. Individual susceptibility can vary greatly, and even trace amounts are dangerous to some people. Symptoms of *ciguatera* poisoning begin with tingling sensations in the lips and tongue that later spread to the hands and feet. Such tingling may develop into numbness. Reversed temperature sensations, where hot feels cold and vice versa, can also occur. Gastrointestinal disturbance, fever, profuse sweating, aches in the joints, and other intermediate symptoms can then lead to nervous-system impairment—temporary blindness, extreme behavioral irritability, convulsions, and paralysis.

Ciguatera occurs sporadically worldwide in the tropics. Intense outbreaks have been noted in parts of the Caribbean and around western tropical Pacific islands. Hawaii and the Pacific coast of Central America rarely experience *ciguatera* incidents.

A few kinds of fishes seem to harbor hallucinogenic substances, again, probably derived from algae in the food chain. An example in Hawaii involves the tasty and popular white goatfish, *Mulloidichthys samoensis*, fairly easy prey for a spearfisherman. Complaints of hallucinations and strange dreams following the eating of the fish seem to be most common in the summer months. One of the sensations noted by individuals experiencing a goatfish "high" is an inversion of the body—a feeling that one's head is below the feet. Recovery is rapid after a few hours, and no serious or lasting effects have been noted. Dr. Eugenie Clark, in her first book, *Lady With a Spear*, mentioned similar hallucinogenic reactions induced by eating a species of rabbitfish in the western tropical Pacific. So far, the underlying pharmacology of these unusual intoxicating experiences has not been resolved. Neither of us has ever eaten a hallucinogenic fish, so we don't know whether to recommend it. It's unlikely that *Mulloidichthys* will ever supplant *Cannabis* for social acceptability. "Fish head" is an even less appealing appellation than "pot head."

Having once swum back to shore or boat with a hearty meal's worth or more of fine eating fish in tow, you will probably agree with us that actively prowling and pursuing your game through the magical forests of the sea is much more satisfying than sitting above the surface holding a rod or handline, waiting for the fish to take the initiative. Good hunting!

Chapter 17

An Underwater Rogues Gallery

O F THE VARIOUS serious hazards faced by divers, or just plain swimmers for that matter, biological dangers are nowhere near the top of the list. Minor cuts, scrapes, and punctures aside, the chance of serious injury from an encounter with a dangerous aquatic organism is extremely small. The water is just not teeming with evil critters ready to pounce on the unwary diver.

Of the dangerous aquatic organisms that do exist, sharks and killer whales are by far the most impressive and potentially aggressive, but not necessarily the most dangerous. These large predators are discussed later in this chapter. The overwhelming majority of a diver's natural enemies are totally passive, and injury is a matter of self-infliction that can usually be avoided.

Freshwater Creatures

Naegleria. Quite likely the most dangerous aquatic creature (and the rarest diving threat) in North America is one that can barely be seen without a microscope. Anybody who took biology in high school remembers watching a tiny ameba slinking through a drop of water on a glass slide. Rest assured that you were watching a harmless species, but maybe you remember being told that some types are parasitic in humans. Most of these cause problems in the gastrointestinal tract—amebic dysentery in mild or severe forms. These amebas are picked up on contaminated food, however, not by swimmers. The worst ameba parasites of all are not intestinal; they invade the nervous system (spinal cord and brain). Part of the life cycle of such organisms is spent in warm, usually stagnant, bodies of fresh water, primarily in the southeastern United States. These amebas (several species of the genus *Naegleria*) apparently enter the bodies of swimmers through the tissue-thin linings of the nose and mouth. Once in the host, they make their way to the nervous system and rapidly divide and multiply. The ensuing disease, known as amebic meningitis, is nearly always fatal.

Each year, a small number of people are stricken with amebic meningitis after swimming in bodies of fresh water from Virginia to the Gulf States. The only scuba diving fatality from this cause known to us occurred in Florida. Ponds and lakes are not the only potential trouble spots, however. In 1973, researchers discovered a large *Naegleria* population in a municipal swimming pool in Virginia. A number of deaths from amebic meningitis had mysteriously occurred in this area during several preceding years. In the pool, the biological investigators found a very dense infestation of the deadly amebas well back in a crack just below the waterline. Their theory was that the infestation was the focus of periodic dispersions of the amebas through the pool, perhaps due to turbulence whenever the pool was drained and refilled. Deep within the crack itself, the remaining organisms largely escaped the effects of chlorine and other disinfectants.

Divers are unlikely to encounter *Naegleria* in its typical habitat of algae-rich, low-visibility water. Those who keep their masks on and mouthpieces in place are even less prone to an ameba attack. The chance of contracting amebic meningitis is truly small, perhaps smaller than that of being bitten by a shark, but if you are involved in diver instruction in an outdoor pool, the ameba connection may give you a lever with the city fathers, or the "Y," to keep the pool in tip-top condition.

The Loathsome Leech. Leeches probably make the top ten in everyone's list of aquatic nightmares— shades of Humphrey Bogart staggering through the blood-sucking swamps in *The African Queen*. Actually, even the most sanguine leeches are less offensive than mosquitoes. If a leech is left to feed in peace, it will considerately remove the anticoagulant injected in its host initially in order to keep the blood flowing. Mosquitoes do not follow through in this regard, and the result is an itchy welt, the body's response to the foreign protein in the anticoagulant. Certain leeches have had a long-honored role in classical medical practice, serving as sanitary, controlled, and cali-brated devices for the removal of infected blood. Some leeches, for example the large species in the clear lakes of eastern Canada, are beautifully pat-terned in black, red, and yellow, and they are elegant, sinusoidal swimmers. Many leeches feed exclusively on fish or turtles and cannot even be induced to bite a person. If one should be so inclined, it will take about three minutes or so to carry out the operation, that is, if you don't notice it sitting on your skin. Next time you spot free-swimming leeches on a freshwater dive, overcome the first "yeccch" impulse and spend some time observing these lithe, active dancers as they per-form their ballet of the lakes.

Alligators and Crocodiles. Unlike leeches, alligators and crocodiles are capable of considerable blood-letting. Crocodiles, in particular, are greatly feared by people in some parts of the world. The threat to div-ers from these big reptiles in North America, how-ever, is virtually nil. Alligators rarely appear in decent diving waters, and even when they do, they are rarely large enough and bold enough to approach an adult human in the water. Children, though, are at some risk from large alligators, as a few recent inci-dents in Florida have shown. It seems the problem of potential alligator bite has become especially acute where some well-meaning idiots have been allowed to feed gators. Like bears in other regions, these are wild beasts and will definitely bite the hand that feeds—then the arm—then the. . . .

True crocodiles, too, with a few exceptions, are rarely found in choice diving environments. The exceptions could be met by traveling divers, however. For example, the large (up to 20 feet long) Indo-Pacific saltwater crocodile ranges through the Palau Islands and is reportedly more feared there than sharks. In South Florida (chiefly around Key Largo and the wild shores of Everglades National Park), the American crocodile, found in waters from fresh to fully marine, is growing in numbers, but is still too rare to pose more than a negligible hazard.

The only other menacing reptiles in fresh water are the snapping turtles and the cottonmouth water moccasin, a venomous snake. Common snapping turtles will never attack a diver, or even stand their ground and fight, for that matter. The big alligator snapper, a different species, inhabits turbid, silt-choked rivers in the Mississippi Valley, and if you somehow find yourself diving in this uninviting habitat, you have our sympathy. The cottonmouth snake, a denizen of weedy southern swamps, is one of the least likely of the aquatic reptiles to be met by a diver.

Far south of the U.S. border, freshwater diving must be an uncommon sport. At least one rarely hears of it, and that's probably not because of the piranhas, anacondas, electric eels, or even freshwater sharks (in Lake Nicaragua). It's probably because the ocean diving down that way is so spectacular.

Ocean Creatures: The Northern and Temperate Seas

The Shy Octopus. In classical maritime literature, such as Victor Hugo's *Toilers of the Deep*, the octopus is billed as one of the most threatening creatures in the sea. Just the opposite is true, whether you meet the huge, harmless Pacific Northwest species (largest in the world) or the tiny, highly venomous blue-ringed octopus in Australia. Note that while the blue-ringed octopus can be deadly to humans, the animals are universally shy; a person is bitten only after considerable effort on his or her part toward that end.

Different species of octopus occur in both cold water and in the tropics. We are including them here because the West Coast giant species (*Octopus dofleini*) ranges from Oregon to southern Alaska. These big, active molluscs, whose "intelligence" is comparable, perhaps, to that of a dog or cat, have been greatly reduced in numbers in Puget Sound and the adjoining environs by hunting and harassment perpetrated primarily by the ever-growing population of scuba divers. The state of Washington is now considering serious preservation efforts, among them special octopus sanctuaries, where divers will be permitted to look and take photographs, but not touch the bashful monsters.

Octopuses are carnivores with broad tastes is seafood, but they seem to prefer crabs and other crustaceans. Most species of octopus reach sexual maturity within a year. The mating ritual involves a male inserting part of one arm, bearing sperm done up in membranous packets, into the female's genital opening. The specialized sexual portion of the male's arm detaches and remains with the female, whereupon the male dies. Shortly after mating, eggs are deposited in a protected place by the female, who conscientiously guards them and keeps them clean and well aerated by circulating water over them with her siphon. Finally, she assists dozens to hundreds of her babies to hatch and speeds them on their way with carefully directed jets of water. Worn out and starved from constant maternal vigilance, the female octopus dies after her young have been ushered into the world.

The Slimy Menace. While even the largest North American octopus is harmless and will actively avoid a diver, the same cannot quite be said for another group of tentacle-bearing marine creatures, which occasionally become distressingly numerous in favored diving waters. These are the swimming (or drifting) cnidarians, or coelenterates, also known as jellyfishes. Cold, temperate waters harbor the largest species, those belonging to the genus *Cyanea*. In the North Atlantic, they grow to an incredible size—10 feet across the "bell," with dangling tentacles over 50 feet long. The main populations stay in cold water of the open ocean between eastern Canada and Iceland, but occasionally shifts in summer winds and currents bring baby *Cyanea* (about washtub size, with 15-foot tentacles) south as far as New Jersey. At such times, they seem to concentrate in the narrow funnel of Long Island Sound, especially along Rhode Island and Connecticut shores.

Fortunately, few people are severely allergic to *Cyanea* stings and a moderate rash where tentacles touch naked skin is the usual result. A full wetsuit affords full protection, but few divers, wetsuited or not, are not revolted by bumping into a very large jellyfish.

Farther south, a variety of smaller species of jellyfishes appears seasonally to nettle swimmers and divers. One of the worst of these is the so-called sea nettle (*Chrysaora*), common in Chesapeake Bay during the summer. Fortunately, the sea nettle seems to concentrate more in turbid, brackish water rather than near the open sea where conditions are more attractive for diving.

Along the East Coast from Florida to Cape Cod, the greatest threat from a "jellyfish" comes occasionally during the summer months when unusual wind conditions drive the Portuguese man-of-war (*Physalia*) inshore from its normal drifting path along the Gulf Stream. Man-of-war stings are very painful; even the slightest contact with a tentacle hurts considerably more than a bee sting. This is due to the penetration into the skin of hundreds to thousands of microscopic, hollow, venom-containing threads. Untreated, the pain from a minor brush with *Physalia* usually fades away after half an hour, but some people experience dangerous allergic reactions to the venom and require hospitalization. The first sign of a severe reaction is pain in axial lymph nodes, either in the groin or armpits, depending on the site of contact (most people are stung on arms or legs). Limbs may become numb and temporarily paralyzed. If you are swimming in deep water when stung, head toward shore or your boat immediately. A friend who was stung in several places on the leg while snorkeling offshore barely made it to shallow water before being effectively paralyzed from the waist down. He managed to crawl halfway out of the water, but for more than half an hour was unable to stand up.

In mild cases, off-the-shelf antihistamines will alleviate pain and other reactions to a jellyfish sting. A little meat tenderizer (this destroys the toxin, which is a protein) and rubbing alcohol applied to the site of the sting also helps. The latter two substances, applied together, are recommended for use on children who have been stung. If you dive in man-of-war territory, carry these first-aid items in your dive bag. The widespread practice of using sand to rub vigorously the area of the sting should be avoided. This action causes any undischarged stinging cells to fire into the skin, and may introduce extra venom from discharged cells that didn't fully penetrate in the first place. As mentioned in Chapter 1, a Portuguese man-of-war usually stands out when seen from below against the silvered undersurface, so an ascending diver can avoid a painful blunder by looking up while approaching the ceiling.

The Aggressive Goosefish. Divers along the Northeast Coast fairly frequently spot goosefishes (*Lophius*), gruesomely ugly bottom fishes, most often in summer when many of these creatures come in from the outer continental shelf to lurk near the shoreline. The goosefish looks like the most sluggish animal that ever wore fins (see Chapter 13 for a description of an encounter), but tweak the tail of a resting individual and you will probably find yourself backpedaling with frantic haste as the huge head, full of needle-sharp teeth, whips around almost faster than you can blink. Fortunately, the fish is not a sprint swimmer, and after a few spasmodic flaps in your direction, it will settle down to the bottom again. Only one person we know of has suffered the ignominious fate of a true goosefish attack. This diver was wearing bright yellow fins, one of which was seized, totally without provocation on the part of the diver, by a large goosefish. The incident happened in about 20 feet of water as the diver swam along the base of a rock jetty. He suddenly felt something severely weighing on one fin and mightily retarding his progress and, looking back, saw the fish's mouth engulfing most of his full-sized fin. With what he remembered as mainly disgust, but also a modicum of concern for a visible row of teeth quite close to his ankle, the diver ascended slowly, trying to shake loose the loathsome creature's bulldoglike grip. The fish finally let go at the surface and drifted down again out of sight.

Sting Rays and Electric Fishes. Sting rays are primarily a shallow-water problem, inflicting painful punctures on barefoot waders. Normally, such wounds are sustained only on smooth sandy bottom in quiet water. Sting rays rarely visit the surf zone or areas of strong surge. If you have to wade through their territory, avoiding sting rays is easy. Just do the sting-ray shuffle. That is, slide your feet forward along the sand with each step. This way you will tickle anything lurking there with your toes and scare it up out of the sand ahead of you instead of suddenly placing your tender foot right down on top of it. Some experienced coastal explorers report that stomping hard on the sand every few steps transmits vibrations that scare up rays well ahead of you. Thus, a combination of the shuffle and the stomp may be the safest way to dance your way through the shallows. In a few areas, rays occasionally congregate in such numbers that they form a virtual living minefield.

The ray's defensive reaction, of course, is to whip up its tail at the object attacking it. Near the base of the tail (never at the tip) is a stout spine, or two in some species, that readily pierces human flesh. A sting-ray spine does inject venom into the wound it makes; the venom flows from a small venom sac in the base of the tail down a deep groove into the wound. Most of the time, however, ray venom is not highly toxic to humans, although it is very painful. Sting-ray wounds have a tendency to become infected, a more serious threat to health than the injected venom. The spines of some species of ray have serrated edges, increasing the trauma of the injury.

Very large rays are sometimes seen in deeper water, lying in the sand, often with a shallow layer of sand dusted over them so that only the barest diamond outline of the creature shows through. Best not go close to a large ray. Bizarre cases of free divers being hit in the abdomen and other parts of the anatomy by ray spines have occasionally been reported. In such cases, the divers must have brushed right over a half-buried, resting fish.

Along the California coast, not only sting rays but related fish called torpedo rays make life potentially interesting for divers. Contact with a torpedo ray, for example transmitted through a metal spear handle, can be a shocking experience—electrically, that is. The fish produces an electrical field around itself by means of chemical reactions within special bodily tissues, actually modified muscles. These rays carry what amount to powerful organic batteries, capable of a maximum output in a very large specimen of about 50 volts delivered across the animal's skin in a momentary 50-amp current. Power output is thus up to 2500 watts. Such a shock is capable of killing a person. An average-sized fish, however, delivering an average electrical discharge will only briefly stun a careless diver. Of course, a neoprene wetsuit insulates electrically as well as thermally. If you wish to pet a torpedo ray, just be sure you are wearing your neoprene dive gloves.

Off the Atlantic coast, divers sometimes come upon a different kind of electric fish, the stargazer. A stargazer vaguely resembles a not-so-flattened goosefish, but does not reach quite as large a size. Also averaging smaller than a torpedo ray, the stargazer, nevertheless, can deliver a surprising jolt.

California Scorpionfishes. In southern California, one of the hazards to a diver intent on bottom photography or on searching for lobsters or abalone is a fish that is well camouflaged to blend into scruffy bottom and that stands its ground when confronted by even the largest diver. This cold-water member of the scorpionfish family has the same sort of venomous spines as its more widely known tropical relatives. The point of contact with a diver is often the hand. Aquanauts in the U.S. Navy's Sealab program found to their dismay that numerous scorpionfish took up residence at the entrance to their underwater habitat. Several of the Navy men, including former astronaut Scott Carpenter, were stung. Fortunately, the divers were not seriously poisoned; the venom of this species is not as potent as that of some of the tropical members of the family.

Creatures of the Tropical Seas

Much-embellished tales of the South Seas often give first-time visitors to the tropics an image of aquamarine hell—waters crowded with ravenous sharks, ferocious barracudas, vicious morays, and a host of other evil creatures, large and small, waiting in ambush at every turn of the reef and lurking under every rock. All this is vintage Hollywood bilge. One can swim for years and many miles through tropical seas without experiencing the slightest threat from the natives. While it is true that a somewhat greater variety of potentially noxious marine creatures exists in the tropics as compared to that in cooler waters, these creatures are rarely met, rarely act offensively, and rarely cause damage that is more than skin deep.

The Wicked Urchins. Nearly every diver in the tropics has seen the big purple or black *Diadema* urchins, poking spines of knitting-needle length out from crevices in the reef or among rocks, or else clustered in the shallows around the margins of bays and coves. Actually, the uniformly dark-colored animals are the adults, and similarly armed juveniles, usually with a salt-and-pepper coloration, can be found in the vicinity. These urchins have the longest spines of their tribe and may induce a slightly toxic reaction in the skin of humans who make an uncomfortably close approach.

Surprisingly, if you study a *Diadema* closely, you will see that the longest spines are rather blunt. You can actually grasp them carefully at the tips in order to pick the animal up. But slightly shorter, much more slender, and nestled in between the long spines are the real weapons—perhaps the sharpest needles in nature. They penetrate human skin at the slightest touch. Moreover, they are serrated and will not pull out readily. Instead, they break when tension is applied. Even the best sliver-extraction technique will butcher the skin in an attempt to remove a *Diadema* spine. It's better, especially if you have suffered the penetration of several or more, to soak the afflicted area with vinegar. The mild acid reaction will begin to dissolve the embedded spines, a process that your body will complete after several days. The typical after-effect is itchiness, which may persist for a week.

A few cases of more severe skin reaction to urchin contact have been reported. One different type of urchin (*Toxopneustes*), a short-spined variety, occurs in the tropical Indo-Pacific region and has been responsible for toxic reactions serious enough to be treated by a physician.

Fire Coral, Fireworms, and Red-Hot Sponges. If God had anticipated the full range of human endeavors that have begun to flourish in the late twentieth century, perhaps He would have given us wings and scales, the latter to protect our very tender skins from nasty brushes with things that live in the sea.

Fire coral is a peculiar type of growth (not a true coral, due to strange vagaries in its growth and reproduction). Typically brownish or yellowish, it grows upright in a structure resembling a thick sheet of cardboard with undulating, rounded vertical folds and stubby branches. Most people react to contact with fire coral by developing an angry, poison-ivy-like rash. In fact, a variety of fire coral is known as sea poison ivy. In rare cases of extensive contact or allergic reactions, hospitalization may be required.

Fireworms are beautiful greenish, bluish, brownish, or reddish worms of a variety of species, typically found under rocks. These creatures look like furry caterpillars. But be warned: don't pick one up in your bare, water-softened hand. The "fur" consists of thousands of hollow, penetrating hairs, each bearing a tiny amount of concentrated venom that will make your skin itch maddeningly for a week or more. As treatment a rubbing-alcohol soak is usually prescribed.

Sponges can be an insidious source of skin irritation. The kinds to watch out for are rarely the obvious upright or branching types, but rather encrusting varieties, usually yellow or orange and often found on the undersides of rocks. These sponges contain millions of tiny glasslike needles that readily penetrate the skin. Symptoms are burning and intense itching. Like the aftermath of a jellyfish or fire-coral encounter, and unlike that involving an urchin or fireworm, a sponge "attack" leaves no visible trace of the weaponry employed, since the needles are microscopic. Sponge burn responds less readily to treatment than any of the other irritating situations described. Once again, the sufferer should expect a week or so to pass before symptoms fade away.

Cone Shells. Cones are largely tropical, often beautifully colored and patterned marine snails that actively prey on various other small creatures in their communities. Different cone species tend to specialize in their selection of prey, which falls into three major categories: worms, fish, and other snails. In most localities, worm-eating cones outnumber the others. The worm eaters seize their prey with a long proboscis that extends out of the mouth and down into nooks and crannies of the reef, or into a hapless worm's burrow in sediment. The worm-eating species are harmless to humans.

Cones that attack the other two categories of prey, however, do so in a more dramatic manner, employing means which, at times, can be highly damaging to a naive diver or shell collector. These cones harpoon their prey with a specialized, venom-containing hollow tooth. The venom's primary purpose, of course, is to paralyze active prey. Generally, the most severe toxic effect in a human is produced by the large, fish-eating cones, some of which reach 6 inches in length. However, a few large snail eaters are also capable of inflicting a bad sting. Contrary to pseudoscientific hype, such as that served up on Hawaiian whodunits on television, fatal poisonings by cone shells are extremely rare.

Also, even cones that are capable of delivering a powerful sting are often so shy when picked up that they retreat into the shell indefinitely. Moreover, no cone stings instantly like a bee. A knowledgeable person receives plenty of warning of the cone's intention. Always hold a live cone shell by the posterior, or wide end. If you see a thin, whiplike (often pink, orange, or yellow) flexible extension emerge from the anterior (tapered end) of the shell and begin probing about, watch your fingers. This is the proboscis, which holds the tooth harpoon. The tooth is fired by muscular contraction out of the proboscis at high speed, but this will not happen unless the tip of the proboscis makes contact with the target. Don't confuse the long, thin, tapering proboscis with the shorter, stubbier siphon (or breathing tube), which is usually banded or mottled in various colors and is partially slit lengthwise (not a perfectly closed tube).

People who are stung by cones haven't been watching their fingers while holding a temperamental individual, or, not recognizing it, they have put a cone in their swimsuit pocket and forgotten about it—for a few minutes. In case of a sting by a large specimen, it's wise to seek medical attention right away. Keeping the site of the wound as cool as possible (pack it in ice if any is available) is the best first-aid treatment; this is now recommended procedure for venomous snakebite as well. Needless to say, persons who are allergic to insect or other venoms may be severely affected by a cone sting and should handle the live shells with great care.

Caribbean species of cones do not include any with the toxicity and quantity of venom to induce a severe reaction in a healthy adult. In Hawaiian waters, three species, *Conus striatus*, *C. textile*, and *C. marmoreus*, are recognized as highly potent stingers, but are probably not life-threatening to a nonallergic person. The western tropical Pacific and Indo-Pacific regions have the largest numbers of species demanding a respectful attitude on the part of the diver.

Moray Eels. Suddenly coming upon a large moray (usually all you see is the animal's impressive head) lurking in a shadowed, rocky lair is one of the more hair-raising of underwater thrills. But these creatures, while not exactly harmless, are nearly always benign. This is especially true of the bigger ones, which face you with an unimpeachable air of self-confidence. The slow, steady champing of the jaws as the eel breathes, showing just enough of the teeth to readily intimidate the beholder's imagination, seems to imply, "I choose not to negotiate."

Morays are primarily tropical, favoring a coral-reef environment, although at least one species inhabits the fairly cool waters of southern California, where it frequents bouldery terrain in and around kelp beds. If a diver is unbiased regarding slinky shapes and slimy textures, morays are among the most beautiful and admirably adapted reef fishes. Many species are strikingly patterned in exotic colors. They have extremely flexible skeletons and lack gill covers, permitting them to force their way, forward and backward, through very narrow passages, nooks, and crannies in a reef.

Unprovoked attacks by morays on people are rare, although they have occurred, usually in shallow water, and nearly always by fairly small eels. Unfortunately, even a 3-foot moray generates enough force in its jaws to break bones in a human hand and severely damage muscle tissue in an arm or leg. Morays are attracted to speared fish, and, in the presence of blood, some species do exhibit a kind of feeding frenzy, biting objects at random. Keeping your catch buoyed at the surface, where morays do not go, will eliminate the problem. The classical moray injury involves a diver reaching into a hole or under a rock where he can't see everything that may lie hidden within. The watchword here is: "Never!" You could lose your hand to an otherwise perfectly placid, friendly, proprietary moray, who simply will not tolerate violation of his or her personal space. Veteran tropical lobster hunters are aware that a holed-up lobster with one antenna pointing outward and one back into the hole behind itself is keeping tabs on two potential enemies. There is a moray back there, and in this situation trying to catch the lobster with your hands may not be worth the risk.

Tropical Scorpionfishes. The most venomous fishes in the world ocean inhabit the shallow reefs and reef flats of the Indo-Pacific region. These are the drab-to-ugly little stonefishes, related to the larger but less potent California scorpionfish. Surprisingly, within the same family exist some of the most beautifully bizarre of fishes, plumed and colorful, but also venomous—the lionfishes, zebrafishes, and turkeyfishes. Sometimes these names are used interchangeably for various species. The threat to a diver from these small bottom dwellers of clear tropical waters stems from a behavioral trait common to all scorpionfishes. They have acquired an evolutionary confidence in their defense mechanism and often simply fail to get out of your way. Typically, they wait until you are right beside them, even touching them in a few cases, before making a slight revealing movement. While waders on the reef flats can avoid being stung by wearing tennis shoes, divers should look to their hands. It is possible to put your hand right on one, and the venomous spines can pierce a thin glove. The best means of avoiding a very painful and (in the Indo-Pacific, including western Micronesia) potentially lethal experience is to move slowly and deliberately along the reef; do not use your hands indiscriminately to pull yourself along the bottom. Slow movement will give the fish time to react to your presence. Often, one will "flush" from the bottom just ahead of you, and make a short swimming hop of a foot or so as it displays its colors (even drab species usually have bright color patches behind the pectoral fins, which are flared as a warning to potential predators) and flourishes its spiny, loaded weaponry.

Barracudas, Giant Clams, and Sea Snakes. Each of the creatures in the heading of this section has a certain lethal lore associated with it, and none of the horror stories seems to be true. The only serious threat a diver is likely to experience from this trio would come, accidentally, from a large barracuda. Without exception, an attack on a diver would be due to a mistake on the part of the fish. It is well known that barracudas are attracted to shiny metallic objects. Their favored prey are small silvery fishes, and snorkelers and divers wearing reflecting bracelets, buckles, medals, and similar objects are more likely to be followed and approached by a barracuda than an individual without such a flashy underwater presence. Reportedly, a few divers have been struck and on rare occasions bitten by small barracudas mistaking a shiny object on the person for its prey. Speared fish also attract barracudas, and tales of fish snatching by these toothy carnivores are common in the Caribbean. Nevertheless, according to tropical ichthyologists, such as Perry Gilbert, formerly of Cornell University and more recently director of the Mote Marine Laboratory near Sarasota, Florida, no barracuda would ever consider a human as an item of prey. The worst-case accidental attack involving a barracuda attracted to a shiny object might involve the fish severing a major blood vessel as it struck the site of the reflection. Protecting yourself from this highly remote possibility is simple: when in barracuda country, don't wear anything shiny on your arms or legs.

The old South Pacific legend of divers being trapped by the leg or arm in the shell of a giant clam *(Tridacna)* is another stock scenario of the Hollywood School of Diving. First of all, such clams, which lie partly embedded in (or overgrown by) the mass of a coral reef, rarely open their shells widely enough to accommodate a naked human foot, let alone one wearing a swim fin. It is possible to get your hand and forearm inside, whereupon the shell will slowly close on it, but not with a grip sufficient to trap even a weak person who is determined to withdraw his arm. Divers in the South Seas will occasionally see a native person with his hand in just this position. A moment later the observer will see the withdrawal of the hand holding a knife, with which the diver has cut the adductor, or closure, muscles of the shell. The shell then remains open, allowing the delicious meat to be scooped out.

Sea Snakes. Sea snakes, which are highly venomous reptiles, occasionally do bite people, but the only known victims have been native fishermen of the Indo-Pacific region who accidentally trapped sea snakes in their nets. Sea snakes range throughout the tropical Pacific and Indian oceans, but do not occur in the Atlantic. Biologists believe that they are restricted by water temperatures below about 65°F (18° C), and thus are unable to migrate around Cape Horn and Cape of Good Hope. Neither have they found their way through the Suez or Panama canals, probably due to the extensive systems of locks and an aversion to the fresh water found in the central stretches of those canals. However, Smithsonian Institution biologists who have studied sea snakes in Panama predict that if a sea-level canal is built anywhere across Central America, the common yellow-bellied sea snake of the eastern Pacific would quickly reach the Caribbean and probably spread as far north as Cape Cod in the summer months.

At present, the yellow-bellied sea snake ranges along the American Pacific coast as far north as the tip of the Baja Peninsula, and it may begin to appear at roughly comparable latitudes off the Mexican mainland. But it is very rare here and only becomes fairly common in Costa Rican and Panamanian waters. Surprisingly, it does not frequent Hawaiian waters, although occasionally a snake may reach those islands after following the slow, wide currents that drift to the west.

Sea snakes typically inhabit drift lines or tidal fronts up to several miles offshore. The drift lines are marked by floating vegetation and debris up to the size of dead trees. The flotsam attracts small fishes, which are preyed upon by the snakes. Except for one dubious report of an unprovoked, aggressive sea snake (at a western Pacific site) published in a popular magazine, swimmers and divers who have encountered these graceful, prettily patterned marine reptiles, and who have merely observed them quietly, have unanimously found them to be benign.

Sharks

Some day you may be diving or snorkeling along a reef's edge when suddenly you become aware of a shark nearby behaving strangely. It holds its body in an unusual rigid posture as it swims back and forth over a short stretch of the reef. It is also shaking its head in wide exaggerated sweeps from side to side, to a human observer seeming to pantomime, "No! No! No!"

Better leave the area quietly and at once. These strange antics are part of a well-documented threat display of the gray reef shark, *Carcharinus menissorah*, a fairly common species averaging 5 to 6 feet in length and inhabiting relatively shallow waters in tropical seas. The rigid posturing and head shaking, which is the most complex known example of warning behavior exhibited by sharks, was first described in 1974 by diving scientists from California State University at Long Beach. Professional shark watchers believe that the threat display is meant to warn intruders away from the gray reef shark's territory, a few hundred square meters of reef and sea floor. If the warning is ignored, the shark quickly becomes aggressive. Some divers have been badly bitten by this species, although none fatally.

So much has been written about sharks and shark attacks that it is hard to avoid repeating all the old but undyingly dramatic stories, many of which can be traced to antiquity. Sharks are spectacular predators and have appeared in accounts of ocean adventures since the dawn of heroic literature, so it is not surprising that the composite, reconstructed, and frequently hypothetical shark is almost inevitably the first entry on a diver's list of dangerous aquatic animals. Yet there is a good chance that someone who dives primarily in cold northern seas may never see a shark. Then again, if you are an active ocean diver, especially in regions such as southern California, the southeastern United States, the Gulf and Caribbean, and Hawaii, sooner or later you will probably see one of these primeval predators gracefully weaving its way toward you out of the blue-green haze.

What should you do? First, it might be comforting to remember three facts, which shark experts have confirmed after years of observation:

1. Sharks never rush in immediately to bite a diver.

2. Most sharks scavenge dead or injured animals. Around you they will be cautious, but perhaps curious.

3. You are much larger than the prey of all but a few very rare individuals of a couple of dangerous species (in most areas frequented by North American divers).

Upon encountering a shark of significant size, reciting a kind of litany from the three facts above may help to quell a sudden witless urge to shoot to the surface and sprint across the water to safety on the beach or boat.

Reactions

In any encounter with a shark over about 3 or 4 feet long, it will behoove you to leave the area, and, if the shark follows, to leave the water. Swim away with smooth, deliberate strokes. Moving confidently through the water is believed to be important, communicating to the shark that you are not an item of prey. Appearing agitated, flustered, or weak—by projecting these states of being through body language—to a large, potentially hungry shark is not in your best interests. Take special care not to thrash or kick violently at the surface. Many observations and experiences related by Cousteau and others suggest that the surface is the most dangerous place to be in the presence of a large shark.

Head toward shore or your boat. Stay close to the bottom for as long as possible. If a long, straight-up, open-water ascent in the company of a shark is necessary, partners should go up at a normal pace in a back-to-back position. Three or four people can perform this maneuver together. In exceptional cases, after decompression dives, where several sharks are clearly excited and maneuvering close to the divers, or if a large shark appears to be threatening, decompression may have to be waived. If you are forced to miss a decompression stop, even a short one, head for the nearest chamber as soon as you get out of the water. You will probably get there before the onset of the bends, but if not, at least you'll know what to expect.

Occasions

Sharks rarely appear in the vicinity of divers unless certain obvious, almost stereotyped, conditions are present in the diving area. One of these conditions involves spearfishing. A bagful or stringer of punctured small fish leaking blood and appetizing juices will always be a powerful shark attractant. Watch out, in this case, for a shark in murky water. He may get close to you before you see him, his appetite whetted by the scent of his normal injured prey in the water. Sharks also sense low-frequency vibrations, for example those produced by a large wounded fish, for hundreds of yards. Odor trails from wounded fish are believed to be not as far-reaching. Novice spearfishermen should beware of carrying a string or bag of fish attached to their bodies. Instead, they should trail the catch behind at the end of a 20-foot length of buoyed line.

A few diving manuals and popular articles on sharks warn that menstruating women are highly attractive to sharks. We do not agree that a menstrual flow, as normally intercepted by a tampon device, would ever provide a long-range signal to a shark. Only in an extremely close encounter, say within a few inches, might a shark react to the exceedingly minute concentration of blood possibly escaping to the water.

Other identifiable shark attractants include a great deal of commotion made by people at the surface. The snorkeler or diver who flails and slaps his fins half in and half out of the water has been known to call up a shark; a splashy swimming party from a boat with people jumping and diving noisily into the water may also conjure several inquisitive fins; and water skiers are sometimes followed by large sharks—perhaps eyeing the ultimate in trolled lures. Underwater explosions are notorious for attracting sharks, some from perhaps several miles away. A dead, stranded whale, or other large carcass, may attract and excite sharks for a mile or more along the coast. In Hawaii, where shark attack is rare, a dead whale, beached near a surfing area, may have been indirectly responsible for a frustrated great white shark taking a bite out of a surfboard and leaving a tooth as calling card. Fortunately, the surfboard's owner, who was aboard at the time, was uninjured.

Orcas

Except for Eskimos, not many of whom are scuba divers, people who go down to the sea, and beneath its surface, seem to have a surprisingly blasé attitude toward the "killer whales." Indeed, *Orcinus orca*, which attains lengths of more than 25 feet and may weigh 6 or 7 tons, is probably the most formidable predator to evolve on the planet since *Tyrannosaurus rex*. A long-ago relative of the great white shark, the extinct *Carcharodon megalodon*, which left its 5-inch teeth in fossil deposits of the southeastern United States' coastal plain, might have rivaled a big orca in voracity, but present-day great whites seem like minnows beside the cetacean rulers of the sea.

The feeding habits of orcas are disturbing, to say

the least. These creatures are the only marine mammals to clearly prefer warm-blooded prey, chiefly seals and porpoises. Occasionally, a group of orcas will pursue whales of larger species, but disabled or very young individuals are usually the targets of an attack.

Recently, striking photographs have been made of killer whales preying on seals and sea lions and playing with their victims as a cat plays with a mouse. One series of pictures in *Audubon* magazine* documents a game of "catch" with young sea lions as the balls. This behavior, which seems to be common, may help young orcas learn how to catch their prey. In another similar case, a large solitary orca off southern California was observed playing with a dead adult male sea lion, which must have weighed several hundred pounds. The solitary cetacean sport went on for twenty minutes and included several tosses of the carcass high in the air. Needless to say, no smaller marine mammal is safe in open water in the presence of an orca, whose swimming speed can reach 30 knots (exceeded only by large tunas).

What are the implications for human divers vis-à-vis orcas? Somewhat surprisingly, according to marine mammalogist Victor B. Scheffer, an authority on orcas and other whales, there has never been an authenticated attack on *Homo sapiens* by *Orcinus orca*. Harrowing tales have been told by Eskimos and polar explorers of killer whales cooperating in packs to break ice floes in order to get at sled dogs and perhaps humans. This technique has also been reported as a means by which orcas catch walruses and other natural prey resting on the ice. It is possible that humans and dogs are on rare occasion mistaken for something else. There has never been any reason to believe that a diver using scuba or a snorkeler has been attacked by an orca.

Where is a diver most likely to encounter orcas in North American waters? According to Victor Scheffer, Puget Sound in Washington State may harbor the

*J. Wilson, "Killers in the Surf," *Audubon* 77 (1975):2-5

highest population density of killer whales in the world. It also has a large and growing population of divers, boaters, and professional and amateur ocean watchers. Spectacular sightings of orcas in Washington's bays and sounds are not uncommon, for example around the San Juan Islands, where pods of 60 or 70 of the sleek black-and-white predators of all ages have been closely observed in the narrow interisland channels. From shore, it's a thrill only to glimpse a lone, 3- to 4-foot-high dorsal fin, dark and sickle shaped, cutting through the water just out past the kelp fringe. An underwater sighting of an orca is far rarer and much more hair-raising, but so far does not seem to be a cause for alarm.

It is a little surprising, given the large population of both orcas and divers in Puget Sound and adjoining waters, that more underwater contact is not reported. Are the orcas deliberately avoiding scuba divers? This may be the answer, for it is highly likely that orcas detect divers from at least several hundred yards away with their biological sonar. So far, there is not the slightest hint of an orca regarding a diver as potential prey. Is it a plot? Are they just very patiently putting us off our guard and planning a large and special feast all over Puget Sound on some future summer weekend? Maybe we could sell the movie rights to that one!

To cetologists, orcas seem to have a discriminating palate, favoring seal and porpoise meat and a few kinds of fish. Perhaps an occasional killer whale has sampled the flesh of *Homo sapiens*. If so, the word may have spread among these highly social carnivores that the smallish, gangly-legged things taste poorly (a lot like pork, if cannibal lore is to be believed), or maybe worse, especially if the meal consisted of some cigar-chomping, whiskey-guzzling ancient mariner. It might be interesting to see if orcas will accept pork in captivity. Thinking ahead, it might not be such a good idea if this new taste were acquired by a wild population of orcas.

We would like to conclude this chapter with a proposal for peaceful coexistence between divers and the creatures of the sea. When a person comes to feel at home in the water, comfortable with its fluid rhythms and familiar with the ways of its wildlife, fear and apprehension largely give way to wonder and appreciation. While there is no question that sharks, orcas, and many other aquatic creatures demand respect, they are also extremely beautiful in their various ways and marvelously adapted to their ancient world. There are intangible values embodied in all these denizens of the underwater wilderness. One doesn't have to see a shark or scorpionfish to benefit from their existence or to know that, without them, the adventure of diving would be greatly impoverished.

Chapter 18

Undersea Futures

A GLANCE AT THE HISTORICAL record will show that diving for pleasure and profit has developed only very recently in humankind's long relationship with the sea. Like a rising tide, the art and science of diving has swelled from sluggish, uncertain beginnings into a flood of interest, participation, and entrepreneurship. Since antiquity, natural scientists and philosophers have pondered the depths and imagined the conditions and forms of life prevailing there. During the late Middle Ages and early Renaissance, gifted inventors such as Borelli and da Vinci designed crude diving equipment. Workable diving bells made of heavily caulked and reinforced wooden casks were available to Spanish treasure salvors in the seventeenth century. In the Caribbean during this time, attempts were made to recover valuables from sunken galleons at depths approaching 60 feet. The divers typically were prisoners or Indian slaves pressed into service for the occasion. It's unclear to historians whether "professional" divers were then extant as a working class. Perhaps they had a very short life expectancy. Certainly there were no pleasure divers.

Serious and sustained underwater commerce and industry have arisen even more suddenly than aviation. Within a few decades, humans have learned not only to fly the skies and beyond, but to live for comparable periods beneath the surface of the sea. One wonders if the sudden acquisition of new aquatic skills, new behaviors, new perspectives, and a sense of expanded dominion will prove to be a turning point in human development. Will this sea change prove to be as significant as some of the major human migrations of the past, in which, it is theorized, brand new environments and subsequent adaptations led to unforeseen cultural and material advancement?

The State of the Art

We believe that, at least in the near future, the sport of diving will continue to grow rapidly, especially in the vicinity of heavily populated coastal centers. Vigorous, outdoor-loving people will continue to be attracted to the elemental freedom one feels in the underwater wilderness. We predict that in the more crowded parts of North America the adventure of diving will remain more accessible than hang gliding and potentially more satisfying than backpacking, sports that offer similar challenges and rewards.

Increased diver patronage of remote, exotic locations, such as the western tropical Pacific, will depend on future transportation costs and quite possibly on the amount of environmental spoilage that results from incompatible industrial projects, for example, the proposed Palau oil-storage facility. Massive oil spills in the Caribbean in 1979 foreshadow blackened reefs and ruined undersea landscapes wherever supertankers converge. It's just a matter of time. Given the scale of the ships, frenetic shipping schedules, and proliferation of tanker routes in the coming final decades of Big Oil, even the most pristine reefs hundreds of kilometers from a superport might be endangered eventually.

The domestic tropics will probably continue to grow in popularity. New and spectacular diving destinations will undoubtedly be "discovered" and made accessible (not overdeveloped, we hope) in the Caribbean and on the Pacific coast of Central

America. As mentioned earlier, fishwatching appears to be approaching birdwatching in popularity in some areas. Illustrated guidebooks to fishes are extremely popular in many coastal regions. These books are beginning to resemble Peterson's birding guides, and some of them are now printed on plastic pages so that a serious fishwatcher can tuck the book into a pocket of the BC where it will be available for instant reference on the bottom when an unusual fish appears. Some divers may already have started "life lists" of fishes they have observed. Annual Christmas counts of species in limited areas, now very popular with birders, might prove to be a rewarding group activity for dive clubs to coordinate in many coastal or island localities. Northern divers would probably choose to shift the date of the count to July or August. Over the years such assessments of the abundance of fishes in local areas should contribute valuable data on the effectiveness of marine conservation.

Technical developments in sport diving will certainly feature new and improved equipment. The most basic and useful items we foresee include an improved decompression meter that would more closely simulate the uptake and release of nitrogen by the whole body. When perfected, this device would take into account the integrated functions of the body's fast and slow tissues. It will probably be expensive.

We also hope to see breakthroughs in insulating materials and manufacturing techniques that will lead to less expensive unisuits, allowing northern divers of modest financial means to escape in relative comfort to their local underwater wilderness areas at any time of year.

Push-button refinements in diving gear will probably continue to appear. Perhaps the next step beyond the mechanically inflated BC will be a truly automatic BC that responds to changes in depth by inflating or deflating to maintain neutral buoyancy without the diver's conscious effort. Of course, a manual override for inflating and purging the device during an emergency would be included.

Improved devices for underwater communication will probably appear. Presently, accessories for voice transmission between divers tend to be expensive, cumbersome, and prone to breakdowns. Simple and inexpensive devices are available, but transmit garbled, distorted conversations.

We hope to see advances in instruction that will address problems of diving psychology, helping people to be basically at ease in the water. Individuals who perform adequately in a pool may experience anxiety the first few times they enter open water, and an instructor should be prepared to help prevent psychological setbacks at this stage of the learning process. A diver's self-confidence and cooperative attitude are especially important at the vertical extremes of the diving range. Being at home on the surface of a rough sea is essential for a beginner; mature, responsible, cooperative behavior in deep water should be the hallmark of an advanced diver.

A protective attitude toward the underwater environment is another theme we would like to see permeate basic diver training everywhere. Discriminate spearfishing and shell collecting, in which rocks and coral are left as undisturbed as possible, anchors are placed carefully, and picnic trash, used flashbulbs, and other litter are retained, will preserve the beautiful seascapes for others' enjoyment and for yours the next time.

Tighter rules and regulations governing diving are probable from federal, state, and local governments, as well as from within the industry itself. It is the hope of many who make their living in the design, manufacture, and sale of diving equipment, or in diver services such as training and certification, transportation, and guiding, that the industry will remain effectively self-regulating. Thus, the creation of new, clumsy, outside bureaucracies, excessive paperwork, and unnecessarily higher costs for everyone involved in recreational diving would be prevented. So far, the diving industry nationwide has shown itself to be admirably responsible and capable of maintaining high standards in instruction, in renting equipment to qualified customers only, and, perhaps most notably, in voluntarily working to establish a regulation for annual visual inspections of scuba tanks, a procedure that assures a much higher standard of safety than the federally mandated, five-year hydrotests. At tropical resorts and aboard charter boats, new and more restrictive controls on diving will probably appear. After all, no one in charge wants to spoil the fun, or the profits, with an accident.

Shore divers in the more populous coastal states may find access to their favorite beaches and coves more and more restricted. This trend is at least partially due to negative attitudes toward divers on the part of private landowners and town and county officials. We suggest that an increasingly important function of diver associations and clubs be to plan strategies to reverse the rising tide of antidiving sentiment and to ensure that public beaches remain open to divers (many in the Northeast are already closed). Public-relations efforts by dive clubs—for example, coastal litter cleanups; slide presentations in area schools on local marine life; special seasonal outdoor marine science seminars, perhaps featuring aquarium talks, the identification of edible wild seafood and recipe swapping, and crafts projects such as seaweed pressing and mounting or Japanese fish printing (*Gyotaku*)—might soon make your dive club very popular in the community.

If the town fathers fear that hordes of weekend divers, like aquatic Hell's Angels, will descend on small local beaches, terrorizing babies and intimidating 90-pound weaklings, try compromising by offering to set up some sort of limited-use schedule. This concept is being applied to more and more natural areas on land with very gratifying results, as reported by the wilderness users themselves. Sometimes liability for diver accidents is the major worry of those who control access to the water. If this is a problem at your favorite shore-diving spot, offer to devise and sign a strongly worded waiver absolving the coastal proprietor of all responsibility. Get the wording checked by a lawyer so that the document will have as much weight as possible. We hope for and predict the quick reversal of the recent ridiculous tendency to assign negligence to blameless individuals and organizations after some self-destructive damn fool has succeeded in injuring himself.

The State of the Profession

Some amateur divers become so enthusiastic about life under water that they aim to make a career of it. While future prospects for professional underwater activities are varied, there will probably not be a greatly expanded role for scuba divers *per se.* Among the most exciting, though severely limited and intensely competitive, opportunities for underwater explorers are those in oceanography. Spectacular new discoveries will undoubtedly be made in marine biology and geology. Much remains to be fathomed in the areas of the deep geothermal vents, or submarine hot springs, recently found on the ocean floor near the Galapagos and off the Pacific coast of Baja, California. These incredible oases in the nearly universally cold and inhospitable deep sea harbor strange life forms like no other on earth. The discovery of lush, biologically dominated seascapes where no one had imagined they could exist is a little like finding life on another planet.

But these discoveries were made by oceanographers ensconced at atmospheric pressure inside a small research submersible, and this is the way of the future. It's safe to say that no diver will ever swim out into the pitch darkness, feel and taste the strangely mild mineral water, two miles down beside one of the Galapagos submarine vents. No diver will play a beam of light closely over the rugged terrain with its population of foot-long clams, baffling dandelion animals, and ropy pogonophorans, animals that appear to have no mouth, anus, or digestive organs.

Although mixed-gas divers have locked out of pressurized chambers and swum in the twilight zone as deep as 1500 feet, and though tests at very high air pressures have subjected human volunteers to even deeper dives in simulation, it appears that direct human effort will not contribute significantly to deep underwater exploration. Pressure-induced bone disease is considered a real threat to very deep divers, and the cost of a few minutes' work in subsequent days of decompression time is too great. Nevertheless, according to experts such as NOAA fishery scientist Dr. Richard Cooper, it is possible that practical work can be done by divers to depths approaching that of the edge of the continental shelf, about 600 feet.

A semipermanent undersea habitat on the continental shelf could be established roughly contemporaneously with the proposed first permanently inhabited, orbiting space station. But with respect to both of these baby steps away from the natural human environment, direct human exploration and exploitation will be severely and indefinitely curtailed. The giant leaps through both the solar system and deep inner space will be made nearly exclusively by unmanned probes and machines designed for special purposes.

Still, the demand by ocean industries and technologies for professional, ambient pressure diving near the surface may continue to grow. The following is a catalogue of developing areas of interest.

Oil and Gas Exploration. As the world's easily accessible oil runs out, offshore petroleum will be sought in environments that are increasingly inhospitable and dangerous for diving. The stormy Gulf of Alaska and the ice-clogged Beaufort Sea are potential sites for large offshore oil fields. If any industry-related diving is required in such places it will probably not be much fun. The trend in undersea operations of the oil industry, however, is toward more and more one-atmosphere work and "seafloor completion." In these activities, personnel work in special rigid suits or submersible units that lock into sea-floor control chambers at surface air pressure.

Ocean Thermal Energy Conversion (OTEC). If the new floating power plants are successful—at the time of this writing, the first of them is about to be tested off Hawaii—some near-surface diving will probably be required for construction, maintenance, and repair. OTEC installations will be primarily in the tropics, where warm surface water overlies cold deeper layers (the controlled juxtaposition of the two is the source of the power). Of course, the power plants must be situated over very deep water, so divers here will never approach bottom. However, gin-clear, tropical offshore conditions around the huge facilities, which may attract large oceanic fish, curious porpoises, and perhaps turtles from time to time, should afford company professionals some memorable undersea excursions.

Manganese Nodule Mining. Nodules are potato-sized lumps of metallic ore that virtually pave the deep ocean bottom in some areas. Although nodules are largely composed of iron and manganese minerals, their lesser contents of nickel and copper provide the economic incentive for deep sea mining. So far only mining tests have been carried out by several multinational industrial corporations, and full-scale commercial development of this industry is uncertain.

This is another deep-sea operation, so occupational diving, if any, will involve work around the ships, barges, and uppermost parts of the suction dredges, which will extend downward three miles or more.

Offshore Kelp Farming. Some spectacular diving will be available if this industry begins to float. The idea is to grow kelp in huge, deep-water, floating plantations off western North America. The kelp, to be processed into alcohols and methane biofuels, will be sown on nylon mesh artificial bottoms, perhaps 100 feet deep. Some of the kelp plantations could extend for miles, a potential diving paradise attracting large migrant fishes and other marine life in relatively clear offshore water.

Offshore Fish Farming. The raising of large oceanic fish in floating enclosures or bottom pens has been envisioned, but may be impractical. Diving work in this business might be interesting, but the most successful advances in aquaculture will probably be in unexciting, even ugly (for a diver) coastal bays and estuaries, and freshwater ponds.

Despite such potential new and interesting professional opportunities for divers, most of those who earn their living under water will probably continue to do so, along with the rest of us landlubbers, in less than romantic environs. Would-be professional divers should realize that for every lucky talent signed on to help locate a sunken galleon or to perform support work in oceanographic research, many more professional divers are scouring befouled hulls and performing routine salvage in muddy rivers and oily harbors.

Protecting the Future

Every committed diver has a dream of the future. Settings of the dream vary—a dappled glade amidst lush giant kelp; a boat suspended in water so clear it appears to be grazing bottom 30 feet below; an infinite blue vista beyond a wall of living rock—but the basic elements of the dream are always, by implication, the same. Wild, clean, beautiful, living underwater surroundings are as essential to the future of diving as neoprene, which is made from petroleum.

Conservationists intent on saving from despoilation large tracts of pristine natural environment, both under water and above, face a delicate irony. The same forces that provide access and materials essential to explore the remote and beautiful places also threaten them. Modern diving may well lead other outdoor sports in its dependence on supportive technology and industrial processes whose continued growth will destroy that which is ultimately responsible for the diver's enjoyment. Perhaps we, as divers, should look for examples of wasteful and environmentally damaging processes in the industry. Can we cut back to leaner diving lifestyles, assure the lightest personal impact on the shallow seas, and, in the finest diving areas, voluntarily (to paraphrase the wilderness backpacker's creed) take nothing but photos, leave nothing but swirling eddies?

A few specific conservation measures come to mind. First, on a personal level, good care of one's diving gear will keep it functioning for years after more casually treated equipment has turned to dust and rust. More generally, we feel that sport divers who purchase and use underwater power sleds and scooters pose a danger to the environment and at least an embarrassment, though quite possibly a threat, to themselves. This kind of equipment is the underwater version of the ORV and snowmobile, and its proliferation poses a new threat to remote and pristine environments. Motorized explorers cover far more ground, and as can be clearly seen on land, tend to be less respectful of the lovely, silent places than those who have chanced upon a beauty spot by dint of their own efforts. As with the situation on land, the aftermath of hordes of buzzing sea scooters and riders crisscrossing thousands of square yards of reef is likely to be frightened wildlife and a trampled terrain that has been plundered for delicate coral growth and shells.

Another problem with motorized equipment is that it can carry inexperienced, out-of-shape people into remote wilderness areas, beyond the point at which, if the machinery quits, they can make it back on their own resources. Perhaps the already overworked rescue branch of the Coast Guard should begin to consider regulating the sea-scooter traffic. We recommend that divers who want to cover a lot of underwater country on a single airfill try drift diving, and go with an experienced leader.

Now that fuel prices are rapidly going out of sight, sailing vessels may become more common in the diving-charter business. A sailboat might take a little more time to reach the outlying sites, but the trip itself could be more memorable, perhaps even romantic, and certainly less costly.

So much for the good news. The bad news is that the coastal ocean—that is, the continental shelf of North America and the more crowded island coastal zones nearby—as well as many of the finest inland lakes are dying. A few more miles of coastal waters become diseased every year, whether from oil spills, pesticide pollution, heated water from new power plants, overfishing, or ill-advised underwater dredging and mining. Sometimes the disease is checked in time and recovery occurs, but more often conditions gradually get worse and worse. This is a modern societal problem. Up until very recently, the ocean was able to absorb the kinds and amounts of pollutants it received and neutralize them rapidly, but marine scientists worldwide now largely agree that the absorptive limits and recycling abilities of the coastal zones around the more populous and industrialized countries have been exceeded. Tragically, the areas that are dying, although relatively small on a global scale, are among the most productive of fish and other life, and they are the places frequented by divers.

A lot of the problem has to do with the insidious growth of waste, a corollary of our species' search for ever greater convenience, excessive—even self-destructive—bodily comfort, and faster ways to live our lives. These intangibles constitute the trade-offs for which irreplaceable pieces of the environment are given up and lost one after another.

What can divers do about this problem beyond practicing specific, personal conservation measures within the sport? Divers, for the most part, are respectable members of the comfortable, consuming middle class, which has largely spawned the era of environmental trade-off. Divers can do a lot of positive lobbying among nondiving friends and neighbors, informing them of the declining condition and fate of our epicontinental waters. Those who observe the consequences of regional problems—oil spills, fish kills near power plants, diseased marine life around ocean-dumping sites—should let people know. Most such observations still go unreported.

Even the smallest incidents with precise location data, photos, if possible, and samples of the oil, fish, and the like, if possible, should be reported to state and local environmental officials, the nearest office of the Environmental Protection Agency, the Coast Guard, and even local news media. Most coastal environmental degradation is hidden to all except divers. Bringing evidence to light will help convince others of the seriousness and widespread nature of the problem. Divers generally understand the relationship of a healthy aquatic environment to such considerations as climate, future food supplies, and satisfying recreation. To preserve our rationally comfortable and interesting lifestyles, as well as our favorite sport, we should try to help everyone to understand these things.

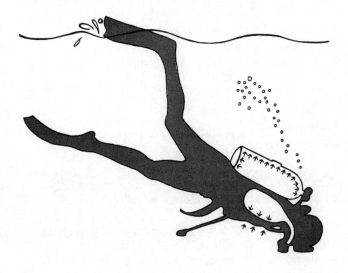

Appendix 1

Measurement and Conversions

Pressure

1 atmosphere = 14.7 pounds per square inch = 760 millimeters of mercury

Temperature

1 degree Celsius (centigrade) = 9/5 or 1.8 degrees Fahrenheit

To convert Celsius to Fahrenheit, use the formula $(C° \times 9/5) + 32 = F°$.

To convert Fahrenheit to Celsius, use the formula $(F° - 32) \times 5/9 = C°$.

Volume

1 cubic foot = 29.9 quarts = 28.3 liters
1 liter = 1.06 quarts

Depth and Distance

1 fathom = 6 feet = 1.8 meters
1 meter = 3.3 feet
1 mile = 5,280 feet = 1.6 kilometers = 0.87 nautical mile
1 mile per hour = 0.87 knot

Weight

1 pound = 0.45 kilogram

Area

1 square meter = 10.76 square feet

Appendix 2

Information and Resources

Diving Instruction & Equipment (including repairs)

Inquire at local dive shops affiliated with one or more of the internationally recognized instructional agencies (NAUI, YMCA, SSI, NASDS, and PADI). Titles of amateur diving courses offered at this writing:

● NAUI: Skin Diving, Basic Scuba, Sport Scuba, Advanced Scuba, Specialty Courses (Cave Diving, Deep Diving, Diving Leadership, Ice Diving, Professional Diving, Search and Recovery, Underwater Environment, Underwater Hunting and Collecting, Underwater Photography, Wreck Diving)

● YMCA: Scuba Diver Course, Advanced Diver Course

● SSI: Advanced Open Water Diver Course (includes basic pool training), Dive Control Specialist Course, Underwater Photography, Dive Rescue

NASDS and PADI did not respond to request for information.

Planning a Dive Vacation

Numerous diving resorts and guided tours to exotic locations are advertised in the magazines *Skin Diver* and *Sport Diver*. Both magazines publish a directory of professional dive shops and the services they offer in the United States, Canada, and other countries.

Fishing and Salvage Regulations

Fish and game laws and salvage regulations vary widely from state to state, and writing ahead for information on regulations is always advisable. The state agencies having jurisdiction over such matters are variously designated as conservation departments, natural resource departments, or fish and game departments. Outside the United States, the most reliable sources of information are national bureaus of tourism, major diving resorts, and boat-chartering companies.

Marine Biology, Ecology, and Underwater Technology

Sea Grant Universities and Colleges

Found in all coastal sections of the country, including the Great Lakes Region, Sea Grant offices on college campuses sponsor programs and publish material devoted to achieving greater public involvement with the aquatic environment.

Public Aquariums and Marine Museums

Educational programs on marine life, undersea geology and archaeology are frequently offered at these facilities in many parts of the United States.

Interpretive Periodicals

Among the more informative periodicals of interest to divers are: *Oceans*, published by the Oceanic Society (San Francisco); *Sea Frontiers*, the International Oceanographic Foundation (Miami); and *Oceanus*, Woods Hole Oceanographic Institution (Woods Hole, Massachusetts).

Conservation Organizations

Groups that are active in oceanic conservation and dissemination of information include:

The Oceanic Society
Building 315
Fort Mason
San Francisco, CA 94123

Other chapters are located in Culver City, California; Seattle, Washington; Atlantic City, New Jersey; and Stamford, Connecticut.

The Cousteau Society
8150 Beverly Blvd.
Los Angeles, CA 90048

The American Littoral Society
Sandy Hook
Highlands, NJ 07732

The Sierra Club is a member of a coalition of groups working toward greater marine and coastal protection. 1980 has been designated as "The Year of the Coast," and many events are scheduled throughout that year. For more information on Year of the Coast events, write:

Year of the Coast
Station S, P.O. Box 2708
Washington, D.C. 20013

Appendix 3

Algae Art

Among the larger varieties of seaweeds such as kelps, divers frequently find beautiful and delicate plants of different species of algae that look as if they belong in a fairy tale. The fantastic forms and patterns of such algae can sometimes be captured on film, if you are careful not to stir up the bottom. Even better, the plants themselves can be preserved as a kind of natural art. Here's how.

Materials You Will Need

- Collecting containers (plastic bags or jars)
- Formaldehyde solution
- Covered bucket for carrying specimens home
- Large shallow tray
- A fairly heavy, high-rag-content paper for mounting
- Heavy blotting paper or absorbent cardboard
- Corrugated cardboard sheets, about 1 ft. by 2 ft.
- 2 exterior plywood boards, about 1 ft. by 2 ft. by 3/4 inch
- Several old newspapers
- Wax paper
- Artist's paint brush
- Small electric fan or "gun"-type hair dryer
- 2 six-foot lengths of rope

Collecting

This is usually as easy as picking flowers. Just be conservation-minded, and don't take more than you can use; if a plant seems exceedingly rare in the area of your dive, leave the specimens alone. As living art forms, they are worth far more to a beholder than any arrangement produced by even the most expert algae artist. Store your specimens in plastic bags or, if they are especially delicate, carry them in closed, water-filled jars, preferably plastic ones that can't break easily.

Preserving

As soon as possible after collection, while they are still fresh, algae specimens should be immersed in 5% formalin (a solution of formaldehyde in water). You can obtain formalin concentrate for little cost at some larger drugstores or hospital supply stores, or a local high school or college biology teacher can refer you to the nearest supplier. You don't need very much: a 5% formalin solution is made by mixing 5 parts concentrate with 95 parts water. Be careful of getting concentrated formalin on your skin. If you do, flush it away immediately with water to avoid embalming that part of your anatomy.

Very thin and delicate varieties of seaweed need only be dipped several times in the solution. Specimens with more bulk should remain in the solution for up to an hour or so.

Mounting

After preserving the algae, you should have ready the shallow tray, half-filled with clean fresh water. Slip the mounting paper into the water and float your algae specimens so that they spread out over the surface of the paper. Now your artistry awaits expression in the arrangement of the algal fronds. You may opt for a lifelike appearance of the plant, or you can create a more abstract pattern. Use a stylus or a small artist's brush to work with fine branches. When the arrangement is just right, drain off the water slowly and carefully. There are several ways to do this. The preferred one is to siphon the water gradually out of the tray using narrow-bore plastic or rubber tubing. Some algae artists merely tip the tray very slowly; others manage to carefully lift the paper free of the water without disturbing the arrangement. Once the mounting paper with its specimens is out of the water, it is kept flat, with the algae face up.

Drying

Place the wet mount, still algae-side up, on a somewhat larger piece of blotter or absorbent cardboard. Then the combined layers (mount plus blotter) should be placed on several sheets of newspaper, which, in turn, should lie atop a still larger (about 1 ft. by 2 ft.) piece of corrugated cardboard. Finally, cover the algae specimens with a piece of wax paper or a clean plastic sheet.

Now the whole "Dagwood" sandwich, consisting of (from the top) wax paper, algae specimens, mounting paper, blotter, newspaper, and corrugated cardboard, is ready to go into a plant press—that is, the sandwich is placed between the two plywood boards, and rope is cinched as tightly as possible around the whole. Several specimens, each done up in a sandwich identical to the one described can be stacked and dried at the same time in the same press. For fastest drying, make sure that the air channels in the corrugated cardboard are all oriented in the same direction. Then a fan or hair dryer can be placed at one end of the press and a flow of air directed straight toward the air channels and through the whole stack.

Each specimen dries through the back of its piece of mounting paper, which contacts the blotter. Moisture is continuously drawn away by the airflow through the corrugated cardboard. As the algae dries, it glues itself permanently to the mounting paper.

Rarely do you find a loose branch that must be glued artificially after a specimen has dried. If a fan or dryer is used, drying takes about two or three days. When your specimens are completely dried, they can be framed, and most kinds of algae will last indefinitely under glass. Some delicate colors (notably reds and pinks) may eventually fade, but often will last for years.

Collectors who want to identify their algae specimens should consult local botany teachers, a library, or a museum for information on recognizing the algae of a given region. Also refer to the sources listed in the bibliography at the end of this book.

In most diving areas, different species of algae appear in different seasons. Once you begin to acquire a green (or yellow, or pink) thumb as an algae artist, you may be stimulated to dive more frequently the year round.

Appendix 4

Japanese Fish Printing

Japanese fish printing, or *Gyotaku*, is an ancient art that has been adapted by ichthyologists in other countries to record scale patterns and surface areas of fishes.

The technique of Gyotaku can be adapted to make impressions of other objects such as shells, coral, and mineral crystals. Usually fish prints are strikingly unusual but precise images of the real thing, with scales and fins faithfully reproduced in pattern and proportion.

Prints made with black ink frequently evoke fossils. Colored inks can be used to render either a realistic or an impressionistic print. Using your imagination can lead you into greater abstraction. The same fish or a variety can be printed several times on a large sheet of paper, resulting in a strange school of skeletal swimmers.

Materials You Will Need

- A very fresh fish with scales firmly in place
- Printer's ink (a water-base type will permit washing the fish clean to start over, or to use different colors)
- A moderately stiff one-half-inch brush
- Plastic modeling clay
- Straight pins
- Printing paper (newsprint is best to start with; the more expensive rice paper is preferred by accomplished artists
- Old newspapers

Technique

First wash the outside of the fish thoroughly with soap and water. A hand soap or dish detergent does the job nicely. Dry the fish completely.

Next place the fish on a table generously covered with clean old newspapers. Build up some modeling clay under the fins and spread the fins over the flattened surface of the clay. Pin the fins to the clay and angle the tops of the pins away from the fish.

Brush a *thin* coat of ink on the side of the fish. Most beginners tend to ink the fish too liberally. If the ink is spread too thickly, the fine patterns of the scales will smudge or turn out solidly blackened on the paper. This is especially critical on a fish with fairly small scales. If you make a mistake with water-base ink, rinse and dry the fish thoroughly, and start again. Do not ink the eye if you wish to achieve a lifelike impression.

When your fish is fully inked, carefully drape a piece of the printing paper over the fish. Using your fingers, gently press the paper into contact with the fish over the entire inked surface. Try to avoid any sliding or slipping of the paper on the fish, since this smudges the print; a paper that jumps slightly on the fish may yield a double print with one image slightly displaced from the other.

Thin-bodied fish are the easiest to work with. If you wish to work with a wide-bodied fish and have trouble bending the paper around its curving flanks, try partially embedding the fish in a tray or dish filled with sand. The inked side of the fish should remain free of sand, but the fish will remain physically stable and stationary, and you can devote all your attention to pressing the paper around the sides.

The final step is usually to paint the eye of your print with a small brush. When you have finished working with a fish, if you have used water-based ink, it can be washed, scaled, and perhaps skinned, and may still be edible. At the very least, it will be appreciated by a cat, and you will appreciate this unique art form where the medium can become the menu.

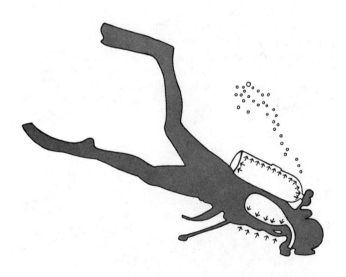

Bibliography

Useful supplementary references for divers.

ABBOTT, R. T. *American Seashells*. Princeton, N.J.: D. Van Nostrand Co., 1954.

ADOLPHSON, J. AND T. BERGHAGE. *Perception and Performance Underwater*. New York: John Wiley & Sons, Inc., 1974.

AMERICAN RED CROSS. *Standard First Aid and Personal Safety*. New York: Doubleday & Co., Inc., 1973.

BRIGHT, T. J. AND L. H. PEQUEGNAT. *Biota of the West Flower Garden Bank*. Houston: Gulf Publishing Co., 1974.

BRITISH SUB-AQUA CLUB. *The Diving Officer's Handbook*. 4th. Edition. London: Riverside Press Ltd., 1973.

CLARK, E. *Lady With a Spear*. New York: Harper and Brothers, 1953.

COUSTEAU, J. Y. *The Silent World*. New York: Harper and Brothers, 1953.

CULLINEY, J. L. *The Forests of the Sea*. San Francisco: Sierra Club Books, 1976.

DAWSON, E. Y. *How to Know the Seaweeds*. Dubuque, Iowa: W.C. Brown Co., 1956.

DUEKER, C. W. *Medical Aspects of Sport Diving*. New York: A. S. Barnes & Co., Inc., 1970.

GOODSON, G. *The Many-Splendored Fishes of Hawaii*. Palos Verdes Estates, Calif.: Marquest Colorguide Books, 1973.

GOODSON, G. *The Many-Splendored Fishes of the Atlantic Coast. Ibid.*

GREENBERG, I. AND J. GREENBERG. *Waterproof Guide to Corals and Fishes of Florida, the Bahamas, and the Caribbean*. Miami: Seahawk Press, 1977.

HALSTEAD. B. W. *Poisonous and Venomous Marine Animals of the World*. Princeton, N.J.: Darwin Press, 1978.

HEDGPETH, J. AND S. HINTON. *Common Seashore Life of Southern California*. Healdsburg, Calif.: Naturegraph Co., 1961.

MADLENER, J. C. *The Sea Vegetable Book*. New York: Clarkson N. Potter, Inc., 1977.

NATIONAL GEOGRAPHIC SOCIETY. *World Beneath the Sea*. 2nd. Edition. Washington, D.C.: The National Geographic Society, 1973.

NATIONAL OCEANIC AND ATMOSPHERIC ADMINISTRATION. *The NOAA Diving Manual*. Washington, D.C.: Manned Undersea Science and Technology Office of NOAA, U.S. Department of Commerce, 1975.

NORTH, W. J. *Underwater California*. Los Angeles: University of California Press, 1977. (Sections on underwater photography by Robert Hollis).

ODUM, H. T., B. J. COPELAND, AND E. A. McMAHAN. *Coastal Ecosystems of the United States*. Washington, D.C.: The Conservation Foundation, 1974.

PEARSE, J. S. AND V. A. GERARD. "Kelp Forests." In *Coastal Ecosystem Management*, edited by J. Clark. New York: John Wiley & Sons, Inc., 1977.

SCHENCK, H. V., JR. AND J. J. McANIFF. *United States Underwater Fatality Statistics—1975*. Washington, D.C.: NOAA, U. S. Department of Commerce, 1977.

TINKER, S. W. *Fishes of Hawaii: A Handbook of the Marine Fishes of Hawaii and the Central Pacific Ocean*. Honolulu: Hawaiian Service Inc., 1978.

UNIVERSITY OF CALIFORNIA. *Gyotaku—Japanese Fish Printing*. Berkeley, Calif.: Sea Grant Marine Advisory Office, Cooperative Extension Program, Publication AXT-445-3,

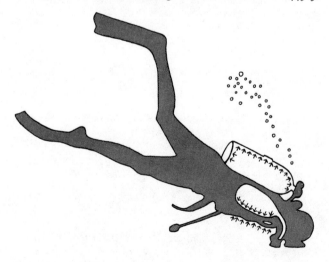

INDEX